The
PERFORMANCE
of HEARTBREAK

The
PERFORMANCE
of HEARTBREAK

and Other Plays

SCOTT CAAN

A Barnacle Book • Rare Bird Books
Los Angeles, Calif.
2015

THIS IS A GENUINE BARNACLE BOOK

A Barnacle Book | Rare Bird Books
453 South Spring Street, Suite 302
Los Angeles, CA 90013
rarebirdbooks.com

For information on performance rights, please contact:
Jonathan Mills, Paradigm Agency
jmills@paradigmagency.com
212.897.6400

For more information, address:

A Barnacle Book | Rare Bird Books
Subsidiary Rights Department
453 South Spring Street, Suite 302, Los Angeles, CA 90013

Set in Dante

Printed in the United States

10 9 8 7 6 5 4 3 2 1

Publisher's Cataloging-in-Publication data
Names: Caan, Scott, 1976-, author.
Title: The Performance of heartbreak : and other plays / by Scott Caan.
Description: A Barnacle Book. | New York ; Los Angeles : Rare Bird Books, 2015.
Identifiers: ISBN 978-1-942600-01-5
Subjects: Relationships—Fiction | Current events—Fiction. | Bisac: Drama /
American.
Classification: LCC PS3553.A24 2015 P47 | DDC 812./54—dc23

For Sheila Marie

Contents

On Scott Caan's Plays

by Michael O'Malley

When athletes compete with honor, they sometimes summon victory. The best athletes do this with a combination of heart and guts, and, hopefully, at crucial moments—their brains. Dedicated athletes who give their all—heart, guts, and brains—on occasion find themselves being lifted off the field on their comrades' shoulders. Winners.

We pat their backs, shake their hands, ask for autographs, and retire their numbers. We buy the products that they endorse, we hang their posters on our walls, build statues of them, and give them keys to our cities. Yet, though we celebrate these winners as if our rooting had somehow helped will their victories to happen, we know deep down that their victories are their's alone to claim.

Thankfully, there are writers like Scott Caan that take an athlete's heart, guts, and brains, and combines them with his spleen—the organ that filters the blood, filters all of our blood, and puts our lives onstage.

When Scott Caan writes, he writes with all his blood pumping for us. So we can know ourselves better. So we can live better lives. Lives where we understand one another. Lives where we feel more united than apart. And, as a result, the victory at the end of his art is a victory for all of us— not just him.

I crave a writer who writes with his heart, who writes about things that *I've* thought or felt but haven't quite known how to put those things or feelings into words. I crave a writer with the guts to take on challenging topics, and one who does it deftly—one who doesn't stop until he's left it all on the field.

Like the best athletes, Scott Caan competes on the page with his heart, guts, and brains, but what wallops you with his writing is his spleen. For the reader and the theatergoer, the applause rings out in gratitude, wonder, and admiration that a fellow human being has plunged to the depths of their imagination, and put it on stage so we can see humanity laid bare.

We need more big-spleened writers with Scott's understanding and empathy for people. We need more writers who don't sneer at sincerity, who honor and adore people who seek the road to redemption and the betterment of self, who strive to connect with others, and who know the meaning of forgiveness and making oneself fully whole. But here's the good news: we've got one here.

Enjoy his plays. Read them. Stage them. Write your own.

He's an inspiration.

Foreword

by Val Lauren

I was ready to leave. Four years of training at Playhouse West had passed and it was the best education I had ever gotten, but I was starting to grow fidgety. A perfect piece of direction or a silent nod of approval from my guru and teacher Robert Carnegie was no longer enough to get me through the week and, in retrospect, I realize that was his plan all along.

It was Saturday early morning and I was chain smoking on the sidewalk in front of the theater, prepping for my scene that was up on stage next—*Does a Tiger Wear a Necktie* by Don Peterson. I was playing Beckam, a reckless kid being held against his will in a youth facility. In the scene, Beckam confronts his counselor and all hell breaks loose. All the pacing, cigarettes, and bad thoughts had worked up a good lather… I was on the verge of capturing that elusive "click" I needed to serve the scene… I could feel the click coming…

That's about when I looked up to see a black Cadillac DeVille barreling directly toward me. It made a quick stop within a few feet of my person and out popped a ball of energy in a grey hoodie. It flew by me and into the front door of the theater.

Before I knew what's what, I was alone again on the sidewalk… now completely distracted. Fifteen minutes of preparation and four cigarettes down the drain. The thoughts that replaced the previous went something like:

…Was that…? What the fuck is Scott Caan doing here? He left before I started at this school and he does movies now…he left before I started what the fuck is Scott Caan doing here…that's a very nice Cadillac…he was the dude that literally stole Varsity Blues *out from under every single actor in that movie and had me running*

out of the theater proud to be a member of Playhouse West what the FUCK is he doing here?...okay, think about your scene think about the scene...you are walking into the counselor's office to demand...that Cadillac would have done some real damage if it hit me what the fuck is Scott doing here?

The front door of the theater opened again and my scene partner waved me in—times up.

My motivation for performing my scene changed in one instant and set me on fire—"Show Scott Caan that you can act."

I feel bad for what I put my poor scene partner through on that day. The abuse was palpable.

After class, I cornered Scott outside with my trusted copy of *Hurly Burly* by David Rabe and asked him to read a scene from it with me and I guess my plan worked—he agreed.

We read right then and there on the sidewalk. An hour passed and we were now performing the thing with and for each other, pacing, smoking, and yelling Rabe's lines on Lankershim Blvd.

That collaboration has been going on ever since and will continue to go on until it won't—which is never ever.

The work that we have since created together, the theater culture that we have been exposed to, and the growth that comes along with it, has been my most cherished experience as an actor and I am thankful for it, for Scott, and for this book, which has been the backbone of everything above.

In this book lies a very particular and peculiar map into the human psyche. A very particular and peculiar music that if played just right, will reveal itself in its entirety—almost. The rest you will find in yourself.

The essential ingredient that is neccessary to making this book work is one and the same with the opportunity it presents—there must be enjoyment.

Author's Note

by Scott Caan

This book contains ten years of plays worked on solely by members of the Playhouse West Repertory Theater Group. *The Performance of Heartbreak, An Epilogue*, and *Day in Life* were all written during a very specific time for me. A string of life-changing events had gotten me to a place, creatively speaking, that I had never been before. As a writer and human being, I wasn't happy. What started as an exercise in therapy turned out to be some of my favorite work, and consequently ended up being what brought me back to the theater where my playwriting started.

This collection represents ten years of hard work done by a very specific group of dedicated, fervently working theater junkies.

Most of the plays in this book have been produced and performed in one way or another, the ones that have not, probably never should be.

Scott Caan
Los Angeles, 2015

I began writing this play on September 11, 2001. It was up on stage just two months later. Although a lot of my views have changed drastically from the ones expressed in the play, it would be an extreme injustice to change a word. So I didn't. Except a few fucks. I took some of them out because it was a bit excessive.

Over black we played an edit of sound bytes. News reports and phone calls gathered from the day. Some silence, and then lights up on the stage.

9/11

A Play in Two Acts

9/11 *was originally produced by The Playhouse West Repertory Theater Company—artistic director Robert Carnegie at Playhouse West Studio Two in North Hollywood, California, December 2001. It was directed by Robert Carnegie; set design by Scott Caan and Val Lauren; stage management, lights, and sound design by Zachariah Moura. The cast was as follows:*

MATTY................. *Mark Pellegrino*
VIC......................... *Val Lauren*
SEAN..................... *Scott Caan*
TONI..................... *Danielle Wolf*
MAN...................... *Doug Cavanough*

9/11

ACT ONE

THE BACK PATIO OF A COFFEE SHOP IN HOLLYWOOD

A few tables, a few plants, it's a pretty simple place. A man in his late twenties, MATTY, sits down at a table drinking coffee and listening to a small transistor radio. News of the World Trade Center attacks blasts from the speaker of Matty's radio.

He switches the radio off.

MATTY: I can't believe this shit... I just can't believe it... Motherfuckers...

A man in his mid-twenties strolls over to the table wearing a perfectly tailored suit and a fedora to match. All style. This is VIC. He pulls up a chair next to Matty.

MATTY: *(Cont'd)* Can you believe this shit?

VIC: It's a tragedy, and no, I cannot... The Giants did not cover, you owe me a dub. You will grab breakfast and we will call it a ball.

MATTY: *(Annoyed)* Fine.

VIC: No, not fine.

MATTY: What?

VIC: I hate it when you do that shit.

MATTY: Shit? What shit?

VIC: I'll tell you what shit.

MATTY: Okay.

VIC: You lay a small one, right? You lay a small one and you think to yourself, *Mr., Vic here is dealing strictly big time, big time.* So, what do you do? You come in big time small time. You come in with something like this, for example, a couple a saw bucks on the Giants. You figure it's a wash, a no brainer for you. If you win, you collect a few dimes and call it a ball, but if you lose, it's nothin' to me, we both know that I am not going to go chasing the cat for a measly twenty bucks. You do it time and time again and I have been meaning to tell you that it agitates me, and that I will not call it kosher no more…you are paying for the freaking meal here.

MATTY: *(Very annoyed)* Fine.

VIC: See that!

MATTY: See what?

VIC: You say fine when I bring it up, then you…

MATTY: Would you shut up… Do you realize what's happening here?

VIC: Yes, I do, and it's been bothering me, what you do, and I'm not going to let you use something like that to defuse the matter at hand.

MATTY: The matter at hand?

VIC: That's right.

MATTY: The matter at hand?

VIC: Right again.

MATTY: The goddamn matter at hand is not the ball, or the wash, or the stupid twenty dollars I owe you. I am not changing the subject to pull you off track here. Do you understand what is happening in the world, in our country?

VIC: Yes, I do. And the president of these United States clearly stated that the best thing that we could do, as Americans, is to try to keep it together. And that's exactly what I am trying to do. Keep it together. My job, as an American, is to not do what you are doing, my friend. I am keeping the world turning. I woke up, I watched the news, and now I am out in the world running my business like a good goddamn American should.

MATTY: Vic?

VIC: What?

MATTY: You're a bookmaker for Christ's sakes.

VIC: That's not the point, Matty. I run a business.

MATTY: An illegal business.

Vic scans the joint to make sure they are alone.

VIC: Please keep your voice down, and who the hell are you to judge me? I mean, what the hell are we talking about here? Big freaking deal…

The Giants did not cover, you owe, and you will buy the meal. That's it! That is all this is.

MATTY: This! This, that's what this is. But there is something else, my friend, a bigger "this." The biggest "this" you and I will ever see in our lifetime. World War Three might have just started and you are talking to me about the fucking Giants.

VIC: Business is business my friend, and the President of the United...

MATTY: Goddamn it, I know what the president said. But he wasn't talking to you. Okay? He was talking to the lawyers, the doctors, the teachers, he wasn't talking to the people who run illegal fucking businesses. What you do in no way services the world, so don't give me some bullshit rap about how you are trying to keep it together here, okay? I am totally fucked up and in utter shock about this whole thing. You don't give a shit. You just want your twenty bucks. Do you realize what happened this morning?

VIC: Yes, I do, and I resent the fact that you say I don't give a shit. I do. I'm just trying not to freak out here, like you are obviously doing.

MATTY: I just don't think you realize the severity of what is going down. And for the record you can stick your twenty dollars right up your ass.

VIC: Don't talk to me in that fashion. Show some damn respect.

MATTY: *(Starting to laugh)* Vic, you know I love you, right?

VIC: Right.

MATTY: Do you also know that I have known you since you were a little kid, and that if I wanted to, I could reach across this table and rip your head off your neck like a little chicken?

VIC: Keep your voice down.

MATTY: Good! I just wanted to get that out of the way... Now the severity of what just happened this morning... Right? That's what I was saying, right?

VIC: I need a cup of coffee.

A YOUNG MAN with a newspaper and a cup of coffee walks on stage. He looks for a place to sit. He listens to Matty and just stares at him.

MATTY: *(To no one)* COFFEE PLEASE! Listen to me! These Arab...fuckin' Arab cocksuckers did not just walk into the Beverly Center and threaten to kill a few people, okay.

Matty notices the frozen young man.

MATTY: *(Cont'd)* What the fuck are you looking at?

YOUNG MAN: *(Walking off stage)* Asshole!

MATTY: They didn't just throw a little piece of dynamite into the dressing room of the Banana Republic, which who knows if that's on the fuckin' schedule for the afternoon, but that's not the point... What these camel-fucking, dirty, low-life...motherfuckers did, was attack, with force, the goddamn epicenter of our country with the strong intent to kill innocent fucking people.

An attractive WAITRESS walks up to the table.

WAITRESS: What can I get you?

VIC: Yes, hello. I would like a cup of black, and one of those muffins with the orange shit in it.

WAITRESS: *(Writing)* Coffee and orange shit... You okay?

MATTY: Yeah, I'm good.

WAITRESS: All right... *(She walks off)*

MATTY: You think this shit is over? It's all done now? No, my friend, this shit has just begun. The whole world is gonna change. The whole world is gonna change and people don't realize.

VIC: Can I say something?

MATTY: What?

VIC: Can I say something without you getting all upset?

MATTY: I don't know, you'll have to say it first.

VIC: I know what happened.

MATTY: I don't think you do.

VIC: Well, I do.

MATTY: Did you watch?

VIC: Yes, I watched.

MATTY: Everything?

VIC: Yes, everything.

MATTY: Did you watch the little fuckin' kid dancing in the streets? Celebrating? I'd like to get on a goddamn helicopter with an AK-47 right now and hover over the West Bank. Target practice. I'd start with that little fuckin' kid. I'd shoot him right in the face. Spray the little fucker's brains all over his grandma, and then kill that bitch, too. Then I'd shoot his mother, his uncle, his brother, sister...

VIC: Matty, Jesus Christ.

MATTY: Fuck them, and fuck our bleeding American hearts. We are too compassionate. You want me to feel fucking sorry for him? You want me to say, "Hey, he doesn't know any better, he's just a kid, give him a break." Fuck him! Kill him now! Kill the little sonofabitch before he grows up to win the terrorist of the year award ten years down the line.

VIC: You just said the word.

MATTY: What word?

VIC: Terrorist.

MATTY: Yeah, so what?

VIC: The point I am trying to make to you, if you would shut up for two seconds, is this... Why do they call them terrorists, Matty? What does that mean? The job of a terrorist is to terrorize. Look at you. You are the textbook definition of a man who has been terrorized. You are letting them win, you are letting these assholes know they are doing their job correctly... Stop it... Excuse me...

MATTY: What are you doing?

Vic pulls a miniature-sized phone out of his pocket. Matty watches.

VIC: *(Into phone)* Vic here... Yeah, I'm open, hold on... *(He pulls out a piece of paper and starts to write)*

MATTY: What are you doing?

VIC: *(Into phone)* All right, a dime on the Viks... Yeah, plus six... Wait no... They are the dog, my bad, minus six.

MATTY: Asshole!

VIC: Okay, a dollar on the Pats... What else?

MATTY: What an asshole.

VIC	MATTY
Two dollars on Hottie... Wait slow the fuck down... Parley Hotlanta, to who... The Jets are a pick 'em... I don't know, Testeverde is a queen, what do you want? (*Reviewing*) All right... Hottie to the Jets for a couple bucks... Viks over the Boys for a big one, and the Pats for a doll... All good? No, I'm not taking the fight... No... No... NO, what are you, a cop, I'm not taking the fight... All right. Cubbies over the Cards for another big one... Jesus Christ, what, you save the best for last? All right, got everything... You're big time, big time, baby... Call it a ball... You're all good...	The trade center fell down and he doesn't care... He's taking bets... (*sarcastic*) the two buildings in Manhattan?— You know the big ones?... The big ones, they don't exist anymore... They blew up... Yeah, planes with terrorists flew into them and they fell to the ground, blew up, and then fell to the ground... Oh yeah, people were in the buildings when they fell down!

VIC: *(To Matty)* WHAT A FUCKIN' WHALE...*(He puts the phone away)*

MATTY: I can't believe it.

VIC: *(Excited)* I can't believe it either. This guy is the biggest whale known to man. What a degenerate this guy is.

The waitress brings over the coffee and the muffin and sets it on the table.

WAITRESS: Anything else?

VIC: Just keep it hot.

WAITRESS: Right. *(She walks away)*

VIC: I mean this is the kind of guy's phone you tap to find out who he's betting on, then bet the farm the other way.

MATTY: Unbelievable!

VIC: No shit. This guy could not pick a winner at the Special Olympics. He just paid my bills for the next month.

MATTY: What an asshole.

VIC: What do you mean?

MATTY: This asshole is calling his bookie. Has everybody lost their minds completely…? What a scumbag.

VIC: You know what? You need to stop. I see what you're doing and you need to stop it.

MATTY: No, no, no! The entire world is going into the shit house, and this lowlife is worried about the Tampa Bay Buc-a-fuckin-eers.

VIC: You are a terrorized human being and I want you to stop it.

MATTY: And you're taking part in it.

VIC: Stop it.

MATTY: You're the fuckin' ringleader.

VIC: What should I do? Go home and think?

MATTY: Why not?

VIC: I will not fall victim to these circumstances. I will not be terrorized.

MATTY: Oh, shut up!

VIC: Tell me what I am saying that does not make sense?

MATTY: It doesn't make sense.

VIC: You are a liar. Nobody likes a liar, Matty.

MATTY: First of all, if you're talking about being a good American, the conversation stops here. I will not entertain that humongous pile of horse shit. I will, in fact, for your sake, entertain, your little, excuse me, small-minded terrorist theory.

VIC: I will get up and I will take the coffee to go! Please keep your voice down, and put a hat on the insults.

MATTY: I'll try to be polite.

VIC: Sarcasm has no place either.

MATTY: Would you like to hear what I have to say?

VIC: No!

MATTY: Would you listen anyway?

VIC: Sure.

MATTY: Great! What the fuck was I saying?

VIC: I don't know! Must not have been very important.

MATTY: No, it was.

VIC: Can we please just call it a ball on this whole fucked up topic here?

MATTY: No, we cannot.

VIC: Fine.

Matty rests his head into his arms for a few seconds.

MATTY: I remember!

VIC: Great!

MATTY: Your theory on terrorism.

VIC: Here we go.

MATTY: If I were actually scared, I guess what you are saying would have some validity.

VIC: What?

MATTY: That means it would be valid.

VIC: I know what the fuck validity means, asshole.

MATTY: Then what, what?

VIC: What, what, what?

MATTY: You said what! What the hell were you saying what to? I began to speak and you said what.

VIC: I don't fuckin' know.

MATTY: You're driving me crazy, you know that?

VIC: You're doing fine by yourself.

MATTY: Can I just say what the hell I am trying to say?

VIC: Sure, I'll try not to say what.

MATTY: If I were actually scared, your theory on terrorism would make sense.

VIC: You mean it would have some validity. It would be valid.

MATTY: Right.

VIC: I now remember why I said what, but I'm just going to drop it.

MATTY: Great! I'm not scared! I have not been terrorized. I'm pissed off, righteously pissed off, and I wanna kick somebody's ass. I'm not frightened! I want revenge. To me there is a difference between mourning and giving in to the terrorism. It's not like it's an event that has thrown me into a little scared place. It's healthy to grieve. We've experienced a tragedy here, and it's okay to grieve over it. I mean, I don't know if I'm actually grieving, or venting, or whatever, but it has definitely moved me, and my life is not the same.

VIC: That is all fine. All I was saying is that people should continue with their lives. There is nothing we can do. And I think it would be unhealthy to have everyone stop living normally.

MATTY: But nothing's normal.

VIC: You are making it that way.

MATTY: No, the fuckin' assholes who flew the airplanes into the buildings are making it that way.

VIC: Fine! But you are helping... Hold on.

Vic takes his phone out of his pocket again.

VIC: *(Cont'd, into phone)* Vic here.

MATTY: I can't talk to you anymore. I can't talk to you anymore!

VIC: *(Into phone)* No, I'm not taking the fight.

MATTY: You're unbelievable.

VIC: *(Into phone)* What's with everybody's concern with me and my goddamned decision to not take action on the fight... I don't know Tommy, stick the fight in your freakin' ear.

MATTY: Lowlifes, all of them.

VIC: *(Into phone)* Excuse me. *(To Matty, covering the phone)* You know what? Shut the fuck up. I don't want to hear it anymore.

MATTY: Well you're gonna hear it. You're gonna hear it all...

VIC: But I don't wanna.

MATTY: You're gonna hear it until my point has been made, you degenerate son of a bitch.

VIC: That's enough! *(Back into phone)* Tommy, I'm going to have to return momentarily.

VIC: *(Cont'd, he hangs up the phone)* Now I'm a degenerate? I'm a degenerate you self-righteous, hypocritical fuck?

MATTY: Hypocrite? I'm a hypocrite?

VIC: If I'm a degenerate, then you are a hypocrite.

MATTY: You know what? Take the bets, run your business. I don't give a shit. You are unreachable. You are a lost cause. I'm done with you.

VIC: Do you gamble, Matty?

MATTY: Shut up.

VIC: Do you gamble with me?

MATTY: Shut up, you fuckin' parasite.

VIC: You shut up, you gambling, hypocritical cocksucker.

SEAN, mid-twenties, Matty's younger brother, walks up to the table and sits down. He looks disheveled.

SEAN: Dude, I am having the worst fucking day. *(To Matty)* What's up, bro?

MATTY: *(Standing up)* UN-FUCKING-BELIEVABLE!

Sean watches as Matty gets up from the table and walks away.

SEAN: What the hell was that?

VIC: I don't know what the hell that was. You know, I try to be a good person and for the most part I think I do a pretty good job of it. Your brother makes me feel like I'm a piece of shit, and I'm not a piece of shit… Am I piece of shit, Sean?

SEAN: I don't think so.

VIC: Thank you. I'm not. But this fuckin' guy is crazy. I mean, what the hell does he want from me? What the hell does he want. The planes flew into the buildings, and they burnt down. I didn't do it… I mean, I might as well have, the way the freakin' guy treats me. I don't know. You know he needs to be talking to a freakin' therapist is what he needs, or be checked into a mental institution or something… I don't know.

SEAN: What are you talking about?

VIC: I'm talking about…

Matty storms back on stage.

MATTY: *(With a tear in his eye)* If they fuck with Disneyland, I swear to God I will sign up tomorrow and kill people.

VIC and SEAN: *(Simultaneously)* What?

Matty: *(Cont'd)* They closed Disneyland.

VIC: Matty…

MATTY: You shut up! I'm not talking to you.

Sean stands up.

SEAN: How 'bout me? Will someone talk to me? English?

MATTY: You shut up, too, 'cause I'm not talking to you either.

Matty storms off stage

VIC: See that, you see that shit? Fuckin' psychopathic.

SEAN: Can I...

VIC: You can't talk to a human being when he is in a state such as that. It's impossible, there is no communication...

SEAN: *(Still standing)* What the fuck is going on here?

Matty storms back on stage.

MATTY: I'll tell you what's going on. Your buddy here, the glamorized criminal, is driving me crazy.

VIC: Glamorize this.

MATTY: You're a cockroach. You know that?

VIC: Rats like you keep cockroaches like us in business, you motherfucker.

Sean sits back down.

SEAN: I quit... I don't even care. It's fine.

MATTY: That's right, sit down. 'Cause I've got something for your ass.

Vic picks up his phone again.

VIC: *(Into phone)* Vic here...

MATTY: Scumbag.

VIC: *(Walking off stage)* Fuck you.

Matty sits down next to his brother.

MATTY: You know what I want to know about? I want to know about your bad day. I want to know about my little brother's bad day. I want the details. I want to know what it is like to be you today. I mean, how bad was it? Was it hot when you got up? Did you have a bad sleep. Did you shit yourself on the way to breakfast. WHAT?

SEAN: I just…

MATTY: You know what? I don't want to hear about it. I can't believe I'm sitting here talking to you about your bad day.

SEAN: You're talking to yourself about my bad day.

MATTY: No, I'm talking to myself in general. I gotta sit here and go back and forth with that mongoloid friend of yours, with the hope that when you show up, I will have a little support. And for the lack of brain cells that little motherfucker has, he somehow has the ability to drive me out of my mind.

SEAN: He's actually smart.

MATTY: Apparently. Now what do you do? You show up, and basically in so many words express to me, unintentionally, of course, that you are no different than he is. You're the same.

SEAN: How did I do that?

MATTY: By saying, "I am having the worst day."

SEAN: I think you're digging a little deep there.

MATTY: Oh, I don't! It says it all. It says everything. It shows how all the hard work I have put into raising you to be the good goddamn American that our father once was, rest in peace, has just gone straight into the downward spiral of a gas station bathroom. Osmosis! Through the years, the stupidity has sunk in. He has rubbed his dummy vibes all over your brain, and you are now as clueless as he is… That's it! I'm not letting you see him anymore.

SEAN: What the fuck are you talking about, dude? What the hell did I do? I just walked in and said I was having a bad day. Is that not all right? Why am I being condemned for this? I don't know what the hell you guys are talking about. Mental patients, criminals, planes into buildings… Fuckin' Disneyland! I feel like I walked into a goddamned Jerry Bruckheimer film… *(Calming down)* I mean obviously I've missed something here.

MATTY: You don't know what's going, do you?

SEAN: Well, thank the lord… Can't slide nothin' by you, can I?

The waitress walks on stage.

WAITRESS: Do you need a minute?

SEAN: No, I'm not gonna eat… I'll be sick if I eat. I'll just have a cup of coffee, please.

WAITRESS: Did your friend leave?

SEAN: *(Long pause)* I don't know.

She just stands there and stares at Sean.

SEAN: Great.

She walks off. Sean is charmed.

SEAN: *(Cont'd)* That was strange.

MATTY: I can't believe it. I don't know if this is bad or good. Do you ever watch the news?

SEAN: Not really, no.

MATTY: But you have a television?

SEAN: Yes, I do.

MATTY: It was never on recently?

SEAN: Dude, do you want my fuckin' TV or something?

MATTY: No, I don't want your TV.

SEAN: Then, what is your trip?

MATTY: My trip?

SEAN: Yes.

MATTY: *(Pause)* Speaking of trips. Do you remember when we went to New York for the '96 World Series?

SEAN: Yes.

MATTY: Do you also remember the two really tall buildings that stood on the lower part of that island?

SEAN: What island?

MATTY: New York! The island of Manhattan! New York.

SEAN: You know what, dude, I don't need your hostility. I'm sorry I can't figure out the code in which you are speaking to me, but so you know, it's really annoying. And although the last time I said it I got chastised, I'm gonna say what the hell, and say it again. I'm having a really bad day. I have been walking for the last six hours. Walking! Amber, at three forty-five in the morning, in a very passive-aggressive manner, tells me to get out of her house, for the record, I didn't do anything wrong, but whatever. So, I go downstairs and my car won't start. I reach into my pocket, I have no wallet. Now I guess the right thing to do would be to go upstairs and see if I left it at Amber's, but I'm scared at this point. She scares me! I'm cold, I'm depressed, I'm scared of my fucking girlfriend, or at this point, ex-girlfriend, so I figure I'll walk it off. And I do! But where to? My house right? I mean, where the hell else am I gonna go? Fifteen miles at four o'clock in the morning, walking, but I make it. The sun's coming up, all I'm thinking about is a shower and some sleep... Guess what? No keys. Don't got those either. Left 'em in the fucking car at Amber's. You're not home. So, what do you do? Fuck it, right? You turn back and go get your keys. Why? Because you're a fucking man and that's what men do! You walk! Now if you had your wallet or even a fucking quarter, you make a phone call to a friend. But you know what? I liked it. In fact, I loved it! The misery, the pain, mental and physical, of walking two hundred blocks, depressed about my girlfriend who tortures me, as the sun came up, seemed like a great idea at the time. So there I am, head down, and walking. Again. More like dragging at this point. I remember actually praying to God that it would rain just so I could really feel it. Ya know? But I make it. I get back. I'm literally crawling and then guess what? My car's not there. It's gone. Someone stole it. I mean, who the fuck steals a 1987 Corolla... No one! That's the point. No shit, I would have been happy if a Mac truck came by doing eighty. I would have tried to see what it felt like to get hit by a truck. So it was either try to run across the freeway repeatedly until I didn't make it, or WALK here to meet you guys. I chose the latter. In search of a helping hand and maybe just a little bit of love. And what do I get? DICK!

Matty takes it all in.

MATTY: Are you done?

SEAN: Yep.

MATTY: Good, 'cause I really wanted to hear you out.

SEAN: Thank you.

MATTY: The World Trade Center and the Pentagon were attacked this morning by camel-fucking, low-life, Arab, terrorist cocksuckers. They hijacked and flew American airplanes carrying hundreds of American people into the three buildings, causing them to collapse and kill thousands. American thousands! Basically declaring war on our country... But anyway, back to your bad day... Your car, it was?

The waitress walks back onstage carrying a cup of coffee. She sets it on the table.

WAITRESS: You okay?

SEAN: What?

WAITRESS: Would you like anything else?

SEAN: No... No, thank you.

WAITRESS: Well, let me know if you do.

She walks back off stage.

SEAN: I didn't know, dude... I'm sorry.

MATTY: How could you not know?

SEAN: I don't know. I told you what I was doing... Jesus Christ!

MATTY: Do you have any clue what is going to happen now?

SEAN: I haven't really had time to think... Jesus Christ. What happened? I mean, how many people are dead?

MATTY: They don't even fuckin' know yet, but a lot. It might not be over. Big buildings and landmarks all over America are closing down. The airports. There is not a single airplane in the sky right now. People are fucked up. This is the first time in history, aside from Pearl Harbor, that America has been attacked. We're probably going to war.

SEAN: Holy shit!

MATTY: I want to sign up.

SEAN: No, you don't!

MATTY: Yes, I do.

SEAN: You sign up, I'll shoot your kneecaps before you go. Anyway, we're not gonna go to war. We don't need to do that. We're America. Why don't we just drop a big bomb?

MATTY: Where? Nobody's admitting to it.

SEAN: Well, fuck 'em all. Bomb the whole goddamn continent. Let's just make Israel an island. Or, fuck it, let's just go over there with a bunch of cargo planes and pick up all the Jews... Give 'em Hawaii or something and then just drop the big one.

MATTY: I fuckin' agree. But it's not that easy.

SEAN: Why not?

MATTY: I'm just happy to see you're on my goddamn side with this. You are my blood. Thank God.

SEAN: What?

MATTY: That fuckin' asshole Vic doesn't even give a shit... He's taking bets.

SEAN: Ohh... He owes me money. The Giants lost... It's all good, we'll make him buy breakfast and call it a ball... *(Seeing Matty's look)* What?

Vic walks back onstage holding his phone.

VIC: I can't believe it.

MATTY: What can't you believe?

VIC: What the fuck is happening here. That's what I can't believe.

MATTY: Thank you... Finally!

VIC: *(To Sean)* Do you realize what's happening?

SEAN: Well, now I do.

VIC: I can't fuckin' believe it.

MATTY: Sinking in now? What are you on? Delayed time? Have another cup of coffee. Join us!

VIC: They closed down all sporting events for the rest of the week. What the fuck is the matter with these people?

Matty jumps out of his seat and lunges for Vic.

MATTY: I swear to God...

Sean steps in between the two of them holding Matty back.

SEAN: What the fuck?

VIC: Get that fuckin' animal away from me.

MATTY: Fuckin' scumbag.

VIC: You need to see a doctor; you know that?

Matty lunges at Vic again. Sean pulls him away.

SEAN: What the fuck is going on? Jesus Christ, Matty.

MATTY: That man is just too ignorant to be around right now.

VIC: Fuck you, you fuckin' hypocrite.

SEAN: Hold on! I don't know what the fuck you're talking about, but as far as the man's IQ goes, that's your opinion, which you're entitled to, but you can't kick his ass because he's stupid.

VIC: I'm not stupid, asshole.

SEAN: I'm not calling you stupid.

MATTY: You know what? You're right. Live and let live. He wants to be stupid, it's none of my business.

VIC: Watch it!

MATTY: Watch what, you little pissant!

SEAN: Matty, you're being an asshole here!

MATTY: Don't you take his side. Don't you dare take his side.

SEAN: I'm not taking his side.

VIC: Don't take his fuckin' side.

SEAN: Goddamn it! I'm not on anybody's fuckin' side. I don't even know what the hell the problem is. I'm just trying to keep it real here. Now do you think it maybe would be possible that we all sit down, like gentlemen, and have a conversation? We are in a restaurant, nobody's here, fine, but still it is a place of business. Now let's just bring it down a notch. Can we do that? Just sit down? Matty? Vic…?

VIC: Sit down? I'm not gonna sit down and get my brain pounded in.

SEAN: Matty's not gonna hurt your brain.

MATTY: It'd be like beating a dead horse.

VIC: What the hell does that mean?

SEAN: Matty, sit!

MATTY: He sits down, I'll sit down.

SEAN: Vic?

VIC: Ditto. He sits down, I'll sit…

SEAN: How about on the count of three we all sit down? Huh?

Long pause.

MATTY: *(Sitting down)* This is ridiculous… I'm not five.

Vic and Sean both sit down.

SEAN: Okay, what's the problem?

MATTY: This asshole...

SEAN: You know what, it's not gonna work if you do it like that.

VIC: Thank you very much.

MATTY: Fine. Okay, I have a problem with the fact that HE could basically care less about the state...

VIC: Stop right there, objection...

SEAN: Overruled!

VIC: Your honor, the witness's testimony is bullshit. It is a matter of opinion whether or not I give a shit.

SEAN: Okay, here's the problem. If you don't let him speak, I will never be able to find out what it is you do or do not give a shit about.

MATTY: Thank you.

SEAN: I also will not be able to hear your side of the story if you don't let him finish first.

MATTY: Thank you, again.

SEAN: On that same note, when it is his turn to speak, Matty, you then will have to keep your comments to yourself. All good?

MATTY: Fine, but I would like to have it noted that I have not interrupted him.

VIC: I haven't spoken yet.

MATTY: Coincidentally, you haven't, but with that being the fact I have the right to say that I would have let you finish if you had been speaking.

VIC: You believe that, you believe in the Tooth Fairy.

SEAN: Okay, here's the deal, everyone is clear, no cross talk. Matty gets to tell his side of the story and then Vic gets to tell his. Everyone cool?

VIC: Fine with me.

MATTY: Great. So what was I saying before I was rudely interrupted...

VIC: Fuck you!

Matty stands up.

SEAN: Wait, Matty... Vic, please.

VIC: Sorry.

SEAN: Continue.

MATTY: *(Sitting back down)* I am having anxiety, I just want you to know.

SEAN: You'll be fine.

MATTY: *(Calming himself)* Okay, for the last time, I have a very big problem with the fact that we, as Americans, are in the middle of a crisis situation here and this…this…person is more worried about balancing his books than the goddamn fall of our nation.

Vic raises his hand.

MATTY: *(Cont'd)* Now if…

Vic has his hand raised, waving it in Sean's face.

SEAN: Matty, I'm sorry… Hold on… *(To Vic)* What is it?

VIC: Can I please make one little point here and then I will let him continue?

SEAN: *(Turning to Matty)* Matty, would you mind if he made one little point here and then he will let you continue?

MATTY: For the record, I am the cooperative one here.

SEAN: Noted and appreciated… What is it, Vic?

VIC: First of all, you're being dramatic. Second of all, I just cannot sit here and listen to this aggressive assault on my character without saying something. It's not human, Sean.

SEAN: But you will have your turn when he is done.

VIC: Can I just go first then? I think that would help me out a lot.

SEAN: Matty, would you mind if he spoke first?

MATTY: Yes, I mind.

VIC: Come on, Mr. Cooperation.

MATTY: I started this conversation, like a gentleman, I don't even know how long ago and he keeps interrupting me… I just don't think it would be fair.

SEAN: You'd be the bigger man if you let him speak first.

Long pause.

MATTY: Fine.

VIC: Great, I'm the small guy. Let's let the small guy talk first.

SEAN: You're not the small guy.

VIC: I don't care if I am... I'm the small guy, okay.

SEAN: Great.

VIC: The small guys says, the way I deal with something is of no business of yours, my friend...

MATTY: But you don't give a shit, I'm in your vicinity, it becomes my business.

SEAN: Cross talk.

VIC: Can I speak now please, big man? I thought it was my turn.

MATTY: You haven't shut up yet. You've been speaking.

SEAN: Matty.

VIC: Bullshit, you've been speaking.

SEAN: Vic.

MATTY: *(Standing up)* I can't do it. You know what? You are not even an American, you know that? That's right! You don't give a fuck about what happened... People are dead, asshole, but your phone is ringing.

VIC: *(Standing up)* Oh, now I'm not an American? I keep my emotions to myself, asshole... I've got a business, unlike you, you, you...

Sean jumps out of his seat and leaps onto the table.

SEAN: HEY... STOP IT! WE'RE IN A RESTAURANT. WE'RE IN A GODDAMN RESTAURANT!

VIC: *(Slowly coming off of his rant)* Jesus Christ, Sean, we're in a restaurant for crying out loud. Get off the table.

SEAN: *(Getting down)* Sorry.

MATTY: Jesus! Now you're the one who's screaming.

SEAN: Fine, I apologize.

VIC: Crazy runs in the family, I see.

MATTY: That's patriotism, asshole.

VIC: That's coo-coo shit, it ain't patriotism.

MATTY: *(Getting up)* I'm gonna kill him.

SEAN: *(Holding Matty)* Wait!

VIC: *(Backing up)* When was the last time you waved an American flag?

MATTY and SEAN: *(Simultaneously)* What?

VIC: *(Cont'd)* You need a goddamn tragedy to wave a flag.

MATTY: What are you talking about?

SEAN: Yeah, what the fuck are you talking about?

VIC: You're a front runner. You only bet on the Jets when they're in first place.

SEAN: Good time to make a bet, I'd say!

VIC: Thank you.

MATTY: Oh, I get it... I see what you're doing.

SEAN: Wanna explain it to me?

MATTY: I can't believe my patriotism is being graded by Vic the bookie.

VIC: Well, take a look, pal, 'cause it is...

MATTY: By a man who gives more of a shit about Dodger stadium being closed down than he does the crumbling of New York City. Am I losing my mind? Is it me? Am I wrong? What the fuck here? He's pissed about the goddamn sporting events, Sean! I wanna kill somebody.

SEAN: I see that.

MATTY: Am I crazy?

SEAN: I don't think so.

VIC: He wants to kill somebody and you don't think he's crazy! Maybe the both of you should go to group.

MATTY: I don't even know what the hell I'm talking about anymore.

VIC: The show must go on to Matty.

MATTY: What did you just say?

VIC: The show must go on.

MATTY: I heard it, I wanna know what the fuck it means.

SEAN: So do I!

VIC: It's a term used in the theater. It means no matter what happens, you do your show. You're sick, sorry, you gotta show up. Your girlfriend left you?

SEAN: That's a good one.

VIC: Sorry, you gotta show up. The World Trade Center blew up, sorry...

MATTY: Stop! I can't hear it anymore.

VIC: The truth is a motherfucker, I know.

MATTY: Oh, go call somebody.

SEAN: Yeah, go make a phone call, dude.

VIC: I ain't got nobody to call, Sean. Who do you want me to call? God bless PacBell, but I got no one to reach out and touch. Okay? They are all on his trip. The whole world apparently.

MATTY: I'm not on a trip, pal, I give a fuck. *(Standing with a hand over his heart)* A good God Bless American fuck.

VIC: Let me ask you a question, Mr. Jefferson. If you give such a fuck, how come you're sitting here ordering croissants and cappuccinos, huh?

MATTY and SEAN: *(Simultaneously)* What?

VIC: *(Cont'd)* If you're such a great fuckin' American, what are you doing here?

MATTY: I come here to get my mind together, I need a little distraction.

VIC: I got a distraction for you! Join the army!

MATTY: I just might, asshole.

SEAN: *(Standing up)* No, you won't. Okay, that's enough. You're not going to the army. Vic, obviously he is not taking this very well so you have to be a little compassionate.

VIC: He's been attacking me all morning.

MATTY: I'm not attacking you.

SEAN: Matty, you have to let him deal with things the way he wants to. You can't control that! He's got a good point. *(Reacting to Matty's look)* Not a great point.

VIC: Hey.

Sean turns to Vic and starts to whisper something to him.

MATTY: Oh, that's great. I'm the big, bad wolf, huh...? I'm the bad guy here? Don't you dare whisper behind my back, you patronizing little shit. It's bad enough that you agree with the little gimp.

VIC: I got your gimp right here.

SEAN: I said he had a point. I didn't say I agreed with it.

MATTY: Whatever.

SEAN: And don't call me names. I'm not him.

VIC: What's that supposed to mean, asshole?

SEAN: Oh, fuck both of you, man. Matty, you're my brother. I love you. Vic, you're my best friend. I love you. I'm just trying to keep the peace here. Would both of you please get off my, and each other's, dicks for a second. You're different. People are different! That's okay. We live in America, a place where you're entitled to your own opinion… To some extent anyway. Bro, you gotta let him do his own thing, although you might think it's wrong. And you, you have got to work on your people skills.

VIC: I got people skills.

SEAN: You add fire to the flame.

VIC: I don't add fire to the flame. I deal with people every day. I am a people person. A person of the people, if you will.

SEAN: I will. You're great with people.

VIC: Thank you.

SEAN: How bout a hug? *(Vic steps toward Sean)* Not me! HIM!

Matty looks at Sean as if to say, "You gotta be kidding me." Before Sean has a chance to speak, Vic runs over to Matty and gives him a big hug. He wraps his arms around Matty and dangles him by his waist.

SEAN: *(Cont'd)* Hug back.

Matty gives up and puts an awkward hang on Vic's shoulder.

SEAN: *(Cont'd)* See how nice…

VIC: Call it a ball…

MATTY: I'm gonna go get some Alka-seltzer…

VIC: You're going across the street?

MATTY: Yeah.

VIC: Good! Get me a pack of Dentine, and some smokes with that money you owe me, just kidding.

Matty stares at Vic as he walks off stage.

VIC: *(Cont'd)* Just breaking balls, my friend…

From offstage, a cup comes flying toward Vic's head. He ducks.

VIC: (*Cont'd, sitting back down*) Jesus Christ, I am not kidding, that man needs help. I mean, he genuinely worries me. If I got bad people skills, he's a fuckin' social retard... I mean, what do you think? Am I in left field over here? I mean, am I playing a different sport or what?

SEAN: I don't know, dude. He gets agro sometimes.

VIC: Agro? What the hell do you mean agro?

SEAN: Aggressive! He's very aggressive.

VIC: I know what the hell it means but it doesn't serve justice to the man's condition.

SEAN: Just stop, all right?

VIC: No! The man has a condition! He's like a polar bear or something.

SEAN: How's that?

VIC: It's like he's got two different personalities. One minute he's all smiles and thumbs up and then the next he's thumbs down with a frown. I mean, you know?

SEAN: Right! And that's like a polar bear how?

VIC: I don't know, I saw a special on wild life or the science channel or some shit. Maybe it was a koala. I don't know! Some bear stands for fucked up in the head. It's a condition, that people have!

SEAN: Oh, right! Well, I don't think he's like a polar bear. I just think he gets emotional, he's very opinionated. You know one time he was gonna kick my ass 'cause I said that Chevy was just a better built car than a Ford?

VIC: See that, small time?

SEAN: Which is obviously a no-brainer. Ford can't touch Chevy, but from years of dealing, and living with such an opinionated man, you learn to let it go... Hence, people skills.

VIC: Fuck you on that, but wait a minute, not small time, big time, big time in fact. I'm seeing a pattern here.

SEAN: A what?

VIC: A pattern.

SEAN: You're seeing a pattern, like you're hallucinating, what? Reds and blues?

VIC: No, asshole, a pattern. Chevy...Ford.

SEAN: Cars.

VIC: That's right. American cars.

SEAN: No comparison?

VIC: Forget the comparison. Keep the pattern.

SEAN: Not seeing it.

VIC: Oh, I am.

SEAN: How's it look?

VIC: Great. You still can't see it?

SEAN: Nope.

VIC: Look closer, 'cause I can see it clear.

SEAN: Do you?

VIC: The rain is gone, my friend.

SEAN: And what can you see?

VIC: Your brother has what I would call "American," very specific, "American Polar Bear disease."

SEAN: Really?

VIC: Think about it! These are the things that set him off. American cars and American disasters. Other American things that we will, I'm sure, discover through further research, but for now this is what we have. Cars and planes. Planes and cars... Wait a minute! I'm seeing another pattern. Holy shit! It's things that are American, that also take fuel... Wait another minute, maybe I'm reaching now, let's backtrack for a second...

SEAN: You're not reaching now, you're reaching in general. That's enough, stop it. My brother is not bipolar...

VIC: That's it! Bipolar, that's it!

SEAN: Right, he has no illness associated to cars or planes, or to anything American for that matter. He's just a passionate guy. When he feels strongly about something, he forms an opinion, and that opinion becomes law. Don't try to fight it 'cause you will lose, just get on the bus.

VIC: Fuck that. I don't want to get on the bus, I got my own opinions.

SEAN: Fine, then argue.

VIC: You're missing the point here, Sean. The man's impossible.

SEAN: You're missing the point. I'm not gonna sit here and listen to you talk shit behind my brother's back, let's just end it.

VIC: Fine, it's a ball... But for the record, I'm fucked out! I'm not talking shit! I care, therefore I am.

SEAN: Great!

A LADY walks on stage holding a dozen individually wrapped roses. She walks up to Vic.

LADY: (*Accent*) Would you like to buy a rose?

Long pause.

VIC: What do I look like, a fuckin' faggot?

SEAN: Dude!

The lady turns to Sean.

LADY: Would you like to buy a rose?

VIC: Hey, lady, señorita, nobody wants the fuckin' roses.

SEAN: Vic, stop! Miss, we don't need any roses, but thank you!

LADY: No rose?

VIC: I can't take it, Sean.

SEAN: Whatever!

VIC: (*Standing up and pulling out a money clip*) How's this, lady? I'll give you five dollars to just go away and leave me alone.

She takes the money and pulls a rose out of the bunch.

VIC: (*Cont'd*) No, I don't want the rose... I don't want...

She insists.

VIC: (*Cont'd*) Okay... That's very nice... Thank you!

The lady walks offstage.

VIC: (*Cont'd*) Those people drive me crazy. If I want a rose, I'll go to the flower shop.

The lady walks back on stage.

LADY: Roses?

VIC: (*Stands up*) NO! No roses! I'll tell you what! Here's twenty dollars. Don't bother anybody else today, all right? Give me the roses.

She hands him the roses and walks offstage.

LADY: Thank you!

VIC: You're welcome!

Vic walks back to the table holding the whole bouquet of roses. He throws them on the table.

VIC: (*Cont'd*) Great, I've worked up an appetite, let's eat. You hungry?

SEAN: No, I'll puke if I eat.

VIC: What's the problem?

SEAN: I don't want to talk about it.

VIC: What's the matter?

SEAN: I don't know. I don't want to talk about it.

VIC: Well, what's the problem?

SEAN: The problem is I don't want to talk about it.

VIC: That's very unhealthy.

SEAN: No, doctor. I'll tell you what's unhealthy. It's unhealthy to ask someone repeatedly what's wrong with them when they keep insisting that they don't want to talk about it. It's unhealthy because not only are you not helping, but you're creating another problem on top of the original.

VIC: Well, that's what I want to talk about. The original. I'm not trying to cause another problem.

SEAN: I know that. But I don't want to talk about it.

VIC: The original?

SEAN: No!

VIC: Then what?

SEAN: What?

VIC: What don't you want to talk about?

SEAN: ANYTHING, DUDE!

VIC: Fine, but you don't need to snap. I just care!

SEAN: And therefore you are!

VIC: Exactly.

SEAN: Great.

VIC: Good! Just so we understand each other.

SEAN: I don't understand anything.

VIC: Was that a fishing reel?

SEAN: What?

VIC: Well, you're saying some things, like you don't want to talk about it, which I clearly respect, but then you say other things that I take to be your way of letting me know that in actuality you do wanna talk. And I will play along and swallow that hook, but I just wanna make sure first that there's actually a hook there in the water. The water being this general area.

SEAN: I don't know, dude.

VIC: Express, Sean.

SEAN: I got problems.

VIC: A man is dead without them.

SEAN: Yeah, well, it feels selfish.

VIC: What do you mean?

SEAN: I mean very serious things have gone down in the world today and it just seems selfish to talk about my miniscule problems.

VIC: Well, that's a good thing.

SEAN: To be selfish?

VIC: No, to be yourself at a time like this. You're a very self-absorbed kind of guy.

SEAN: No, I'm not.

VIC: I mean that in the nicest way possible. What I mean is that you care about yourself. A LOT.

SEAN: Right.

VIC: No, that's not what I mean. You care very much about what happens to you.

SEAN: That's the same thing, it's just worded nicer.

VIC: I'm getting all screwed up here and it's not coming out right.

SEAN: Just forget it. I'm a self-absorbed asshole.

VIC: No! Look, what I mean is that you don't walk around with a lack of thought. You think for yourself, and for other people. You care, you're a thinker. You think a lot. And I think, at a time like this, it is good to feel the things that you normally feel. It's good to feel! No matter what the circumstances. I mean, don't act like your brother. Don't shut down! Feel! Grieve over the loss, if you must, but then come back to reality and live. Feel…! Please feel.

SEAN: I'm feeling.

VIC: Now, express.

SEAN: Okay, I just…

Vic pulls his phone out of his pocket.

VIC: Hold on one second. (*Into phone*) Vic here… I know, can you believe that shit?… It's fuckin' ridiculous, I know… Well, the good news is, we still got the fight… Of course I'm taking the fight, who said I wasn't taking the fight… Fuck him, what do you think I am?… All right, a couple of bucks on the Cuban… All good? It's a ball.

Vic hangs up the phone and puts it away.

VIC: (*Cont'd*) Sorry.

SEAN: That's pretty rude.

VIC: What do you want me to do?

SEAN: I don't know, we're in the middle of something here.

VIC: Hey pal, I gotta pay the bills. Okay? You have any idea how fucked I'm gonna be with this whole thing? Who knows how long this shit's gonna last?

SEAN: Well, it's just that I was having a hard time saying something, and I was just about to get into it, and then the phone rings. You pick it up. It's a little annoying.

VIC: Well, I don't mean to annoy you, but business is business.

SEAN: I understand that, it's just…

VIC: I care!

SEAN: I know that, but…

VIC: I could never be accused of not caring…

SEAN: No, you couldn't, but…

VIC: It's just that I have things, too, Sean.

SEAN: Of course, but…

VIC: So you understand!

SEAN: Right!

VIC: But, more importantly, you were saying.

Sean takes a deep breath.

SEAN: Amber.

VIC: What about her?

SEAN: She just…

Vic pulls his phone out of his pocket again.

VIC: Hold on one second. (*Into phone*) Vic here… What? What when? Get the fuck outta here… Those motherfuckers! What the hell is the matter with these people? (*To Sean*) I'll be right back. (*Walking offstage talking into the phone*) How the fuck could they cancel the fight? This fight is so important… (*O.S.*) BUT HE'S CUBAN!

LIGHTS OUT

ACT TWO—*a few hours later*

NOTE: *Through this next scene a WOMAN, at some point, should walk onstage and sit down. She should be waiting for service and do whatever she feels, without any dialogue, as to work off the situation. The situation being that she gets no service. Sean and the waitress get so involved with their conversation that they, particularly the waitress, pay no attention to the waiting customer. Eventually the customer must leave before the scene is over.*

Lights up, music fades.

Toni, the waitress, cleans off one of the tables. Sean enters from the bathroom.

SEAN: Hey.

TONI: Hey.

SEAN: I'm sorry about the mess this morning.

TONI: It's okay.

SEAN: And all the noise and everything else.

TONI: It's no big deal.

SEAN: Yeah. We eat here every day. We're, for the most part, pretty decent people. I mean we don't usually scream or yell and destroy shit. I mean, that's not our normal behavior. I mean, I'm not neccessarily normal in general. I mean, I'm not crazy or anything. I'm just not normal like boring normal. But who's normal anyway? Maybe you are. I don't want to, I mean, I don't even know you, you may be normal. I don't want to jump to any conclusions. I don't want to insult you. Boy, I sound like an idiot right now. I'm just gonna shut up.

TONI: It's fine. You sound fine.

SEAN: Thanks. I was just trying to say that I feel a little off is all.

TONI: It's understandable. So do I.

SEAN: Yeah…weird day.

TONI: Weird first day.

SEAN: Oh, you just started working here?

TONI: Yeah.

SEAN: Yeah, we eat here every day. I've never seen you before.

TONI: That's probably because it's my first day.

SEAN: Yeah. No, it's just that we come here every day. Which I've told you three times now. You're gonna have to excuse me. I'm a complete idiot right now.

TONI: No, you're not. You're just…

SEAN: An idiot. It's fine.

Toni offers Sean her hand.

TONI: Toni.

Sean takes her hand.

SEAN: Sean.

TONI: Nice to meet you, Sean.

SEAN: Nice to meet you, Toni. Toni! I love it when girls have boy names.

TONI: Really?

SEAN: I mean, you don't look like a boy.

TONI: Oh no?

SEAN: Is it even possible that I could say any more stupid shit right now?

TONI: It's okay. I think you're cute.

SEAN: And I think you're very cute… But I want you to know that something is very wrong with me right now, because, on top of being cute, I can usually be pretty charming, as well.

TONI: Are you trying to charm me?

He takes a beat to think about it.

SEAN: I don't know what the hell I'm doing. I mean, would that be wrong if I was? If I was flirting with you, would that be wrong?

TONI: I don't know. Why would it be?

SEAN: For a lot of reasons. To start with, I might have a girlfriend. I mean, that's up in the air. The fact that I hate her and she tortures me is irrelevant. But let's just put that aside for a couple of seconds. Let's just say that today is Tuesday.

TONI: We don't even have to say it. It's a fact. It is Tuesday.

SEAN: No, I mean like a regular Tuesday. If today were a regular Tuesday. I'd be flirting indefinitely. No doubt. On any other day. But I'm guilty. I feel guilty. Do you even wanna hear this?

TONI: Yeah.

SEAN: Good, 'cause I gotta let it out.

TONI: Go ahead.

SEAN: Thanks. I feel guilty because I'm thinking about my own shit. I keep trying to tell myself that on a day like today, who cares about my miniscule problems, but it's not working, it's making me think about them even more. And the more I think about them, the more shallow and self-obsessed I feel. I mean, I'm feeling it right now. Every word that comes out of my mouth drives me one step closer to being a complete asshole. As I speak, I'm telling myself to shut up… Anyway, the answer to your question is… What was your question exactly?

TONI: I don't know. Did I ask one?

SEAN: I think so… Flirting! Are we flirting?

TONI: I guess so.

SEAN: And that's okay?

TONI: Why not?

SEAN: That was the question.

She smiles, quietly gets a kick out of him, and then continues.

TONI: Well, I think you shouldn't feel bad. Or selfish, or guilty. For thinking about yourself. Flirting with me when you have a girlfriend's a different story… But about how you feel, I think it's normal. I've been sort of feeling the same way. All day it's like I'm in this cloud. I'm confused, I'm sad, confused about why I'm sad. I've only been here for a few days now, so I don't really even know anybody. I feel pretty alone. Thinking about how I'm all alone. That's selfish.

SEAN: I don't think so.

TONI: Right. And I don't think it's so bad that you feel the way you feel.

SEAN: All right, keep going, I'm getting better.

TONI: I just moved here from Texas, but I'm originally from New York, and my mom's still out there. And that's another reason I feel selfish. All day long, all I can think about is how she's feeling. How she's alone,

I'm alone, how I wish I could be there with her... I'm more worried about her than I am about what happened. And she lives all the way up in the Bronx.

SEAN: Which is where the Yankees play and is far, far away from the lower part of that island...that island being Manhattan.

TONI: Right.

SEAN: Sorry, I just wanted you to know that I understood you and that I knew where the Bronx was.

TONI: Right.

SEAN: Is your mom okay?

TONI: Yeah, she's okay. She's freaked out a little bit.

SEAN: That's understandable.

TONI: Yeah, but my point was that it's normal to feel however it is you're feeling.

SEAN: Because you feel the same way?

TONI: Not exactly the same way, but yeah.

SEAN: Close enough.

TONI: I don't have a girlfriend.

SEAN: Oh, right...right...you said you felt alone. Do you feel alone?

TONI: Yeah.

SEAN: If you had a girlfriend, would you feel alone?

TONI: If I was you, maybe I would.

SEAN: You're not me.

TONI: I like guys, not girls.

SEAN: You're making this very difficult. If you had a boyfriend... Do you have a boyfriend?

TONI: No.

SEAN: Good. If you did, would you feel alone?

TONI: No, I guess not.

SEAN: Then I wouldn't either, I officially don't have a girlfriend, and I don't want to discuss it further.

TONI: Fine. I'm over it.

SEAN: Good... Would you like to cuddle with me tonight and not feel alone? Take it from there and see what happens.

Long pause.

TONI: Why not?

SEAN: That's a great answer.

TONI: I'm glad you liked it.

SEAN: I did. Should we leave now and get started.

TONI: I don't get off until six.

SEAN: No one's here. Let's just leave.

TONI: I'd love to, but I can't. I've been wanting to leave all day.

SEAN: Sorry, I'm just excited.

TONI: Can you wait a little while?

SEAN: Yeah, but I'm a little fragile right now, so don't take advantage.

TONI: Okay.

She starts to leave.

TONI: (*Cont'd*) I'm gonna get back to work... Hey, I'm glad we talked.

SEAN: Yes, it is. But we're gonna cuddle, too, right?

TONI: Yeah, but can we start with a ride home. Can you give me a ride home?

SEAN: Yes... Wait, no... I have no car... I mean, I have a car, I just don't know where it is...

TONI: Okay.

SEAN: It's a long story.

TONI: You could tell me while you walk me home.

He looks horrified.

TONI: (*Cont'd*) It's only a couple of miles.

He smiles.

SEAN: I'd love to walk you home.

TONI: Good.

Toni heads toward the door.

TONI: (*Cont'd*) You know, I walked here this morning, it wasn't so nice. Maybe the walk home will be nicer.

SEAN: I know what you mean!

She waves and exits.

Sean walks around the stage for a few beats, and then sits back down.

SEAN: (*Cont'd*) Everything's going to be fine!

MATTY: (*O.S.*) Get away from me, you fuckin' asshole.

SEAN: Almost everything.

Matty walks back on stage followed by Vic. Matty looks like he is going to explode.

VIC: (*Approaching Matty*) Why don't you just calm down!

MATTY: (*Gathering his things off the table*) Sean, keep him the fuck away from me, I swear to God. I'm not fuckin' playing right now.

SEAN: Vic, back up… Matty, what the hell are you doing?

MATTY: (*Upset, for real*) Opinions are opinions, Sean, I guess I can deal with that, but when this motherfucker crosses a line and takes…

VIC: I'm trying to keep you from killing the fuckin' guy.

MATTY: It's called betrayal, buddy.

VIC: You're twice his fuckin' size, should I just stand there and let watch you beat his fuckin' head in?

MATTY: I don't give a fuck how big he was! If he was six-six, I would have done the same thing.

SEAN: Matty, what did you do?

VIC: Tell him! See what he thinks!

MATTY: (*Proudly*) I just beat the shit out of some Arab cocksucker in the parking lot. Do you have a problem with that?

SEAN: I don't know what happened.

MATTY: Well, then I'll tell you... I'm walking back from the liquor store and I see this GUY! He's giving me looks. He's not American-looking. He ain't fucking European-looking either. He's got brown fucking skin and a beard down to here. Ya get me so far?

SEAN: He's from the Middle East?

MATTY: That's right! This Middle Eastern, terrorist-looking asshole is giving me looks.

VIC: Who's giving you looks? You were calling them camel-fuckers all morning.

MATTY: 'Cause that's what they are. They are bad people. I call bad people bad names.

VIC: How the fuck do you know what he is?

SEAN: Vic, shut the fuck up.

MATTY: I don't give a fuck what he is. Fuck them all. Fuck him and fuck the rest of 'em.

VIC: That's great!

SEAN: So, what happened?

MATTY: So, he's giving me this look, so I say, "Hey man, God bless America!" Isn't that what I said, Vic?

VIC: I don't recall exactly what you said, I was standing...

MATTY: Well, that's what I said! God bless America, and when I said it to him, he mumbled something in his greasy fuckin' language and walked away.

VIC: And that's the part. How do you know what the fuck he said?

MATTY: Well, it sure as shit wasn't the Pledge of Allegiance.

VIC: But how do you know? How do you know who the hell he was? He wasn't wearing a turban.

SEAN: So, what happened? He says something in not-English, and then what?

VIC: I'll tell you what. Your brother runs over and smacks the guy in the mouth.

MATTY: Damn straight I did.

VIC: And then he proceeds to kick the living shit out of him...

MATTY: And then this motherfucker runs over to the piece of shit's rescue, and pulls me off the fuckin' guy.

SEAN: What happened to the guy?

MATTY: I don't know! I was too busy trying not to kick my so-called lifelong friend's ass here that the little motherfucker got up and ran away.

VIC: And thank God, you might have killed him.

MATTY: I wanted to! I wanted to kill him.

SEAN: Matty!

MATTY: I did!

VIC: For what? For saying something that you didn't understand? How do you know what he said?

MATTY: How the fuck do you know what he said? How do you know that he wasn't about to plant a bomb down the street?

VIC: I don't, but neither do you. I do believe in this country, you are innocent until proven guilty.

MATTY: But he isn't from this fuckin' country.

VIC: How do you know? How the fuck do you know where he's from?

MATTY: Instinct, motherfucker…

VIC: Oh, that's great.

MATTY: Fuck instinct. Ray Charles could see he's not from this country.

VIC: You see, Sean?

MATTY: I reacted off of his action. It's all I needed. He grunted and turned his back to me.

VIC: Maybe he was scared of you.

MATTY: And you call yourself a friend. I can't believe you stuck up for this guy. Even if I was dead wrong…

VIC: You were.

MATTY: You're supposed to have my back anyway.

VIC: I do have your back! You didn't need any help. What, should I help you kick his ass?

SEAN: All right, look. Matty, get your shit. Let's get the fuck outta here. We will continue this conversation elsewhere. This guy might have called the police…

MATTY: Let him call. I'm not going anywhere.

SEAN: Use your head. I kow you're mad, but use your fuckin' head. Now, let's go! Vic, meet us at our place.

MATTY: First of all, I don't want to talk to him, he's not coming to our place, second of all, I'M NOT MOVING!

VIC: You don't want to talk to me anymore. We're not friends now?

SEAN: Of course you're friends.

VIC: (*Emotional*) No, fuck it! You don't like me anymore? I stuck up for that guy, so you wouldn't kill him, now you hate me? Ten fuckin' years, and now you hate me all of a sudden?

SEAN: He's just upset, Vic.

VIC: No, he means it. And that's okay. But I got something to say. What if that guy had blonde hair and blue eyes?

MATTY: What?

VIC: What if he reacted that way to you and he had blonde hair and blue eyes? Like your brother here. What if he was an Aryan like you? Would you have slapped him?

MATTY: What, are you calling me a fuckin' Nazi?

VIC: Fuckin' right I am. Now answer the question.

MATTY: I should smack you right in the face.

VIC: Be my guest. Just answer the question first.

SEAN: Let's get the fuck outta here, please.

MATTY: No, I'll answer the question.

VIC: Thank you.

MATTY: No! The answer is no! I wouldn't have thought twice! I would have walked away, and not thought twice. You want to call it racism, go ahead, but I think that my skepticism of a man of looks like that at a time like this and his reaction to what I said, the motherfucker got what he deserved. So, call it what you want.

VIC: You want to know what he said? He said peace. You said God Bless America and he said peace.

MATTY: How the fuck do you know?

VIC: 'Cause I speak his language.

MATTY: What?

SEAN: Oh shit!

VIC: That's right. I know what he said and I also know what he feels like. I'm an American! I've lived here my whole life. New York, Chicago, and Los Angeles, but my father was born in Afghanistan. That's right. I'm half of what you hate. You want to know why I stuck up for that guy, 'cause I don't imagine what it's like to be him, I am him. Or maybe I'm wrong! Maybe he was a terrorist. Maybe he was on his way to blow something up, but I'm not gonna blow nothing up so I gotta give him the benefit of the doubt. My whole life I'm scared of shit like this! That's why I lie about who I am. So that guy's got a bigger set of balls than me, I guess. You don't know what it's like to be me. To know that people would look at me differently if they really knew where I came from, and believe me, they would. I saw it with my pop growing up. Why do you think we moved so much? You think people just started hating Persians and Afghanis this morning, I don't think you do. I think you know that people have hated them, us, me, for as long as long can go. But I want to let you know something, if there was a war tomorrow, and we had to go over there and fight those motherfuckers, I'd be standing straight with an M-16 in my hands and an American flag strapped to my back. My father left that country to become an American and that's what he is, and that's what I am. I wish people could understand that, but they don't. So not even the closest people in the world to me know who I really am.

After what feels like forever.

SEAN: I knew.

MATTY: What?

SEAN: I knew. I've known for years.

MATTY: I'm fucked up right now.

VIC: Sorry.

MATTY: What the fuck is happening? How the fuck did you know?

SEAN: I figured it out a long time ago, but who cares anyway?

MATTY: Well, I think I fuckin' care… I don't know what about, though. Wait a minute… How could you not tell me?

SEAN: 'Cause who gives a shit? I know that I had a hard time with it when I figured it out, and it took a lot for me to get over it.

MATTY: Did you know he knew?

VIC: Nope.

SEAN: I didn't want to embarass him. It's bad enough he's got to live a lie his whole life. I just kept it to myself.

MATTY: Wait. I'm still fuckin' pissed here, but I don't know about what.

SEAN: Look, you love the guy. Who gives a shit where he's from or where his dad's from, or his uncle or whatever? Who cares? That's what happened to me when I found out. I didn't know whether I was mad 'cause he lied or because I was a bigot or what. But what I did figure out is that it doesn't matter. He's your brother! And I also figured out he must have had a really good reason for lying about it, because he's too good of a guy to lie for no reason. Yeah, at first, I was like, "Fuck that fuckin' camel-jockey motherfucker." Sorry, but then I was like, "Wait, this is my friend, my best friend!" My best friend, who gives a shit! I'd kill for him and he'd kill for you. And at the end of the day, nothing else matters.

MATTY: So, I guess that I'm just the big fuckin' asshole then, huh?

A MAN walks onstage carrying a plate with some food. He sits down at a table on the other side of the stage and begins to eat his food.

SEAN: Yes... No, I mean that...

MATTY: Am I the asshole, Sean?

SEAN: No, you're just confused.

VIC: And angry.

SEAN: And angry.

MATTY: I'm joining the fuckin' army. Out of sheer confusion, I'm signing up tomorrow.

SEAN: Would you stop saying that?

MATTY: Why? What difference does it make? Nothing is really making that much sense to me right now, Sean!

SEAN: So, you're gonna go join the army. "Hey, I'm confused, give me a gun!" That's great.

MATTY: I'm fuckin' serious right now.

SEAN: So am I!

VIC: Can I say something?

SEAN: Yes, thank you, please do.

VIC: If you're serious about this, I want you to know, as your friend, I have your back.

SEAN: Shut the fuck up, Vic.

VIC: I mean it! He wants to go fight for what he truly believes in, I say you can't stop the man.

SEAN: Who the fuck are you, dude?

VIC: Look, I said a lot of things today, but if he feels so strongly about it, then I say so be it.

MATTY: Thank you... I think!

SEAN: Fuck you, I think.

VIC: Look, the man says he wants to kill people. He's been saying it all day long! I say let's make sure he's killing the right people.

MATTY: Oh, I get it!

SEAN: Hey, look, Vic. I have no problem with killing people in general! Like, if other people want to kill other people, that's fine with me. I just don't want my brother involved. Is that okay?

MAN: I was just gonna say listen to the smart guy right up until that last comment.

SEAN: Excuse me?

MAN: Yeah, you were speaking the truth right up until you said the no problem with killing people part.

SEAN: Right! Well, I appreciate your concern...

MATTY: (*To Vic*) I'm serious about this.

VIC: As you should be, and I support what you...

SEAN: Hey! Shut up, Vic!

MAN: You guys all need to change the way you think.

SEAN: You shut up too, please. Sorry to be rude, but this is a family matter. Okay? Mind your business.

MAN: Okay, but you sound like you need help. And your friend there definitely needs help.

VIC: Who the fuck are you?

MAN: Just a peaceful soul who can see beyond violence.

VIC: What are you, fuckin' John Lennon?

MATTY: Hey, buddy. Why don't you do yourself a favor and eat your meal, all right?

MAN: That's what I'm doing, brother. Just eating a meal and trying to help a friend.

MATTY: Oh, yeah. How's that?

MAN: Talking about war and killing people? What we need to do is come together.

SEAN: It's actually John Lennon. Good call!

MATTY: You know what? That's right! As Americans, we need to come together.

MAN: Wrong, my friend. As human beings, we need to come together.

MATTY: And how do you suppose we do that, brother?

MAN: Change our ways. Violence breeds violence.

VIC: Yeah, and sticking your nose in other people's business breeds ass kicking.

MATTY: What should we do then? Huh? Sit back and do nothing? "It's a shame what happened, really hope it won't happen again, but violence breeds violence." So we'll just take the loss on this one? Is that, sort of what...

MAN: We need to find a new approach.

MATTY: And what might that approach be? Two wrongs don't make a right?

MAN: It's a good start! We as Americans see the world as a square, we need to start looking at the circle.

VIC: What the fuck does that mean?

MAN: It means we need to stop and take a look at what we put out there. People in the world, other parts of the world, not just our precious America, need help, and they cry out! Maybe if we would think more about those things, what happened this morning might not have taken place.

SEAN: My man, you really need to stop right there, and mind your own business, seriously, just end it. Go back to Canada or something.

MATTY: Wait just a fuckin' second, are you trying to imply that what happened this morning is our fault?

MAN: If the shoe fits.

MATTY: (*Standing up*) Let's see if this shoe fits, mother...

SEAN: Matty, stop! Let the idiot be.

MAN: Idiot? I thought you were the passivist?

SEAN: Hey, I'd like to kick your ass, too, but I got a date tonight.

MAN: Good, that's great, kick my ass. Kick everybody's ass. We're America. The brave, the wealthy, the powerful. I'll tell you what! We need to get out of that mentality. We need to start dealing with these people, the so-called little people, with some compassion. For years they have been begging for our help, and what do we do, we sit back and do nothing. It's a shame that it takes something big like this to wake us up. And it's a shame that we have no clue how to do it right once we've awoken.

SEAN: That's really profound.

MATTY: I'm having a real hard time listening to this shit.

MAN: I'm sorry.

MATTY: So, what's the answer? You sound like you got it all figured out.

MAN: I do.

MATTY: Well, what the fuck are you doing here? Go tell someone!

MAN: I've been telling people.

MATTY: So, what is it?

MAN: The answer?

MATTY: Yeah.

MAN: You tell me.

MATTY: Bomb the motherfuckers. Kill 'em all! That's my answer.

MAN: Yeah! Let's strong arm them. It's real easy to strong arm other little countries, so why don't we?

MATTY: You want to know why we strong arm other countries, because we earned the right to. You fuck with us, these are the repercussions.

MAN: Yeah, well those rights we earned got us a few thousand dead this morning, and we'll just repeat the pattern, won't we?

MATTY: What the fuck did we do, though? We didn't do anything.

MAN: You just answered your own question. We didn't do anything. All those people are asking for is a hug.

MATTY: Oh, that just fuckin' did it. They want a hug! Did you hear that, Sean?

SEAN: I don't think so.

MAN: It's a metaphor.

MATTY: No. They want a hug! Well, all they had to do was ask. And what you're saying is that for the lack of hug giving on our part, we get what we deserve?

MAN: Well, it goes a little deeper than that. But, basically, yes.

MATTY: Well, you're a fuckin' genius. And what we should do now is retaliate with a plethora of open arms, right? Fly over there and drop a hug bomb?

MAN: (*Standing up*) Well, I guess some people are just unreachable.

MATTY: That's right! Them! They're unreachable. People like the ones that took those planes this morning can only be dealt with one way. And we all, deep down, know what that way is. Kill 'em. Why? 'Cause they are unreachable, ignorant assholes.

MAN: Say what you want, but I'm ashamed to be American today, and if you ask me, you are the ignorant ones.

MATTY: (*Moving toward the man*) I'm gonna kick his fuckin' ass.

Vic jumps in and holds Matty back.

VIC: You want to know something, you dumb, peaceful cocksucker? I'm proud to be an American. You want to know why? 'Cause I'm guaranteed, constitutionally guaranteed, the pursuit of happiness. Yeah sure, we fuck up, everyone fucks up. But this country, America, is by far the best the world has been able to do. I mean, you show me a country that bombs a motherfucker, and then feeds their kids at the same time. Who does that? We do! Why? 'Cause that's how we fuckin' do it. The reason this country is great is not because of our wealth, or success, or power, or whatever bullshit you were saying, but it's because of the people who live here. We're a bunch of immigrants, Polacks, Wops, Micks, Jews, and yes, camelfuckers, and the reason we're the leaders of the free world is because we worked for it. Pulled ourselves up by our goddamned bootstraps and made it happen. Fuck complaining! Handle your shit, and that's what we do! There are bad people in this world, hopefully we can find out who they are, and then deal with them accordingly. They have to be dealt with! And who's gonna do it? We are! Why? Because we can! And again, that's how we fuckin' do it!

MATTY: YEAH, MOTHERFUCKER!

SEAN: HOW YOU LIKE ME NOW, BITCH?

MAN: Well, I can see that there's no getting through to you people.

The man gathers his things and walks offstage.

VIC: (*Kicking him in the ass*) Go on, ya motherfucker.

Vic turns back to Matty and Sean… Matty walks over to Vic and throws his arms around him.

SEAN: (*Joining the hug*) That shit was fly!

Matty and Vic slowly break out of the hug.

VIC: You know what really gets me?… We been sitting in this place for the last eight hours… Let's get outta here! GI Joe, pay the bill already.

MATTY: Wait, we still have a major issue here, okay?

SEAN: Please, no more issues. I've had enough issues today.

MATTY: No, no. I still have a problem with him, and it has nothing to do with the fact that he's a camelfucker.

VIC: I got your camelfucker right here, asshole.

MATTY: Before we leave, I want it known that I'm not paying the bill. I never bet any money on the Giants.

VIC: You most certainly did.

MATTY: No, I didn't. I hate the fuckin' Giants, I'd never bet on them. I'm a Jets fan.

VIC: (*Pulling out a sheet of paper*) One of you bet on the Giants, I know that. I got it on the books.

SEAN: I bet the Giants game, and they lost.

VIC: Oh, it was you. My bad, but either way, it's a ball, one of you can buy the meal.

SEAN: Check the books, slick, I bet the other way.

Vic carefully looks at the books.

VIC: Sonofabitch!

MATTY: What?

VIC: I guess the meal's on me.

MATTY: Hah!

VIC: I can't believe this shit...

Sean sits down.

SEAN: I'm hungry all of a sudden.

Matty joins him.

MATTY: Me, too!

VIC: Fuck you both!

MATTY: I'm starving! I haven't had a thing all day. I'm gonna eat a lot. WAITRESS!

SEAN: Toni!

Lights begin to fade.

VIC: Sean, don't order too much, because I'm not gonna be pulling in much dough for the next little while, and more importantly, it's late. Your metabolism is getting slower...

Lights out! Frank Sinatra's "New York, New York" plays.

THE END

I wrote A Man and His Barbecue *as a gift for my father's sixtieth birthday. Originally, I had no intentions of ever seeing the parody performed until after I gave it to him. He loved it, and insisted on finding a way to have it produced.*

So, I decided to write a short collection of one-acts that would lead up to the couple in the parody. The characters and the tone of the plays would be completely different from the original, but the idea being: two people would meet, fall in love, break up, long for each other, and then end up back together.

For some ridiculous reason, I find it interesting that we often find ourselves paying particularly close attention to our romantic lives during holidays. The feeling of being alone, in love, or going through a breakup always seems to feel enhanced during these times. Though just another day of the year, whatever's going on automatically carries more weight and seems more dramatic just because a baby's born, someone dies, or something's discovered on that specific date. (Or, of course, if Hallmark decides it's a good idea for us to celebrate.)

Minor Holidays

Four One-Act Plays About Love

Minor Holidays *was originally produced by The Playhouse West Repertory Theater Company—artistic director, Robert Carnegie, at Playhouse West Studio Two, North Hollywood, California, March 2002. It was directed by Scott Caan; stage management, lights, and sound design by Zachariah Moura; set design by the lovely Molly and her three assistants. The cast was as follows:*

They Meet *aka* The Kiss
MAN..................... *Mark Pellegrino*
WOMAN............. *Laura Katz*

How It Works *aka* Tom & Jerry
TOM..................... *Kenny Moskow*
JERRY................... *Chris Mancuso*

The Pain *aka* The Shrew
PATRICK............. *Val Lauren*
KYLE.................... *Vince Jolivette*

The End *aka* A Man and His Barbecue
WOMAN............. *Robyn Cohen*
MAN.................... *Scott Caan*

They Meet
AKA

The Kiss

Minor Holidays—They Meet

LIGHTS UP

A bedroom with a table and chairs up onstage.

A MAN sits on the edge of the bed smoking a cigarette. He looks like he's contemplating putting a bullet in his head despite the New Year's Eve party hat he's wearing.

The sounds of the party are heard offstage.

WOMAN: (*O.S.*) ASSHOLE! Fucking kill you!

A WOMAN enters, stage left. She notices she's not alone.

WOMAN: What an asshole.

MAN: Yeah?

WOMAN: Yeah.

MAN: All right.

Long pause. She scans the room.

WOMAN: Do you wanna know why?

MAN: Why what?

WOMAN: Why he's an asshole.

MAN: I guess. If you want to tell me.

WOMAN: Whatever.

MAN: Okay. Whatever.

WOMAN: Yes or no?

MANL Excuse me?

WOMAN: Yes or no?

MAN: Yes or no what?

WOMAN: Yes or no, do you want to hear about the asshole.

MAN: Sure, lady, yeah. I'd love to hear all about it.

WOMAN: *Lady?*

MAN: Yeah, *lady!*

WOMAN: That's what you say? *Lady?*

MAN: I don't know. What should I say?

WOMAN: Well, not *lady.* Who says *lady?* I mean, that's what you say? *Lady?* Lady's just so…I mean… *Lady?*

MAN: Fine! Miss, ma'am…honey…baby…whatever.

WOMAN: Sorry, guy!

MAN: All right, look, I apologize. Okay! I'm sorry, I didn't mean to… It's just that I'm sort of in a…

WOMAN: Happy New Year!

MAN: Yeah! Happy New Year to you, too.

She sits down at the table and starts to pour herself a drink.

WOMAN: Right.

MAN: Right.

They just stare at each other for a few seconds. The Woman studies him and then leans in.

WOMAN: So, do you want me to tell you about the asshole or not?

MAN: Look, *lady,* it seems like you're dying to tell me about the asshole. So, if that's what you want to do, then go ahead and do it. Please! I'm gonna have to be honest, though, I won't know which asshole we're talking about. I've seen a lot of them since I got here. In fact, to be more honest, as far as I'm concerned, they are all assholes. If they were not, they wouldn't be here. This is an asshole party… Anyway, I don't want to be rude, but if you wanna tell me something, please just go ahead and tell me.

WOMAN: What about you?

MAN: What about me?

WOMAN: Well, you're here. Are you an asshole?

MAN: Probably. Yeah!

WOMAN: Are you really?

MAN: I don't know.

WOMAN: You don't know? Is life tough for you? Hate the holidays? It's the holidays, isn't it?

He just stares at her, dumbfounded.

WOMAN: What's the matter?

MAN: Excuse me?

WOMAN: Oh, I see! You're just sad in general.

He just keeps staring.

WOMAN: Is that it?

MAN: Is what it?

WOMAN: Are you just sad in general because you're an asshole?

MAN: You're a monster.

WOMAN: Excuse me?

MAN: You are. You're a monster. It's fine, though, because I'm clearly starting to get a kick out of it. But you are clearly a mean lady.

WOMAN: And you're a mean man.

MAN: How am I a mean man? What did I do?

WOMAN: You just called me a monster.

MAN: Right! Because that's how you're being.

WOMAN: NO! You don't do that. You don't tell someone you don't even know that they are a monster. That they are a mean lady. You don't do that. You don't even know me.

MAN: No, you're right. I don't, but I think I am a very good judge of character, and from the few minutes or so I have known you…

WOMAN: You think I'm mean.

MAN: Yes, I do.

WOMAN: Why? Because I was trying to start up a conversation? I'm trying to talk to you. I'm being social. You're the mean one. I'm trying to be sweet and talk, and you call me names.

MAN: I'm sorry, I completely misunderstood sweet and social for… Something else.

WOMAN: Okay… I accept your apology. I'm not mean, I'm sweet.

MAN: I'm sure you are. Maybe I'm a little judgemental. Jumped the gun a little bit.

WOMAN: It's okay. But so you know, judgement is a terrible thing.

MAN: Yes, it is. I know that. And I'm working on it!

WOMAN: Well, that's good. I'm glad I could help.

MAN: I'm glad you could help, too… Thank you.

WOMAN: You're welcome.

They stare at each other.

WOMAN: Tracy.

MAN: Hi, Tracy.

WOMAN: (*Pointing to herself*) Sweet.

MAN: (*Pointing to himself*) Theodore. Judgemental asshole. But, working on it.

WOMAN: That's really your name? Theodore?

MAN: No, it's Fred, actually.

WOMAN: Really?

MAN: No, Theodore is really my name. Why?

WOMAN: Well, I guess it's better than Fred.

MAN: Oh, I get it. You don't like my name?

WOMAN: It's not that I don't like it. It's just… I mean, is that what your friends call you?

MAN: Don't have a lot of those.

WOMAN: Well, if you did, would you let them call you Theodore?

MAN: You know, I'm starting to do the judgement thing again. I can feel it. I'm trying real hard, but… You know what I mean?

WOMAN: Well, how bout Teddy?

MAN: How bout Trace?

WOMAN: Trace is fine. You want to call me Trace, you can call me Trace.

MAN: I don't want to call you Trace.

WOMAN: And I don't want to call you Theodore.

MAN: Well, that's a bummer. 'Cause that's my name. I didn't pick it, but I got it. Sort of got used to it, too. So…?

WOMAN: Well, what's wrong with Teddy?

MAN: I guess there's nothing really wrong with it, it's just not my name. I mean, you might as well call me Fred.

WOMAN: I'm definitely not calling you Fred.

MAN: Well, that's good. Now we're getting somewhere... Here! I'll explain! Save us a lot of trouble. See, usually what ends up happening is that you go from a Teddy, to the inevitable and very unfortunate, Ted. And that's just a bummer. For me. I mean, it's bound to happen one day or another, and I would just flat out hate to have that happen to me. Being a Ted is something I have been consciously avoiding my entire life. In fact, on top of that, in my entire life, I've never even met one Ted I liked. Even a little bit. All idiots in one specific way or another! Every single one of them. Call me stereotypical, call me crazy, call me judgemental, but whatever you do, please don't call me Ted. Okay?

WOMAN: Okay.

MAN: Great.

WOMAN: If I promise for the rest of my life to never call you Ted, can I call you Teddy?

Long pause.

MAN: Sure.

She gets up and sits next to him on the couch.

WOMAN: You're right, we are getting somewhere.

MAN: Well, praise the Lord.

She stands.

WOMAN: Oh no! You're one of those, aren't you?

MAN: I'm sorry? One of whats?

WOMAN: Are you Jewish?

MAN: No!

WOMAN: Then you're one of those.

MAN: Those? Oh, those. You mean not Jewish, those?

WOMAN: Yeah.

MAN: I'm sorry, is that not okay?

WOMAN: I guess it's all right.

MAN: You guess. You are amazing. You know that?

WOMAN: Thank you... Look, I just think Jewish people are better. In general. Just better people. I mean no offense.

MAN: No, no, no! Please.

WOMAN: And, I also think that they should stick together. I'm not against mixing, really, I just think it's an accident waiting to happen.

MAN: Mixing?

WOMAN: Yeah.

MAN: So, I take it you're Jewish?

WOMAN: Very.

MAN: That's cool. I've personally never really had a problem with mixing. But that's just me.

WOMAN: Well, what are you then?

MAN: You mean, as opposed to Jewish?

WOMAN: Mm hmm.

MAN: I'm not really religious.

WOMAN: Oh, well, that's good. Good for me, anyway. You're open!

MAN: I guess you could say that.

WOMAN: I did.

MAN: Yes, you did.

She stands over him and begins to grill him with rapid fire questioning.

WOMAN: So, if you're not religious, why did you praise the Lord?

MAN: You know, I don't remember.

WOMAN: Do you pray?

MAN: Only when I want something.

WOMAN: Who do you pray to?

MAN: I don't know.

WOMAN: Well, is it internal or do you actually speak?

MAN: How about we be done with religion for now?

WOMAN: Okay! Why are you here?

MAN: Why are you here?

WOMAN: I don't know. Maybe to meet you... Are you lonely?

MAN: Pretty much, yeah.

She moves away.

WOMAN: Is that why you're here? 'Cause if it is, you're barking up the wrong tree.

MAN: You're the most interesting woman I have ever met in my life.

She moves back toward the couch.

WOMAN: Thanks, Teddy.

MAN: No, seriously. I just asked you why you were here and you told me that you were "maybe here to meet me," and then in almost the same sentence, you said if I were here to meet someone that I was barking up the wrong tree.

WOMAN: I was right here, Teddy. I know what I said.

MAN: So, which is it? Am I barking up the wrong tree or did you come here to meet me?

WOMAN: I don't even know you.

MAN: Right. What was I thinking.

WOMAN: I mean, how should I know?

MAN: I don't know, you said it.

WOMAN: I said what?

MAN: Never mind.

WOMAN: Wait a minute. Are you hitting on me?

MAN: You know, I don't really know how to answer that.

WOMAN: What does that mean?

MAN: Well...

WOMAN: Seems to me like a straightforward question.

MAN: Yeah...

WOMAN: Are you or are you not?

MAN: Well...

WOMAN: I mean, I didn't mean to stump you. I was just curious...

MAN: Okay, but...

WOMAN: I mean, was I aggressive when I asked? I didn't mean to scare you. Did I scare you?

MAN: No, you...

WOMAN: I mean, there's no wrong answer. I'm not gonna be mad either way. It's not like you have...

MAN: Will you shut up for a second?

Pause.

WOMAN: Okay, I'm not gonna take that personally.

MAN: Good. I meant nothing by it. I just wanted you to stop talking for a second.

WOMAN: Right, I got that.

MAN: Your question. Was I hitting on you? My answer? I don't know. Or to be exact, I don't know how to answer that. I think that's what I said.

WOMAN: Yeah, Teddy. That's exactly what you said. It only happened a few seconds ago, I was right here. I'm a smart woman. My ears work fine. You don't have to repeat previous conversations to keep me in the loop. Let's just try to move forward when we talk.

MAN: Why mean? Why condescending and mean?

She looks up to the heavens.

WOMAN: He tells me to shut up and I'm the mean one?

MAN: I'm right here. I really hate that.

WOMAN: And I really hate it when smart men think they have to go back and repeat entire conversations so that stupid women can remember what they said.

MAN: That's not why I was doing that.

WOMAN: Then why were you doing that?

MAN: Because I am a smart man. And I want it known that I remember everything.

WOMAN: Good. 'Cause I'm not a stupid woman, and so do I.

MAN: Done. Understood. My apologies.

WOMAN: Great. So were you hitting on me?

MAN: No!

WOMAN: Well! I guess I was doing better before.

She walks away and sits back down at the table. He studies her. She looks away.

MAN: Look, truth be told, I still don't know how to answer that one, I just didn't want to repeat myself. Again.

She re-engages.

WOMAN: Do you find me interesting?

MAN: Very.

WOMAN: Do you find me attractive?

MAN: Absolutely.

WOMAN: We agree that I'm smart, or at least as smart as you. At this point anyway.

MAN: Sure.

WOMAN: Then why aren't you hitting on me? I mean, what else do you want? It seems to me like the three most important elements are all in place. Why aren't you hitting on me?

MAN: I don't know. Maybe I am. Or I was. Or I still am. I don't know.

WOMAN: You're confusing.

MAN: No, *you're* confusing. And that's why I'm not hitting on you.

WOMAN: Figure it out, pal. Either you are or you're not.

MAN: You know what? You just helped me figure it out.

WOMAN: For the record, I've helped you twice now, and I've only known you for a matter of minutes. Another reason why you should be hitting on me.

MAN: See, there's the first part.

WOMAN: What?

MAN: Okay. Here's the grand, overwhelming explanation.

WOMAN: Thank god.

MAN: And there's the second. Every time you say something, something implying that you would like me to move forward, not two seconds later, you hit me with something that moves me back. So, I'm confused. You confuse me. I can't get a clear read here. I don't know what the right move is. My life? Pretty much sucks at this point. I'm unhappy, I'm alone! I'd love to meet an interesting, attractive, intelligent woman. You! Apparently all of the above. But I'm fragile right now. So as perfect as it seems, under the circumstances of course, I'm not in a place where I feel comfortable to just throw myself out there without a net. You, being the net. What I mean is that in order for it to work, I'm going to need some reciprocity. You sway. Back and forth. I'm never really sure if you're gonna return the love. And while existing in this present state, that being one with a great lack of courage, I just can't justify a strong move forward. I wish I could. I wish I felt better in general. But for now this is how I feel. I'd love to hit on you. And I mean, really hit on you. Really give it my all. But, like I said, I'm fragile right now... I feel it just wouldn't be fair to me.

Pause.

WOMAN: That was a mouthful.

MAN: Yes, it was.

WOMAN: So, let me get this straight. You want a guarantee.

MAN: I didn't say that.

WOMAN: No, you said you needed reciprocity. I believe a net is what you said.

MAN: I know what I said.

WOMAN: Well, what's a net? A net is a guarantee.

MAN: No, a net in this case is reciprocity. I don't need a guarantee that it's going to work. I just need to know that we're on the same page.

WOMAN: So, you're saying you need some reciprocity.

MAN: That's what I said.

WOMAN: I remember.

They share the moment.

MAN: So, I have it?

She just stares at him.

MAN: *(Cont'd)* I think you're very interesting, beautiful, and smart! What do you think?

WOMAN: About what?

He stares at her as if to say, "Come on!"

WOMAN: Just kidding.

MAN: Well.

WOMAN: I think you're cool.

MAN: Cool? That's what I get? Cool? You get interesting, beautiful, and smart, and I get cool?

WOMAN: You know what I mean?

MAN: No, I don't. What's cool? What? Cool like the Fonz? Cool like how? What's cool?

WOMAN: I think you're hot.

MAN: Okay, that's…cool.

WOMAN: But I'm not sure.

MAN: You're not sure about what?

WOMAN: About us.

MAN: Oh, us. Well, that's okay. I'm not looking for a guarantee or anything. Just some reciprocity.

They stare at each other. She looks away. She looks back. He's still staring. She looks away again. Then after a few seconds, she looks back, studies him for a few more seconds, and then moves to the couch and sits down next to him.

WOMAN: Maybe we should kiss?

MAN: How's that?

WOMAN: Well, if we kiss, we'll know if we should be together or not. Or at least if it's possible. See, usually you waste all the time of first dates and phone conversations, anticipating the kiss. You could be totally into someone, and then the second you kiss, you realize it's not going to work. I think it's just a big waste of time. If you meet someone and all the intials seem to be in place, interesting, intelligent, blah, blah, blah, then you should just kiss them right away. Save yourself a lot of time. If the kiss isn't there, then it's over anyway. That's how people should introduce themselves. With a big, wet kiss.

MAN: Have you done this before?

WOMAN: I might have.

MAN: Didn't work out?

WOMAN: No. I mean, the kiss was good but he ended up being a coke addict. Not really my thing.

MAN: What is your thing?

WOMAN: I don't know.

MAN: You don't find anything intriguing about the anticipation? The idea of really liking someone and really wanting to kiss them, but waiting? Not because you have to wait, but because it's fun?

WOMAN: Yeah, when I was twenty. Before I became jaded and knew better.

MAN: Lots of red flags going up here.

WOMAN: Look, do you want to kiss me or not? If you don't, fine. I don't want to sit here and try to talk you into it. I'm a pretty and very classy lady. I'm not gonna sit here and beg.

MAN: I'm just talking.

WOMAN: Well, stop! Do you want to kiss or not?

MAN: Yes, I do.

WOMAN: 'Cause then we'll know.

MAN: Right… Should we stand up?

WOMAN: Would you like to?

MAN: Sure.

They both stand. He awkwardly moves toward her. He attempts to put his hand on her waist.

MAN: Is that okay? The hand there?

WOMAN: Yeah, that's fine.

MAN: We could do no touch if you want.

WOMAN: No, the hand's fine.

MAN: Okay.

He puts his hand on her waist. And the other on the back of her head.

WOMAN: That one's good for sure.

MAN: Good.

As he pulls her in closer, almost touching her lips, a crowd of people are heard offstage.

CROWD (*O.S.*) Ten, nine, eight, seven...

MAN: We might as well wait.

WOMAN: Okay.

They stare at each other, with their lips centimeters apart.

CROWD: Six, five, four, three, two, one...

They kiss, as the sounds of cheering party people hoot and holler in the background.

They break out of a long, passionate kiss.

WOMAN: (*Pleased*) Happy New Year.

MAN: (*Pleased as well*) Yeah, definitely.

THE END

How It Works
AKA

Tom and Jerry

Minor Holidays—How It Works

LIGHTS FADE UP ON

An empty apartment. Aside from some furniture, of course.

WOMAN (*V.O.*) Tom?

The front door to the apartment slowly opens. A WOMAN in a costume, that we will later learn is that of Ginger, from Gilligan's Island, *walks through the door. This is JERRY.*

JERRY: Tom?

TOM: (*O.S.*) Jerry?

JERRY: Baby, your door was open.

Jerry starts to look around the apartment.

TOM: (*O.S.*) I know. I left it open for you.

JERRY: Well, what if I was a crazy person?

TOM: (*O.S.*) Then I'd fight you.

JERRY: What if I was stronger than you and I had a gun?

TOM: (*O.S.*) Then I'd stay in here.

JERRY: You should just keep the door locked.

TOM: (*O.S.*) It's fine! We're not in Compton… I knew you were coming.

JERRY: Well, maybe you should just give me a key.

Jerry picks up a piece of paper.

JERRY: Tom?

TOM: Yeah.

JERRY: Did you hear what I said?

Tom walks onstage wearing a Popeye costume.

TOM: What?

JERRY: I said that you should just… What the hell is that?

Tom looks around.

TOM: What the hell is what?

JERRY: That! What you're wearing.

TOM: Oh, it's my costume. You like it?

JERRY: Do I like it?

TOM: I'm Popeye!

JERRY: I can see that.

TOM: Yeah! I wore it last year… I had it from last year… You don't like Popeye?

JERRY: Umm…it's not anything really against Popeye in general.

TOM: Well, what's the problem, then?

JERRY: Well, what happened to Gilligan?

TOM: Oh, Gilligan! Right! Well, honey, you know I thought about it a little bit and I just decided I didn't want to be Gilligan.

JERRY: When? When did you decide this?

TOM: I don't know. Today? Why? What's the problem?

JERRY: What's the problem? I don't know. Look at me! I'm wearing the problem, Tom. I'm Ginger.

TOM: Yeah, you look great.

JERRY: Well, I'm glad you think so, but we still have a problem.

TOM: Why? What's the problem? You look great! I look great. At least, I think so anyway.

JERRY: I think you look fine. It's not that.

TOM: Then what is it? What's the big deal?

JERRY: The big deal is this. You're popeye, everyone knows who you are. Without Gilligan, who the hell am I? I'm the what-do-you-think-she-is costume all night. Everyone is going to be like, who are you?

TOM: So, you tell them. Or wear a sign. I don't know. What's the big deal?

JERRY: Wear a sign? Did you just tell me to wear a sign?

TOM: I was kidding. Why are you freaking out?

JERRY: I didn't want to have to tell people what I am, Tom… Sort of kills it for me. See, that's why you're Gilligan. It just makes sense. They go together.

TOM: I know, but I didn't like it.

JERRY: You didn't like it? All of a sudden you didn't like it. I talked to you last night. You liked it. You liked it last night! Why are you doing this to me now?

TOM: Well, to be perfectly honest, honey, I didn't really think it was that big of a deal.

JERRY: Well, it is. It is that big of a deal, Tom. I don't get it. I just don't understand why you would do this to me now. Why would you wait till now?

TOM: As opposed to when? When should I have told you? Yesterday you said that you would be Ginger, and that it would be cute if I was Gilligan. I said we'll see. I woke up, had a normal day, thought about it, I don't want to be Gilligan.

JERRY: That's great. That's just great. Are you aware of the work I had to put forth piecing my Ginger together?

TOM: All's not lost! Be Ginger!

JERRY: I don't want to be Ginger without Gilligan.

TOM: And I don't want to be Gilligan.

JERRY: Why are you doing this to me?

TOM: Why am I doing this to you? What the hell am I doing? Why do I have to be Gilligan? I don't want to be Gilligan. Why is that not okay? Gilligan's an asshole.

JERRY: He is? He wasn't an asshole last night.

TOM: Sure, he was.

JERRY: Besides…it's Halloween, Tom! Who cares if you're an asshole?

TOM: Well, I sort of do… And besides, honey, it's really not that big of a deal to me. If I would have known how seriously you were gonna take this, I would have just been Gilligan.

JERRY: Really?

TOM: Yes, really. Come on.

JERRY: Then be Gilligan.

TOM: I can't… I don't have time to… Piece it together.

Jerry walks offstage.

TOM: What are you doing?

JERRY: (*O.S.*) I'm helping you.

TOM: With what?

JERRY: (*O.S.*) FOUND IT!

Jerry comes back on stage holding a red shirt with a white collar.

JERRY: How's this? Change that to this and you're all pieced.

Tom just stares at the exact replica of the Gilligan's Island *shirt Jerry is holding in her hand.*

TOM: You know, I don't really think that fits. Where was that?

JERRY: In the hamper.

TOM: Really?

JERRY: Put it on. Same hat, same pants, shoes are good too. You're all set.

TOM: Was that really in the hamper? The trash can is hamper adjacent, you know. I think I threw it away because it didn't fit.

JERRY: Whatever, Tom!

Jerry throws the shirt in Tom's face.

TOM: Whoa, whoa, whoa! We don't throw things at each other. We don't throw things in people's faces.

JERRY: Don't talk to me like I'm five, okay?

TOM: Well, stop acting like it.

JERRY: Put the shirt on.

TOM: What?

JERRY: Put the shirt on right now.

TOM: It doesn't fit.

JERRY: Tom!

TOM: It's dirty.

JERRY: TOM!

TOM: All right! I'm not gonna be Gilligan. Bottom line! Are you happy? You got me. I don't wanna be Gilligan, I wanna be Popeye! I'm Popeye. I said it before, it obviously wasn't good enough.

JERRY: So, you lied?

TOM: I didn't lie! I just moved around the details a little bit.

JERRY: Why? Why did you move around the details?

TOM: So that you wouldn't think I was trying to sabotage your Halloween. All I said was that it wasn't that big of a deal to me. The truth? It really isn't. So I didn't lie.

JERRY: Then put it on. If it's not that big of a deal, put the dirty, oversized, red shirt on.

TOM: It is not that big of a deal, I would just rather be Popeye! Okay?

JERRY: Then be Popeye, Popeye! I'll be the idiot with the what-are-you-costume all night, but that's fine. I don't even care anymore. I know what this is about. Aye aye, Popeye! Read you loud and clear.

TOM: Read me loud and clear about what?

JERRY: The whole point of us having matching costumes is that we are together. We are a couple. GIlligan goes with Ginger, Mickey and Minnie, Chachie loves Joanie. Do you see what I am saying?

TOM: No, I don't.

JERRY: Chachie doesn't love Joanie. That's what I'm saying.

TOM: Do you want me to be Chachie? 'Cause I'll be Chachie. At least Chachie's not an asshole.

JERRY: I don't want you to be Chachie, you moron. I want you to be Gilligan.

TOM: Moron? Did you just call me a moron?

JERRY: Gilligan loves Ginger. Chachie loves Joanie. Do you get it? He loves Joanie. Not Ginger. Not Chachie and Ginger. Not Joanie and Gilligan. Not Joanie and Popeye. Not Popeye and Ginger. Because Popeye doesn't love Ginger. It's Ginger and Gilligan. THEY'RE IN LOVE. Is it clear, Tom?

TOM: Yeah, really clear. You're fucking crazy.

JERRY: I want you to listen to me. And I'll try to speak slowly so that you can understand. I know what this is about. This is not about a costume. You don't want to be seen as a couple. You don't want to be attached. You want to be Popeye. Why? 'Cause Popeye's a man. A ladies' man.

He's a stud, right? That's what you want to be seen as. You don't want to be Gilligan. 'Cause what does that mean? What's Gilligan? Sweet, passive, lonely, loyal, needs a woman like Ginger. Dying to get married. Dying to marry the woman of his dreams. A woman like Ginger. And you, Popeye, don't want that.

TOM: First of all, you just insulted me. A lot. But more importantly than that, simultaneously, while insulting, I think, in just a few simple sentences, you've managed to make me question your mental stability. As a whole. Almost a year now, and in just a few simple words, all of a sudden, I think you're fucking crazy.

JERRY: Oh, now I'm crazy?

TOM: Yes. And don't call me a moron, ever.

JERRY: Am I out of my mind, Tom?

TOM: Well, that was the most ridiculous thing I have ever heard in my life. Did you even hear yourself? I can't even imagine the method, the steps it would take, in which your brain could come up with something like that. It's actually pretty amazing. If you take out the crazy part, it's incredible; so you know what? Let me join you. I got an idea! Why don't you be Olive Oyl?

JERRY: I don't want to be Olive Oyl, Tom. But tell me, what's soooo crazy?

TOM: I apologize, you're completely sane. Let's move on. Why not Olive Oyl? I got the socks. We could stop at the rag store and get a fucked-up dress. Put your hair back. We'll be a hit.

JERRY: I'm not going to be Olive Oyl!

TOM: Why not?

JERRY: Well, shit, Tom. I don't know. I mean, she's just so goddamn sexy. I don't know what's wrong with me. I guess I should be beating down the fucking door to be Olive Oyl so I can look flat-out atrocious. She's ugly, Tom. I'd like to be cute.

TOM: But it's Halloween. Who cares?

JERRY: Okay, Tom you made a point. A stupid point, but I guess that still counts. Ten points for Tom. Good work! Are you done now?

TOM: You are unbelievable, you know that?

JERRY: No, you're right. I'll change my costume. Let's either, a) have you search your entire apartment for some white, knee-high stockings while I do my hair and re-do my makeup, then drive all over Los Angeles at ten o'clock at night to try to find me a new dress. Or, b) you could change your shirt.

TOM: The point is this, honey. The reason I don't wanna be Gilligan the loser is the same exact reason that you don't wanna be Olive Oyl, the not-sexy, ugly person. It has nothing to do with me wanting to be thought of as not attached. We are going to the party together. We're going to walk in together. We are going to leave together. I'm Popeye, you're Ginger. Fuck Chachie and fuck Joanie, okay? Fuck 'em, they have nothing to do with anything. This whole thing is absurd and I would like it dropped now. Please. Can we just go?

JERRY: No! My point has obviously not been made.

TOM: Oh, no, it's been made. Made and shut down, but made.

JERRY: Okay? Let's say you go to the bathroom. Some cute girl, let's say Cinderella, is waiting in line to go. She has to tinkle.

TOM: Wait. Where are we now?

JERRY: At the party, Tom!

TOM: Great.

JERRY: She says, "Hey, Popeye. Where's your date?" Maybe she's pushing her tits up. Now if you're Gilligan, she doesn't say that. Nor does she put her tits in your face. "NO!" she says, to herself, it's a shame that Gilligan is here with a Ginger. Oh, well. Guess I better move on. Do you see my point? She knows better! Cinderella knows you are here with me, Ginger.

TOM: First of all, that shit never happens.

JERRY: Sure, it doesn't!

TOM: Second of all, if it did, I say my date is fucking Ginger.

JERRY: Great! Then she says, "Who's that?"

TOM: Oh, Jesus Christ!

JERRY: My point is this, Tom! Cinderella knows you are alone, and that's what you want. Admit it.

TOM: That's… That's just… I can't… BE FUCKING OLIVE OYL!

JERRY: I'm not gonna be Olive Oyl!

TOM: And I'm not gonna be fucking Gilligan. That's it! It's over! We just ended this. It's over! I will no longer let my desire to not go to a party dressed like a fucking bozo take up space in my life. You don't want to go to a party with Popeye? Fine. Then don't go.

Jerry studies him.

JERRY: Why are you doing this?

TOM: I'm not doing anything. I wanna go to a party and get drunk. It seems to me, and I can only speak for myself, so from my side of things, I feel like you're trying to pick a fight.

JERRY: I'm not trying to pick a fight.

TOM: Then why are we fighting? We don't fight. We never fight! I didn't start it. I know that for sure. So I ask you, why are we fighting?

JERRY: You're not gonna like my answer.

TOM: So what? I'll take it anyway.

JERRY: Will you put that shirt on?

TOM: No, I won't.

JERRY: Then that's why we're fighting.

TOM: Well, that's just plain fucking goofy. And I want you to know that I am well aware I hold the power to end this.

JERRY: Yes, you do.

TOM: Sure! Just put the shirt on, right? But I can't. Just on general principles alone. I don't have it in me to put that shirt on. I don't have what it takes to put that shirt on. I don't have the strength in my muscles to make that move. (*Pointing to his heart*) I just don't have it in here.

JERRY: No, I guess you don't...have it in here! I really wanted to believe that you did, though. I wanted to believe it so much And to tell you the truth, I thought you did. But I guess I was wrong.

TOM: Wait a minute. Are we talking about the same thing here?

JERRY: It does not have to be like this.

TOM: No shit!

JERRY: I don't mind issues, Tom. Issues are to be dealt with. I can deal with issues. I mind denial. You want to talk, let's talk. But you don't want to talk. You don't want to be real with me. You wanna hide behind a costume.

TOM: I'm not hiding behind a costume.

JERRY: You don't want to talk. I guess I understand.

TOM: About what? Where's the issues? What am I in denial about? Jerry, you're losing it. This isn't fair, honey. You've made a judgement on me.

Let's put aside that it's a judgement based on fictional characters. But nonetheless, it's still a judgement. You think we have something to talk about? I say here's a good place. Let's start with the fact that you're making things up all of a sudden. You're just creating a problem when one clearly doesn't exist.

JERRY: Am I?

TOM: Clearly.

JERRY: Okay...do you love me, Tom?

TOM: What?

JERRY: It's a simple question. Do you love me?

TOM: I got the question. I just want to know where it's coming from.

JERRY: Okay, I'll get to that. But first, I just want to be clear about where I'm coming from. Here's where I am! Fuck the party. Frankly, fuck Halloween. We're done with that. I'm pissed now.

TOM: Honey.

JERRY: Don't *honey* me. I want to be clear about how I'm creating something that clearly doesn't exist. We've been dating, dating which is the word you have been using for almost a year now. When are we actually together? Boyfriend girlfriend. That's the first question.

TOM: It's just a figure of speech.

JERRY: Forget that one. I have been spending about half of my life here at your house since we started "dating." Where's my shit?

TOM: Excuse me?

JERRY: Where do I get to keep my stuff?

TOM: In the drawer.

JERRY: In the drawer. That's right, I have a drawer. I share the drawer with old socks that you, for some reason or another, do not throw away, but my entire wardrobe fits in a one-by-one foot drawer... That I share with some old socks.

TOM: You want more drawers, I'll give you more drawers. You just have to ask.

JERRY: I don't want to ask. But let's move on. Where do my parents live?

TOM: You're asking me where your parents live?

JERRY: I'm not asking because I don't know. I'm setting you up for something. This is a whole thing.

TOM: Oh, well, in that case.

JERRY: Just play along, Tom. Think of it as exercising out my insanity.

TOM: Honey.

JERRY: If you call me honey one more time, I'm going to throw up all over Popeye... Now answer the question. Where do my parents live?

TOM: Umm...close? They live close.

JERRY: How close?

TOM: This is really, really stupid.

JERRY: Three blocks away. My parents live three blocks away.

TOM: Give or take a couple... Yeah, a few blocks. So what?

JERRY: What does my mom look like?

TOM: What?

JERRY: Anybody that says "what" can hear, Tom. Explain to me what my mom looks like.

TOM: I would say something like you. But older.

JERRY: Specifically. What does my mom look like?

TOM: I don't know.

JERRY: That's probably because you've never met her. Do you see what I'm getting at? Why have you never met my mom?

TOM: Look, just for the record, by that same rational, why do I know where your parents live? Because I have been to their house. I went there and spoke to your father. I went into his home. We spoke. Your mother just happened to be out. Where's the effort on her part?

JERRY: I'm not even going to humor that.

TOM: Okay, you wanna play. You wanna play, but offense only. Defense isn't your thing, I get it.

JERRY: Is any of this making an impact on you? At all? I mean, even a little?

TOM: Sure! You're attacking me. Out of the blue! An apparent, pent-up attack on your part. Drawers, parents, what do they look like. Not to mention that you're speaking to me like I'm a child. But what else tonight? Keys to my apartment, the words I chose to use...

JERRY: Whoa, whoa, whoa!

TOM: What?

JERRY: Keys to your apartment? Did I ask you for keys to your apartment?

TOM: Oh, whatever… You said it when you got here and I pretended not to hear you. You caught me! Fine! You get my point, though!

Jerry starts to gather her things.

TOM: What are you doing?

JERRY: I'm leaving. I don't want to be around you right now.

TOM: Jerry?

Jerry drops her things.

JERRY: I don't want to talk anymore, Tom. But I am going to give you one more chance, because I do love you. And for the record, "me, too" isn't going to cut it anymore. We can talk about that later. But for now, this is your last chance! We can start over right now… I'm ready to grow with you. I will accept what you were, and hopefully I can become part of what you change into. I'm praying you make the right choice… Put the shirt on!

Tom looks down at the shirt.

TOM: Or what?

JERRY: Or it's over!

TOM: Are you serious?

Jerry walks offstage and returns with a drawer full of clothes in her hands.

JERRY: How do I look, Tom? You have a decision to make. That's all there is to it. This is how relationships work. You meet, you're happy. Then things come up. You either talk about them or you don't. When you choose not to talk about them, they rest. They don't go away, they rest. They sleep, underneath the following year or so of false happiness, they sleep. They're like bears. They're hibernating. And when they wake up, they're pissed off and hungry. You and I are the world. And our feelings are sleepy, little grizzly bears. And you know what? They just woke up. This is what happens. One day, inevitably, there's an explosion. Where all the problems and issues, that were just happily napping, wake up. And that's what's happening. It may sound stupid to you but our explosion is a costume. Just a minor holiday, Tom! Now

I'm not blaming you. In fact, it's my fault for not speaking up earlier, but, nonetheless, this is where we are. This is the point of no return. The bears are up. What are you gonna do? Sleep time is over. You wanna take it to the next level or not. I say I'm worth it. I say it's time to give Popeye a rest. A long one. In fact, kill him. He no longer has a place in your life. It's time to be a real man. A real man named Gilligan.

TOM: I don't know what to say... You've just made it so black and white! I mean, to be really honest with you, if you wanna know the truth, I have some sleepy bears, too.

JERRY: What are your sleepy bears, Tom?

TOM: Well, to start with, I really hate ultimatums. And that's what you're giving me. This is clearly, clearly a controlling... Controlling ultimatum.

JERRY: I'm leaving, Tom.

TOM: Wait a minute.

JERRY: What?

TOM: What do you want?

JERRY: In general.

TOM: Yes.

JERRY: I want more, Tom. I want more than what I'm getting.

TOM: So, then what you are saying is that I am not good enough.

JERRY: If that's how you want to take it.

TOM: That's what you said, basically.

JERRY: No, that's not what I said.

TOM: Then what are you saying?

JERRY: That I want more.

TOM: More than me?

JERRY: More than what you are giving.

TOM: Well, I'm doing my best.

JERRY: It's not good enough.

TOM: Well, that's a bummer. 'Cause I am what I am.

JERRY: Yes, you are... Happy Halloween, Tom.

Jerry heads for the door.

TOM: Wait, wait, wait! I just wanna know one thing.

JERRY: What?

TOM: Did we just break up because of a costume?

Jerry looks around the apartment, then looks at Tom.

JERRY: No!

Jerry walks offstage leaving Tom alone.

THE END

The Pain

AKA

The Shrew

Minor Holidays—The Pain

LIGHTS UP

A man in his late twenties, PATRICK, walks onto the stage. He stares into a mirror as he buttons up his shirt.

A knock at the door of his apartment. He walks over to the door and opens it.

Standing on the other side of the door is his best friend, KYLE.

Patrick analyzes Kyle for a few seconds.

PATRICK: How's the kid?

KYLE: The kid's good.

PATRICK: I believe the kid.

KYLE: The kid is speaking the truth.

PATRICK: Lemme get the profile.

Kyle turns sideways.

PATRICK: Is the kid back?

KYLE: I think so.

PATRICK: You think so?

KYLE: Yeah, I think so.

PATRICK: No, no, no, no! The kid doesn't think, the kid knows. The kid walks in. He looks around. He sees her. He knows. He doesn't think. He knows. He says, "Excuse me, miss…you're very beautiful…I'm the kid." And then he knows. So I'll ask again. Is the kid back?

KYLE: Yes, the kid is back.

PATRICK: You know what you look like right now?

KYLE: What do I look like right now?

PATRICK: You look like a hungry animal…a cougar…you're a cougar.

KYLE: I feel a little cougar-ish.

PATRICK: You do, don't you. You look like a fucking man, pal. Welcome.

The boys walk into the room. Kyle sits down.

KYLE: It's gonna get ugly, isn't it?

PATRICK: So disgusting, and I can't wait.

Patrick continues to get dressed.

PATRICK: Dark, though. Really dark. But you're ready?

KYLE: I am.

PATRICK: I mean ten years and God didn't want to let it happen because he knew.

KYLE: He did, he knew.

PATRICK: He knew what would happen. He knew the extent of the ugly.

KYLE: The dark.

PATRICK: The possibilities of the dark. The numbers, the debauchery within the numbers. The sins. Why is he letting it happen now? I don't know and I don't care. I just want to enjoy. Take advantage of the mistake.

KYLE: Wait.

PATRICK: What?

KYLE: You think he made a mistake?

PATRICK: No! I'd like to scratch that from the record. God makes no mistakes. He just wasn't ready, and now he is.

KYLE: (*Contemplating*) Ten years, man.

PATRICK: And now he's ready. We're ready. Oh my god, it's gonna get ugly.

KYLE: How ugly do you think it's gonna get?

PATRICK: You and I, both single at the same time. Are you kidding me.

KYLE: Oh my god. The debauchery.

PATRICK: The sin. It's time. Ten years we've been waiting for this day to come. This is like an apocalypse. Do you know that? It's all coming together to end in this huge pile of demented evil. You've done your share and I've definitely done my share, but together. It's just... It's just wrong.

KYLE: Wait.

PATRICK: What?

KYLE: You think it's wrong?

PATRICK: No, no, no! Not wrong, you're right. Evil! Evil and wrong, totally different.

KYLE: Same ballpark though.

PATRICK: No, no, no! Similar game, totally different ballpark... Totally different. Similar game. Like baseball and cricket. You got bats, hats, balls, some goofy socks, but not the same game... What are we talking about here?

KYLE: Evil.

PATRICK: That's right! Pure evil and it's going down. And there's no holding back. The promise land awaits, my friend. These chains will hold me down no more. For ten years now, either I've had a girlfriend or you've had a girlfriend. We're free to roam, together. We were cursed. God did it, now he undid it. And I think it's a miracle.

KYLE: Yes, it is. Speaking of that though, have you talked to your girl?

PATRICK: Wow, dude! She's not my girl, she's my ex-girl, and I would appreciate you not bringing that up. This is a joyous time.

KYLE: I was just making sure.

PATRICK: You didn't call yours, did you?

KYLE: My what?

PATRICK: Your "ex"-girl.

KYLE: No.

PATRICK: Good! Why are we talking about this. I don't wanna be here.

KYLE: Well, it's bound to come up.

PATRICK: No, it's not bound to come up. You brought it up. You hold that power. You also hold the power to not bring it up. Exercise that.

KYLE: I'm not saying I wanna talk about it but I think fighting not talking about it when I feel like talking about it is not a healthy thing.

PATRICK: So, you're saying you wanna talk about it?

KYLE: No, not right now. But so you know, for the future, I feel that it's as if you're always putting the red flag up. Like it's not okay to talk about it. Like you think it's healthier to just ignore it.

PATRICK: Okay. Hold on. Hold on. Take that flag and throw it right out the window. You wanna talk about it, we'll talk about it. But here's my point. Do you wanna talk about it right now?

KYLE: I already said no.

PATRICK: Okay, then here's also my point You are prone to an obsessive compulsive type of behavior. Maybe I'm the emotional blocker type, but whatever, we're on you right now. I'm not the one who locked himself in the house for two weeks.

KYLE: That's nice.

PATRICK: I apologize, but let's just get it all out. My point is this. For you. For your sake, I think it would be better that you strive, and strive hard, to not talk about it. 'Cause even when you don't want to talk about it, which is right now, which you've just told me, here we are talking about it. Me... You're right! I could open up a bit. But once again, we're not talking about me. I'm fine. We're talking about you.

KYLE: Are you fine?

PATRICK: I don't want to talk about it, but yes, I'm fine.

KYLE: All right. You're right. I just think a lot.

PATRICK: No! You obsess a lot. Thinking's okay. You wanna think? Let's think. I'm just saying try not to obsess.

KYLE: Okay.

PATRICK: Good.

KYLE: Can I just ask one question, and then I'll stop.

PATRICK: Sure, about what?

KYLE: Well, what do you think?

PATRICK: Here's what I think. I think the kid was here a minute ago, but he left. Didn't even see him leave, either. No! He just snuck out. There are rules in this house and the kid knows these rules... I know the rules, I'm here...

KYLE: One question!

PATRICK: Rules!

KYLE: One question, please!

PATRICK: Fine! Go!

KYLE: One question, then I'll stop.

PATRICK: Go!

KYLE: I swear to God.

PATRICK: GO!

KYLE: Okay! Jesus... Now, I know you saw Jen the other night.

PATRICK: Yes, I did.

KYLE: What did she say?

PATRICK: That's a really fucking general question. What did she say? I don't know what she said. I didn't have a pen and paper handy.

KYLE: So, you did talk to her?

PATRICK: This is two questions you're asking me now. You know that, right? You said one.

KYLE: One cancels out the other. What did she say?

Patrick takes a moment.

PATRICK: If I answer that question, am I supposed to believe that a plethora of other questions aren't going to follow? Are you manipulating me, Kyle?

KYLE: Manipulating you how?

PATRICK: Well, you made this big deal about one question. One question that you swear to God is all you need to know. I'm ready for a question. One simple question. Not a fucking prelude to a two-hour discussion. Did you really want to ask me a question or did you want to manipulate me into a general area of question?

KYLE: All right. Fuck all that. Was she with a guy? That's the question. That's all I want to know.

PATRICK: Good, simple question. Simple answer. No!

KYLE: She wasn't?

PATRICK: Still no.

KYLE: Who was she with?

PATRICK: Stop it now.

KYLE: Would you tell me if she was with a guy?

PATRICK: Of course, I would.

KYLE: So, she wasn't.

PATRICK: Yes, she wasn't. That's my final answer. What's the matter with you?

KYLE: Okay, that's all I wanted to know.

PATRICK: Great. Now can we please get back to the filth and the fury that I was so excited about, please?

KYLE: Yes.

PATRICK: The evil.

KYLE: Yes.

PATRICK: You're the kid?

KYLE: I'm right here.

PATRICK: You're a fucking killer, pal.

KYLE: I know.

PATRICK: You kill them. You attack them. They're scared of you. But not scared like run away scared. Scared like, "I don't know where to run" scared.

KYLE: But I'm not alone.

PATRICK: No! You're not alone! The Captain's right behind you. The Captain's kill 'em too. Pal, we got uzis. It's the Cougar and the Captain. We're a death squad.

KYLE: Unstoppable.

PATRICK: Not even close. It's illegal is what it is.

KYLE: All right, what's the lineup?

PATRICK: There he is.

KYLE: Line up, line up!

PATRICK: Okay, to start, Katie and Carrie, at the Tea Cup for an appetizer.

KYLE: Katie and Carrie?

PATRICK: Twins, pal... Blonde ones!

KYLE: Stop it.

PATRICK: Who am I?

KYLE: You're the captain.

PATRICK: Right! Never question my orders.

KYLE: Twins?

PATRICK: Beer commercial twins.

KYLE: Shut the fuck up.

PATRICK: Well, not literally, but that level. They're like the stunt doubles. Very close. Shape, size...

KYLE: Wait, fuck!

PATRICK: What fuck?

KYLE: We can't go to the Tea Cup.

PATRICK: Why not?

KYLE: We just can't.

PATRICK: No, we can.

KYLE: Jen goes to the Tea Cup.

PATRICK: So what?

KYLE: What do you mean so what?

PATRICK: I mean, so what! I have really hot twins meeting us at the Tea Cup.

KYLE: I know, but it's bad.

PATRICK: No, it's not bad, it's good.

KYLE: What if Jen's there?

PATRICK: She won't be! It's not like she goes there every night. What are the odds? It's a big place…

KYLE: But what if?

PATRICK: (*Pleading*) No, no, no, no.

KYLE: It's bad.

PATRICK: But it's the twins pal! The Tea Cup twins!

KYLE: It's bad!

PATRICK: It's not!

KYLE: It is!

Patrick is beside himself.

PATRICK: Okay… All right. We skip that? Flake on twins. I just wanna throw this out there! Just for laughs! These are twins that almost gave me the vibe that they kinda would fool around with each other. Possible incestuous relations with twins! But whatever.

KYLE: I'm sorry.

PATRICK: It's okay. It's fine. No big deal. We just go to the Candy Store and pick up there.

KYLE: Nope.

PATRICK: Nope? What's nope?

KYLE: Candy store's bad, too.

Patrick takes a pause.

PATRICK: 'Cause Jen goes there?

KYLE: Yeah.

PATRICK: Well, shit!

KYLE: What?

PATRICK: I just thought of something. We're fucked!

KYLE: Why?

PATRICK: Well, cause we need to get gas, and Jen gets gas sometimes, so…

KYLE: Don't do that.

PATRICK: What, dude? It's a big city. People go places.

KYLE: All right. Let's go to the Vine, then.

PATRICK: Fuck you with the Vine.

KYLE: Why not? Cause your ex-girlfriend goes there?

PATRICK: She fucking works there, asshole.

KYLE Maybe she's got the night off.

PATRICK: All right! Fine! You wanna go to the Vine? You wanna see my sack? We'll go to the Vine. Let's go to the Vine!

KYLE: I don't wanna go to the Vine, I was trying to make a point.

PATRICK: The most invalid point I've ever heard in my life. But fuck it! Let's go there. The Vine it is and I hope Lily's working too. Would that make you feel good?

KYLE: How would it make you feel?

PATRICK: Shut up! Don't do that.

KYLE: Look, I just don't want to run into Jen. Is that okay?

PATRICK: You're going to eventually.

KYLE: Well, I'd like to put it off for as long as possible.

PATRICK: Then go back home, lock the door, and never come out.

KYLE: Why are you snapping at me? Why can't you be understanding?

Why don't you understand that I am in pain over this woman. That I hurt. It's not a small thing. It's a big thing. I'm trying to be the kid. You're trying to help, but in the process, please have a little leniency.

PATRICK: I do.

KYLE: Please.

PATRICK: I am.

KYLE: I know I obsess, I'm working on it.

PATRICK: Yes, you do. And yes you are.

KYLE: I miss her.

PATRICK: No, you don't.

KYLE: Yes, I do.

PATRICK: You don't, you're missing something else. Go to therapy, figure it out, but right now can we please just go have an orgy with twins.

KYLE: Wait a minute. You really think I don't miss her?

PATRICK: I don't know. Maybe you do.

KYLE: Do you miss Lily?

PATRICK: No.

KYLE: Fucking liar.

PATRICK: Fuck you.

KYLE: You miss her. Admit it.

PATRICK: Would you like a partner? Is that what you want? Would you like a commiseration associate? I won't do it. I won't sit here and obsess about my ex-girlfriend. I won't do it.

KYLE: And I won't do what you do. I LOVE JEN.

PATRICK: Great.

KYLE: I MISS JEN!

PATRICK: Fuckin' A.

KYLE: I STILL WANT TO BE WITH JEN!

PATRICK: Well, you shouldn't want to be with Jen!

KYLE: WHY NOT?

PATRICK: Because she's a MEAN-SPIRITED BITCH!

Kyle just stares at Patrick for a few seconds.

PATRICK: I'm sorry.

KYLE: Why did you say that?

PATRICK: I just said it.

KYLE: No, there's a reason you said that.

PATRICK: There's not.

KYLE: What did she say?

PATRICK: She didn't say anything.

KYLE: Then why did you say that?

PATRICK: I just sometimes think that she is.

KYLE: Since when?

PATRICK: Since always.

KYLE: That's not true. When did you think she was mean? You never thought she was mean. You always said she was nice. You said she was perfect for me. She's great, you said.

PATRICK: Okay, so I changed my mind.

KYLE: You can't do that.

PATRICK: What do you mean, I can't do that?

KYLE: She said something and I want to know what she said.

PATRICK: I can't just change my mind about a person.

KYLE: Not for no reason.

PATRICK: I just don't think she's good enough for you is all. You're torturing yourself over a woman who's not good enough.

KYLE: But I just want to know how she became not good enough.

PATRICK: It's just a vibe I get.

KYLE: When did you get this vibe?

PATRICK: Can we stop this, please?

KYLE: No, we can't stop this. You started it, and now I want you to finish it.

PATRICK: How did I start anything? I don't want to talk about this shit! I'm talking about twins. I'm talking about having fun. I'm talking about being single. I'm talking about sex. I'm talking about being single having fun having sex with twins! What did I start?

KYLE: Fine, I started it and now I would like you to finish it... Please!

PATRICK: Come on, pal... Where's the kid?

KYLE: FUCK THE KID! She did something. She said something. You heard something. What is it? I want it right now!

PATRICK: Fuck the kid?

Patrick just stares at Kyle. After a long moment of silence, Kyle heads for the door.

KYLE: Forget it!

Kyle opens the door.

PATRICK: Wait.

KYLE: What?

PATRICK: Sit down.

KYLE: I don't want to.

PATRICK: If I tell you what she said, will you sit down?

Long pause. Kyle heads over to the couch and sits down.

PATRICK: Okay. Now, first of all, I want to explain something to you. I didn't want to say anything because I didn't think I had to.

KYLE: Fine. Now you do. What did she say?

PATRICK: I also didn't want to say anything because I didn't want to hurt your feelings.

KYLE: Fine.

PATRICK: But it's not that big of a deal.

KYLE: Fine.

PATRICK: And the more I think about it, what she said, should not hurt your feelings at all, but in fact, should make you feel better about the fact that you are no longer together.

KYLE: Fine. What did she say?

Patrick takes a breath.

PATRICK: She was just being a little disrespectful, that's all.

KYLE: To you?

PATRICK: No.

KYLE: To me?

PATRICK: Yes.

KYLE: How? How was she being disrespectful?

PATRICK: She spoke about you in a way I felt to be a little disrespectful. And like I said, it's not that big of a deal, it's just something I felt. Like a bad vibe.

KYLE: Words. What were her words?

PATRICK: Specifically, it's not important. It's more of how she was being.

KYLE: Well, how was she being?

PATRICK: I'd say rude… Unkind… Mean-spirited. Yes! Rude, unkind, and mean-spirited.

KYLE: No! No! See, that's not a vibe. A vibe is energy. A vibe is a feeling. A vibe could be the fucking air. Rude, unkind, and mean-spirited is something specific my ex-girlfriend said and I wanna know right now exactly what the fuck it was.

PATRICK: She was speaking of you in a way I did not appreciate.

KYLE: What was that way?

PATRICK: Rude, unkind, and mean-spirited.

KYLE: WHAT DID SHE SAY? STOP FUCKING WITH ME! If you beat around the bush for one more second, I'm going to kill you. I want verbatim. I want word for word, and I want it right now. Verbatim. What were the exact words that came out of her mouth?

PATRICK: She mocked you, okay? She imitated you crying to her. To me, your best friend. She imitated you crying to her on the phone about how you had nowhere to go for the holidays. This is at a restaurant. A public place, and that bitch… I'm sorry but she's a fucking asshole… That bitch mocked you. You wanna do that shit. Tell your friends, tell your parents, tell a homeless guy, but don't tell me. I'm your best friend. Don't do that shit. It's cold-hearted, mean-spirited, bitchy girl bullshit, and you're too good for that. I swear to God, it took everything I had not to reach over the table and punch her right in the face.

Kyle just stares at him.

PATRICK: I shouldn't have told you. I knew I shouldn't have told you, and I wasn't going to.

KYLE: No, I'm glad you told me. It doesn't feel good, but I'm glad you told me.

PATRICK: Good. That's my point. It should feel good.

KYLE: It should?

PATRICK: Well, not good like, "Hey, I'm happy, let's go on the ferris wheel." But good like, "Fuck her, she's an asshole, and now I know." Relief. There should be a sense of relief.

KYLE: That what? A girl I spent three years of my life with, that I thought was in love with me, can just turn around and talk shit about me three weeks after we break up?

PATRICK: No.

KYLE: Then what's relieving? Explain to me the relief?

PATRICK: That a girl, one that you are fantasizing about being so fantastic, is in reality, just an asshole. Relief, in that you are having a bullshit fantasy. She's not great. She sucks! What she did was clearly the actions of an asshole… Only an asshole would do something like that. She's an asshole!

KYLE: Would you stop calling her an asshole.

PATRICK: Why? That's what she is! Be happy, happy that you never have to see her again!

KYLE: Oh my god.

PATRICK: What? That's a good thing… I wish I could hear bad shit about my ex-girlfriend. It would feel great. All I get to hear is, "Ahhh, what happened, she was so good for you. I saw Lily the other day, she really looked amazing, you know she's such a sweet girl." Fuck that shit. That's not what I want to hear. I wanna hear that she's toothless, strung out jonesing for crack, getting gang-banged by the Lakers. Shit like that.

KYLE: Well, you and I are different.

PATRICK: Look, I'm sorry, but you need to get over this, 'cause, plain and simple, she's just not the girl for you.

KYLE: Can I ask you a question?

PATRICK: Anything.

KYLE: If Lily was so great, why did you break up with her?

PATRICK: No. We're not doing that.

KYLE: Why not?

PATRICK: Because we're not.

KYLE: Just please tell me why you broke up with her.

PATRICK: Because I hated her.

KYLE: Then why did you go out with her?

PATRICK: Also, because I hated her. We're not doing this shit.

Kyle stands up.

KYLE: Fine. Then let's just call it a night.

PATRICK: Whoa, whoa, whoa! Why? Because I won't play along? You wanna cry together or something, I don't want to do it.

KYLE: I'll tell you what it is. You want me to take your advice and you want me to listen to you. I can't. I can't listen to you because I don't even know if you're human. I don't want to see you get sad, but I'd like to see something. I mean, we're right here in the same spot. Both newly single, both had girls we really cared about, and now they're gone. You're happy, you wanna go out and sleep with twins. I just don't get it. It makes no sense to me.

PATRICK: It doesn't have to make sense to you.

KYLE: It does if I don't believe it. It looks nice, but I think it's bullshit. I think you're full of shit.

PATRICK: You're an asshole, too. You know that?

KYLE: No, I'm an animal, remember… But you wanna know what kind of animal I am? I'm a shrew. You know what a shrew is?

PATRICK: No, I don't know what a shrew is.

KYLE: A shrew is… Do you wanna know what a shrew is?

PATRICK: Sure.

KYLE: A shrew is a mouse. It's a mouse that has no eyes. Maybe he has eyes, but they're covered by his eyelids that never open. Ever! He's blind. He lives in the dirt. Underground, and he borrows through life fighting everything that gets in his way. He'll fight anything. Big, small, it doesn't matter, he's just pissed. Pissed off that he can't see shit and that he lives in the dirt. He has no friends, nobody loves him, and all he wants to do is fight. So, he fights, and he fights, and then one day when he can't fight anymore, he dies.

PATRICK: And that's you?

KYLE: That's right!

PATRICK: So, you don't have any friends? Nobody loves you?

KYLE: When I'm in my hole? When I'm in the dirt? When I'm alone? No, I don't, and no, nobody does. It's truly an ugly place. And I'm fighting real hard but I can't see anything getting better. I'm miserable, completely one hundred percent miserable.

PATRICK: You're not a shrew.

KYLE: Well, I'm definitely not a cougar.

Patrick takes it in. He walks around the room for a few seconds.

PATRICK: All right, fine. So what do you wanna do?

KYLE: What? Tonight?

PATRICK: No, forget about tonight. Forget about the twins, forget about all of it. It's a shame, but forget it... For now. But first, what do you wanna do? What are you gonna do? Cause you can't go on like this. You certainly can't go back home and lock the door. You'll kill yourself.

KYLE: Do you know that I actually think about that?

PATRICK: What? Killing yourself?

KYLE: Yeah!

PATRICK: Sure.

KYLE: Sure?

PATRICK: Yeah, sure.

KYLE: How in the fuck could you just nonchalant me like that? Did you just hear what I said? I just told you I think about killing myself. Yeah, sure? Yeah sure, like I asked if I could borrow some socks? That's what I get?

PATRICK: Listen, you fucking drama queen. What I meant was that I know what you mean. I could relate. You don't think I think about that shit, too. And I didn't mean to nonchalant you. But I also know how you mean it. You're not sitting there with a gun in your hand, sweating, crying to God you can think of a reason not to pull the trigger, writing fucking suicide notes and shit. You're like in the bathtub. You let all the water drain out after a nice, hot bath. You're feeling sorry for yourself. Sitting there like a big, wet, sobbing slob. And you're thinking, "What if?" Not like you're really gonna do it.

But what if? What if I had a gun and I blew my brains out. Right here in the tub. The white porcelain splattered with blood. Soaking wet, covered in blood, real dramatic, but beautiful. Maybe my ex will come over to drop something off... She'll find me. Naked, bloody, dead... She'll start crying... "Oh my god, what have I done?" She'll hold your bloody, dead body. Tears falling on to your lifeless chest. She's holding your head up. It's great. Then you realize it's Wednesday and that the maid's coming tomorrow. Fucks everything up. God forbid you kill yourself and the maid finds you. That would be awful. She comes in to tidy up the bathroom, sees you in the tub. She starts screaming in Portuguese. Nobody can understand her. You can't even hear her, you're dead. Maybe she freaks out and runs away. Doesn't tell anybody. So you sit there and rot. For God only knows how long. And then, by the time someone does find you, you don't even look sexy anymore... Anyway, the point is, you're fantasizing. Dark, twisted fantasy. But you're not really gonna do it.

Kyle just stares at Patrick.

KYLE: That's amazing. I mean, in mine, the maid calls the police, but that's pretty fucking close.

Patrick smiles.

PATRICK: I think about that shit, too, pal. It's very normal.

KYLE: Yeah?

PATRICK: Look. I'm fucking miserable, too, half the time. Just 'cause I don't talk about it doesn't mean it isn't so. People are people. We go through the same shit. We just deal with it differently. Look, I just don't see the purpose in moping around thinking about what happened all day long. It doesn't make any sense to me. It's over! You say why? 'Cause it just didn't work. That's it. But that's enough! Sure I get sad. Sure I think about killing myself. Big fucking deal. Life goes on. I love Lily. It didn't work. I'm gonna try my best not to think about it.

KYLE: I just can't imagine you being miserable.

PATRICK: You wanna see me cry? I could do it right now for you. I just don't want to.

KYLE: But how do you do it?

PATRICK: I just think real hard about how great she was and boom, tears. You wanna see? Here, I'll do it.

KYLE: No, no, no, no. How do you just shut it off like that? You got a button or something? I can't do that shit.

PATRICK: You just gotta try. It's hard, but you gotta try.

KYLE: What do you think I'm doing? I'm the kid. I'm the cougar and you're the captain. I'm saying it, but I don't believe it. Every other confident word that comes out of my mouth is followed up by a fucking picture of her in my head. Or a body part, or a smile. Her walking to the bed. Her telling me she loves me. Her putting on lipstick… Her nose, and the way it gets when she's cold…

PATRICK: Shut the fuck up! Jesus Christ! You're doing it right now. Stop! It's over! What good does that shit do? Do you like torturing yourself?

KYLE: No!

PATRICK: Then cut it out. You have to make a conscious decision to not think about that stuff. You're gonna drive yourself crazy.

KYLE: I'm trying.

PATRICK: No, you're not. Try harder.

KYLE: Okay.

PATRICK: Okay?

KYLE: Okay! I just got one more question.

PATRICK: Sure you do.

KYLE: I'm serious. I'm serious, and I swear to God this is not a segue. I'm not obsessing, I am calm.

PATRICK: Fine, go.

KYLE: What happens if I don't get better.

PATRICK: What do you mean?

KYLE: What if I stay like this? What if I'm stuck thinking for the rest of my life what could have been? What if I try real hard like you're telling me to try? Conscious, constant effort to keep her out of my mind. And it doesn't go away. What if I stay miserable? Miserable over this woman for the rest of my life. What if the only joy I ever have turns out to be moments? Moments that I don't think about her. Moments where I smile, but underneath my smile is a world of pain that I am constantly avoiding? What then?

PATRICK: Kill yourself.

KYLE: What?

PATRICK: Damn straight! Because, number one, there is no fucking way that is possible, and number two, even if it was, I'm telling you for the last time as your friend, she's not the girl for you. And, if you choose, because it is a choice! Your choice! If you choose to spend the rest of your life obsessing about what could have been with a woman that's clearly not even on your level, then yes, I do believe that you should kill yourself. You know what? Fuck it! Do it right now. If that's the plan. Shit, I'll do it for you. But, pal, she's not for you. And that shit is not gonna happen. And that's more important than anything I just said... Is that what you asked me was not a question. It was a fear. It was an expression of your fear. Your fear of what might happen if you let her go. And that shit... Will go away. The second you let it go... It will go away... I swear to God.

KYLE: That's a good answer.

PATRICK: Thank you.

KYLE: And you're right. I am scared.

PATRICK: That's cool.

KYLE: But one way or another, I just don't see what you see. I'm glad you're clear, and I'm glade someone can see me, but I can't! It sounds great. But it's just sound to me. I'm in here, you're out there. To you, it's simple, but to me, it's just more sound. Sound piled on top of other sound. Voices telling me what to do, what I did, what I should have done. Other voices. Advice, directions. Half the time I can't even get a thought straight. I don't know how you do it. I mean, I'm impressed, and it's encouraging, but it's just not enough. All I see is her, and I don't see it getting any better without her.

PATRICK: Well, I don't know what to say.

KYLE: Neither do I.

PATRICK: I don't know. Maybe you're just not done.

KYLE: Do you really think that?

PATRICK: I don't really know how to answer that.

KYLE: But that makes sense, right?

PATRICK: Sure.

KYLE: No, it does. I mean, that makes sense. If I was done, I mean, really done, I'd be done. If it was really over for me, I wouldn't feel like this. Right?

PATRICK: If that's what you think.

KYLE: You said it.

PATRICK: I'd officially like to retract any statements that could possibly hold me responsible for whatever it is you choose to do here.

KYLE: You're not responsible.

PATRICK: Okay... I just want you to be happy.

KYLE: I know... I think I'm gonna give it another shot.

PATRICK: With Jen?

KYLE: Yes.

PATRICK: Okay.

KYLE: I mean, really give it everything. You know?

PATRICK: Only way to do it.

KYLE: Right?

PATRICK: Sure.

KYLE: I mean, I'm not sure I ever really gave it that. It's hard to see what you're doing when you're doing it. Sometimes you need some space to really see. I mean, how do you ever really know for sure? I'll talk to her. I mean, find out why it didn't work. Figure it out... Together. Then if it's done, we at least know why. See, we didn't really ever do that. It's worth at least that; don't you think?

PATRICK: Why not?

KYLE: It's the holidays... You know?

PATRICK: Yeah.

KYLE: Hey, you know what? I'll give it another shot. If it doesn't work... We got summer. Summer's better anyway, right?

PATRICK: Definitely a better time to be single.

KYLE: Yeah. The beach. Bikinis.

PATRICK: The single summer.

KYLE: Yes! The kid and the captain starring in *The Single Summer.*

PATRICK: Sounds good to me.

KYLE: Me, too. Me, too.

Kyle stands up.

KYLE: You think she'll give it another chance?

PATRICK: Her loss if she doesn't, pal.

KYLE: Good point! You're right. You're right!

Kyle heads for the door.

KYLE: Here I go.

PATRICK: There he goes.

Kyle opens the door, then turns back to Patrick.

KYLE: Hey. I'm sorry about the twins.

PATRICK: Twins... What are twins? Twins are... You know what? I'll handle it myself. Things could be worse, right?

KYLE: Things could be worse! You're the captain, you'll be fine.

Long pause.

PATRICK: So, how's the kid?

KYLE: The kid is good.

PATRICK: I believe the kid.

KYLE: I'll talk to you later.

PATRICK: All right.

Kyle exits. Patrick paces around for a few beats and then walks over to the phone and picks it up.

THE END

The End

AKA

A Man and His Barbecue

Happy Fathers Day
LOVE YOU
SCOTT

Minor Holidays—The End

LIGHTS FADE UP OVER

A beautiful blonde WOMAN running around her perfect home with a broom. The cleaning almost literally turns her on. Almost to the point of orgasm.

You could eat off the floors of this joint.

A big, strong MAN walks through the door. He stands in the doorway demanding her attention.

She notices him and smiles.

MAN: What are you doing?

WOMAN: Cleaning!

MAN: Yes, you are.

WOMAN: Yes, I am. How was your day?

MAN: It was good… You wanna know why?

WOMAN: Yes, I do.

MAN: Yes, you do…it was a good day, because I worked. And do you know what happens when I work?

WOMAN: I think I do.

MAN: I think you do, too.

WOMAN: Tell me.

MAN: Going to.

WOMAN: Okay.

MAN: I make money.

WOMAN: Yes, you do.

MAN: Yes, I do. And then what?

WOMAN: You…

MAN: I…

WOMAN: You…

MAN: I...(*Exploding*)...Take care of my woman with the money I make. I bring home the bacon while she cleans the house, and while she cleans the house, I make the bacon. 'Cause that's how it works, and I love it!

WOMAN: So, do I.

MAN: I know you do! You're a woman and I'm a man.

WOMAN: It's perfect.

MAN: I'm right.

WOMAN: I know you are.

MAN: I'm always right.

WOMAN: So am I.

MAN: I know.

The man takes off his shoes, sits on the couch, and turns on the TV.

The woman brings him a beer.

MAN: You know, I hate you sometimes.

WOMAN: (*Smiling*) You do?

MAN: Oh, yeah. I mean, I know we never argue, but I imagine what it would be like if we did. And it makes me want to kill you. Like I'm at work, the office, and I sit there making up all kinds of bad shit about you, like I imagine you driving me completely out of my mind.

WOMAN: Yeah?

MAN: Yeah... The little things. It's the little things that I imagine you doing that drive me completely crazy. And sometimes I just hate you for it.

WOMAN: Like what?

MAN: Like I'll be having a bad day, and you'll call me in the middle of this hectic meeting, and although it's not important, you'll make it this huge, monster deal, and I'll get on the phone, in the middle of this monstrosity of a day that I'm having, and you'll just start bitching about nothing. Going on and on about something that has nothing to do with anything. And you think that what you are doing is expressing your feelings to the one person in your life that truly understands, but really all you are doing is wasting my time and making me want to commit suicide.

WOMAN: But, honey, I would never do that.

MAN: I know.

WOMAN: You know why?

MAN: Tell me.

WOMAN: Going to.

MAN: Good.

WOMAN: Because if I were to be actually needing the support of someone that I actually thought just loved me unconditionally and could truly understand me, I would never call a man. Let alone my stupid husband... You know why?

MAN: Tell me.

WOMAN: Going to... Because men don't understand anything, let alone the feelings of a sensitive woman. To them, it's bitching and moaning, to us, it's the fact that life has become so boring that the only thing that makes sense to do is to go out and sleep with someone else.

MAN: Would you actually do that?

WOMAN: No, but I think about it all the time.

MAN: So do I.

WOMAN: I'm sure you do... How could you not?

MAN: I saw an ass today like you wouldn't believe.

WOMAN: Really?

MAN: Yeah... Unbelieveable. Firm, round, everything. And the legs attached to it. Foget about it.

WOMAN: I bet.

MAN: You bet.

WOMAN: Would you ever cheat?

MAN: No way.

WOMAN: Would you lie?

MAN: That's a whole other conversation, isn't it?

WOMAN: Yes, it is.

MAN: Yes, it is.

WOMAN: You men are such pigs.

MAN: And you women are so dumb.

WOMAN: You know what's so funny about that?

MAN: Tell me.

WOMAN: Going to.

MAN: Okay.

WOMAN: We think just the same about you.

MAN: Really?

WOMAN: Totally. Men in general? Just plain morons. To think that a man at work is "bringing home the bacon," thinking everything is just great. The wife is home "cleaning," everything is just great. Do you know how many of my girlfriends rob their husbands blind?

MAN: What do you mean?

WOMAN: Well, while the smart businessman is hard at work, the smart businesswoman is home at work. She's not really cleaning. She's got a maid. She's sleeping with the accountant. I don't need to give you the details there, but I'm sure you can use your imagination. But the funny part is, the stupid man is so clueless, and thinks his whole life is just perfect the way he wants it, and he doesn't have the common sense to check his account every once in a while.

MAN: Either that, or he's known about it all along and he doesn't say anything. You know why? 'Cause he's content. He's content with the situation, and it's worth a few bucks to continue banging the balls off of the secretary with the great lower half. Who knows, though?

WOMAN: I love you.

MAN: Love you, too! What's for dinner?

WOMAN: We're going out for dinner.

MAN: Says who?

WOMAN: Says you. Yesterday you said you would take me to dinner for my birthday.

MAN: You thought I forgot.

WOMAN: You did.

MAN: I know.

WOMAN: Asshole.

MAN: Bitch.

WOMAN: Come on, let's get ready.

MAN: Well, actually, honey. It's Monday night. The game and stuff.

WOMAN: I hate when my birthday falls on a Monday.

MAN: So do I. But what are you going to do?

WOMAN: I guess I'll whip something up.

MAN: Yes, you will.

WOMAN: Yes, I will, and you know what?

MAN: Tell me.

WOMAN: Going to... I'm not going to hold it against you.

MAN: Thanks.

WOMAN: I'm not gonna just pretend everything is okay, and take it out on you by giving you the silent treatment for the next couple of days, and every time you ask me what's wrong, just pout and say nothing. I refuse to do that!

MAN: Good!

WOMAN: I could if I wanted to, though.

MAN: I know you could.

WOMAN: I could go on and on about the fact that it's my birthday, and how dare you? I could go on still about how you never take me out, and how the kind of sensitivity and affection I need is completely void, and it's amazing that I don't feel totally taken for granted. But I'm not going to do that.

MAN: Why would you?

WOMAN: I wouldn't.

MAN: I know.

WOMAN: But just so you know, I know why I would, if I did.

MAN: Well, just keep that to yourself and we'll be just fine.

WOMAN: Done.

MAN: Love that!

WOMAN: I know you do!

MAN: What are you gonna make?

WOMAN: I don't know!

MAN: I do!

WOMAN: You do?

MAN: Yes, I do.

WOMAN: Tell me.

MAN: Going to.

WOMAN: Love that.

MAN: You're not going to make anything. You know why?

WOMAN: Nope.

MAN: You wanna know why? Going to… 'Cause it's your birthday!

WOMAN: Baby.

MAN: And you can't cook to save both of our precious lives… Just kidding, but if I wasn't, it would be true.

WOMAN: You love my cooking.

MAN: As long as that's what you think, that's all that matters.

WOMAN: That's what I think.

MAN: Praise Jesus.

WOMAN: Where do we eat?

MAN: It's your birthday, and I'd rather stay here and watch the game anyway. You decide.

WOMAN: No! You decide! You bore me to death and I'd rather go out with my friends, anyhow. It's totally up to you.

MAN: Is that true?

WOMAN: Is what true?

MAN: That I bore you.

WOMAN: Who cares?

MAN: Good point. Not me… What is that?

WOMAN: What?

MAN: Spending time together. You'd think that we'd have the common sense to just eliminate that all together. I mean, we only pretend to enjoy it.

WOMAN: When you're with me, who would you rather be with?

MAN: Anybody!

WOMAN: Me, too. Like, anyone else, it doesn't even matter who.

MAN: It's a shame we live together.

WOMAN: Hey, you win some, you lose some.

MAN: I love you.

WOMAN: I love you, too.

MAN: Hey, for the record, just real quick before we can't decide where we want to go eat because I'm a man and you're a woman, and we don't understand each other, and every time I pick a place to eat and you misconstrue it to be my way of letting you know I hate you, when in reality I just want to get the whole thing over with, and I could basically care less anyway.

WOMAN: Right. Or if, like, I pick a place and you think I picked it specifically because I know you hate it, and all I want to do is make your life more miserable than it already is, and then you come to your senses and realize that you're just making up reasons to truly define your disgust for me, when in reality you were right the first time?

MAN: Exactly.

WOMAN: Continue.

MAN: Thanks. What was I gonna say?

WOMAN: Who cares?

MAN: Good point. Let's go.

WOMAN: Perfect.

MAN: Oh, wait. I remember.

WOMAN: Don't you love that?

MAN: What?

WOMAN: Remembering.

MAN: That all depends.

WOMAN: Yes, it does.

MAN: Do you know what I remembered?

WOMAN: What you were going to say?

MAN: That's right.

WOMAN: Tell me.

MAN: Going to.

WOMAN: Good.

MAN: Food.

WOMAN: Where to go?

MAN: Before where to go. Why I'm going!

WOMAN: Because it's my birthday and you love me.

MAN: You're so cute. No! I'm going because I have no choice. It's what I'm "supposed" to do. (*To himself*) Football, dinner with the wife? Football, dinner with the wife? Insurance seminar, dinner with the wife...? You follow?

WOMAN: Like three fags on a yellow brick road.

MAN: Great.

WOMAN: So, where to, man?

MAN: Like I said.

WOMAN: Like you did, but I'm just the woman, and you're paying.

MAN: You wanna know why?

WOMAN: 'Cause you're the man, and men pay.

MAN: For more than you know, honey.

WOMAN: So, where to?

MAN: It's not gonna stop.

WOMAN: You're probably right.

MAN: I mean, we could starve to death.

WOMAN: Who do you think would die first?

MAN: Who do you think?

WOMAN: Meeeee.

MAN: Somebody give the lady a hand.

WOMAN: And somebody give the man a dick so he can make a discussion.

MAN: Below the belt.

WOMAN: Not much.

They both laugh.

MAN: Your pussy's big.

They laugh even harder.

WOMAN: Where to?

MAN: You're killing me.

WOMAN: You're killing me.

MAN: Speaking of which, do you ever think about killing yourself?

WOMAN: Every day.

MAN: Me, too.

WOMAN: Amazing.

MAN: Let's just do it. Then we wouldn't have to eat.

WOMAN: Ever again.

MAN: Perfect.

WOMAN: I have a gun.

MAN: I didn't know that?

WOMAN: If you only knew the things you didn't know.

MAN: Like the accountant?

WOMAN: Or the secretary?

MAN: You kill me.

WOMAN: I'm going to.

MAN: Get the gun.

The woman runs offstage and returns with a rifle.

MAN: Look at that thing. I can't believe you had such a big gun in the house. How did I not know about such a big gun in my own house. Have there been any other big guns in this house that I should know about?

The woman turns to the audience for the first time.

WOMAN: (*To the audience*): Do I even need to say it?

MAN: Wait, there's a problem.

WOMAN: What's that?

MAN: How do we do it?

WOMAN: What do you mean?

MAN: Someone kills and the other gets killed.

WOMAN: We take turns.

MAN: What if I change my mind after you're done?

WOMAN: Good point… You go first.

MAN: What if you change your mind?

WOMAN: I will once you're dead.

MAN: I know.

WOMAN: I couldn't live without you.

MAN: Liar.

WOMAN: Watch it, buddy.

MAN: What do we do?

WOMAN: You're the man.

MAN: This is true. Give me the gun…

Lights out… BANG! BANG!

THE END

Ten Years Later and...

It had been some time away from Playhouse West. Almost a decade. Val Lauren and I had just finished a production of No Way Around But Through *at Garry Marshall's Falcon Theater. Still buzzed from the run, or maybe it was the beer and weed, we got to talking and thought it would be an interesting experiment to go back to our old theater. We would dig up some of my old unpublished plays, invite current members of the company to work with us, and see what would come of it.*

With over ninety students on the material, we managed three full productions at Playhouse West, all original plays that had never before been performed, and the impetuous for this collection. 100 Days of Yesterday *was the first.*

100 Days of Yesterday

A New Play

100 Days of Yesterday *was originally produced by Samantha Watkins for The Playhouse West Repertory Theater Company—artistic director, Robert Carnegie, at Playhouse West Studio Two, North Hollywood, California, November 2013. It was directed by Val Lauren; set design by Jeff Robinson; stage management, lights, and sound design, Michael Miraula; costumes by Kacy Byxbee; additional crew: Joel Slabo, Darryl Clements, Joslyn Fink, and Ann Schmidt. The cast was as follows:*

WOMAN...................... *Anna Nalick*
MAN............................*Joseph Pease*

100 Days of Yesterday

LIGHTS UP

EXT. PARK— GLOOMY DAY

A WOMAN, 30, sits alone on a park bench. She stares ahead. Something in her eyes tells us she's been through it. Both her beauty and her sadness are stunning.

A MAN, handsome, same age, same look on his face, sits on his own bench, stage right, off behind the woman's.

He stares at the back of the woman's head for a few seconds, and then stands up.

Now standing, he stares for a few more beats and then steps forward. Very slowly, he makes a move toward the woman. He steps in front of the bench she's sitting on and looks off into the distance.

The woman notices him. He stands directly in front of her giving her his back.

The man shifts his weight from one side of his body to the other. He's clearly trying to get her attention.

At first she tries to ignore him, but it's too obvious.

WOMAN: Can I help you with something?

MAN: I don't know. Maybe. Can I ask you a couple questions?

WOMAN: No. Go away.

MAN: It won't take long.

WOMAN: Get out of here.

MAN: I just want to talk to you for a second.

WOMAN: Well, I don't want to talk to you?

MAN: Why not?

WOMAN: Because I don't.

MAN: Well, that's not cool.

WOMAN: Oh, it's not cool?

MAN: I haven't done anything to you.

WOMAN: You're creepy.

MAN: Well, that's not really cool either, is it?

WOMAN: What's your question?

MAN: Can I sit?

WOMAN: Absolutely not. You cannot sit. What's your question?

MAN: Why can't I sit?

WOMAN: Because I don't want you to sit.

MAN: But if we're going to have a conversation...

WOMAN: We're not. You're gonna ask me a question. Which I'm not too keen about it in the first place. But I'm being polite, so don't sit. Be courteous, and ask your question standing.

MAN: Well, I'd like to sit. I'd like to sit and have a conversation. I'm not so literal. Everything is not so literal. Someone says I want to ask you a question, it's like someone else saying I just had a baby. It's a way to start something. I'd like to sit and have a conversation.

WOMAN: Then, like I said, and another reason I don't like answering questions, is just that. I don't want to start something. I don't care to engage. Do you have a question or not?

MAN: I have a whole shitload of questions. As a matter of fact, you'd be surprised by how many things I'd like to know. It's seemingly endless. Can I please sit down and talk to you?

WOMAN: Why? I mean, what's the purpose? I mean, what are we doing anyway? What happens? We sit, we talk. Maybe we even laugh a little bit. It all seems so peaceful and happy. What do you do? Really? I like that band, too. Then what? Give me a break. I know the territory. I'm not in my twenties.

MAN: Neither am I.

WOMAN: I can see that.

MAN: That's nice.

WOMAN: Do yourself a favor.

MAN: No! Why don't you do me a favor?

WOMAN: You want to sit and talk?

MAN: Yes, I do.

WOMAN: Well, be my guest. Hope it works out.

MAN: Hope what works out?

WOMAN: Everything. You sitting or not?

MAN: What's your name?

WOMAN: What difference does it make? I'm the pretty lady in the park.

MAN: Nice to meet you.

The man sits down next to her.

WOMAN: So, what are you doing here?

MAN: I don't know. I just come here. Not much else to do. Or not much I'd like to be doing. You?

WOMAN: I don't know.

MAN: I noticed that. I mean, that's what it looked like, anyway. It's kind of why I wanted to come talk to you. Do you read? I mean, I ask because you don't have a book.

WOMAN: You ask if I read because I don't have a book? I shoot skeet from time to time. Didn't bring my shotgun either. Yes I read. What do you think I am?

MAN: Well, you don't have a book.

WOMAN: I don't have a bowling ball either. What is that?

MAN: I don't know. People come to the park, they read.

WOMAN: Yeah? Where's your book?

MAN: That was my point. I don't have one. Most people do things, you know? I come to sit and think, I guess. Contemplate. Go over stuff. Maybe you're doing the same.

WOMAN: Well, maybe I am.

MAN: Well, that's rare is all I'm saying.

WOMAN: That's ridiculous. People do things when they're not doing anything all the time. Nothing's rare about that. What are you trying to do?

MAN: I'm not trying to do anything. I'm simply acknowledging the fact that we're doing the same thing. You find it to be common, I don't. No big deal. We're doing the same thing.

WOMAN: We have so much in common.

MAN: Maybe we do.

WOMAN: Maybe we don't.

MAN: That's fine with me, too.

WOMAN: Well, I'm glad. Because I'll tell you something, life's not all what it's cracked up to be.

MAN: You don't gotta tell me.

WOMAN: Well, sure I do, look at you.

MAN: Excuse me?

WOMAN: You're here, aren't you?

MAN: I don't follow.

WOMAN: You're ten years old, you want to be a fireman, right?

MAN: No. I didn't.

WOMAN: Whatever, the point is, you're not a fireman. I don't know what you do, but you certainly don't fight fires and pull cats out of trees. Am I right?

MAN: I don't do those things. That's correct.

WOMAN: Okay. So, that's my point. Stuff just happens the way it does, and that's that. You can dream all day and you can imagine things up in your head, but it just doesn't work that way. Am I right?

MAN: Yes.

WOMAN: Okay. So you see a pretty woman in the park, guess what?

MAN: She's even worse off than you are?

WOMAN: Maybe so. You got it?

MAN: I do.

WOMAN: So, what did you want to ask me?

MAN: I'm gonna leave you alone now.

WOMAN: That's fine.

The man stands up.

MAN: It was nice chatting with you.

WOMAN: Now, that's not really true, is it?

The man doesn't have an answer right away.

MAN: No, not really, but I like to think I carry a certain tact. Like sometimes I want to tell people how stupid I think they are. Or just strangle them, but I don't. Nice chatting with you. I'd like to see you later, even though I probably won't.

WOMAN: Would you like to strangle me?

MAN: If you were into that sort of thing, I guess I could be up for it.

The woman sticks her head out.

WOMAN: Be my guest.

The man considers.

MAN: You know what, I don't have time for you.

WOMAN: And I don't have time for you. I never did.

MAN: Fuck you.

WOMAN: No, strangle me. Nice tact by the way.

MAN: There is something really wrong with you. You know what?

WOMAN: Tell me about it, I can't wait.

MAN: I'm a nice guy.

WOMAN: Yeah, well, fuck you, too.

MAN: I apologize for that. I wish I could take it back, but I can't.

WOMAN: Whatever.

MAN: I was just sitting there. Unhappily just sitting alone. That's what I do.

WOMAN: Well, I guess I'll start crying.

MAN: Shut up. Just shut up for a second. I'm a nice person.

WOMAN: You don't gotta tell me. You ooze sweetness. You're a prince.

MAN: I try. That's my point. I didn't come over here to harrass you. Is that what you think?

WOMAN: I think a lot of things.

MAN: Well, tell me what they are?

WOMAN: I don't even know you.

MAN: I can imagine that is something you say often.

WOMAN: Listen, you. I didn't come over there. You came over here. I still don't know why, but I'll take a guess.

MAN: To be nice.

WOMAN: Nothing's nice. Nothing's what it is. It's always some dream. Maybe it's a nice dream, but it never comes true. Intentions are like…

She points at him.

WOMAN: Assholes!

MAN: I had no intentions. And why am I an asshole?

WOMAN: I don't know. You just are. Just like I'm not a nice person.

MAN: I never said you were.

WOMAN: But you just assumed and that's my point. You know what? Get out of here. Don't even sit back down over there. Go home if you have a home. Don't think here. You're distracting the people who actually have something to think about. Better yet, go read a book.

MAN: *You* read a book, you goddamned book reader. You probably got a million stupid bestsellers stacked up on some faux fireplace in your little, repulsive, one-bedroom apartment. Don't you? Tell me I'm wrong.

WOMAN: Not only are you wrong, but you're ugly.

MAN: Okay! That I most certainly am not. Now I know you are full of shit. 'Cause guess what?

WOMAN: What?

MAN: I may be miserable.

WOMAN: Indeed.

MAN: I may be contemplating putting a bullet in my head.

WOMAN: Well, welcome to the club.

MAN: But I know one goddamned thing I am not. And that is unattractive.

WOMAN: Really?

MAN: Look me in the eye, and tell me with a straight face that I am not good-looking.

The woman leans in and stares him down.

WOMAN: You are not good-looking.

MAN: LIAR! INCORRECT! The answer is false. You lose.

WOMAN: You want me to tell you why you are wrong?

MAN: Yes. But keep in mind that I am speaking strictly aesthetics here.

WOMAN: Okay, then you're right. You are just stunning. I mean, it's hard getting past your striking good looks to see the real depth of your stupidity. You are so stupid.

MAN: I never said I wasn't. That's not what we're talking about here.

WOMAN: Do you really think it works that way?

MAN: Stop changing the subject.

WOMAN: It's your soul. You have an ugly soul.

MAN: Oh, yeah, and you have an ugly dress.

WOMAN: Now, I know you're full of shit.

MAN: Oh, you mean that dress is not attractive?

WOMAN: You're saying it's not?

MAN: Truth be told, I don't give a shit, but if you must know, I think you should dye it purple and burn it. This feels great, by the way. I really like you.

WOMAN: You're not so bad yourself.

MAN: Get up.

WOMAN: Excuse me?

MAN: Get up. You are coming with me. Let's go get a coffee.

WOMAN: I don't drink coffee.

MAN: Yes you do. Now get up!

The woman stands up.

BLACK OUT:

LIGHTS UP

INT. COFFEE SHOP—LATE DAY

The man and the woman sit on opposite sides of a table. They each have a cup of coffee.

The woman seems to be looking for something. The man hands her two packets of sugar.

She takes the sugars and pours them into her coffee.

MAN: So, what's your story?

WOMAN: Long story.

MAN: I bet.

The man just stares at her.

WOMAN: That's it?

MAN: Excuse me?

WOMAN: You got me here. Please tell me there's more.

MAN: There's more.

WOMAN: I mean, I'm giving you a shot here.

MAN: Is that what you think?

WOMAN: I mean, the stare's just not going to cut it. What do you got? I'm so interested, and at the same time, I will be so disappointed if you're relying on just your looks.

MAN: This is defense.

WOMAN: You?

MAN: No, you. I ask what your story is and you don't have anything to say. Defence. You look to me. And for the record, I have no interest in you sexually.

WOMAN: That's a lie.

MAN: Maybe it is, maybe it isn't.

WOMAN: So, what's your story?

MAN: Sexually?

WOMAN: I couldn't care less about that, but I'm sure you're amazing. Top notch, no less.

MAN: You bet your ass.

WOMAN: I bet.

MAN: Yeah.

WOMAN: You're boring.

MAN: This is stupid.

WOMAN: I agree. And you lose, 'cause guess what?

MAN: I'm dying.

WOMAN: You might as well be.

MAN: What is your deal?

WOMAN: Okay.

MAN: Okay?

WOMAN: Okay. I'll say something. I'll be the man here. I'll be you and me all at once. I hope you don't make me pick up the check though.

MAN: I wouldn't dream of it.

WOMAN: But you dream.

MAN: Almost done with that too.

WOMAN: What do you want?

MAN: What happened? I thought you were gonna play the roles here. Back to me so soon. I'm fucked, what else do you want to know?

WOMAN: Why?

MAN: Why what?

WOMAN: I gotta go.

MAN: Then go. You know what? Just go. Go ahead! I don't know what the hell we're doing here anyway. I don't care about you, you don't care about me. That's what we live in, so I don't know why this gonna be any different.

WOMAN: All right, fine. I'll stay.

MAN: Where are you from?

WOMAN: Nebraska.

MAN: Nope.

WOMAN: Nope?

MAN: You're not from Nebraska. I've been to Nebraska and you are not Nebraska.

WOMAN: Why's that?

MAN: 'Cause that place is nowhere. You're from a coast. You grew up with stuff. Nebraska's dead. Omaha, Lincoln, somewhere else. I've seen that place.

WOMAN: Maybe I moved young.

MAN: Maybe you did.

WOMAN: Where are you from?

MAN: Right here.

WOMAN: No one's from here.

MAN: I swear to God. Born and raised, and I've been everywhere else and this is where I wanna be. Trust me!

WOMAN: You been to Pittsburgh?

MAN: I like Pittsburgh.

WOMAN: Me, too.

MAN: Is that where you're from?

WOMAN: No.

MAN: So?

WOMAN: I gotta go.

MAN: See ya.

WOMAN: You want to come with me?

MAN: Where are we going?

WOMAN: To my repulsive, little, one-bedroom apartment.

The man thinks about it.

MAN: It's really not that bad.

She seems perplexed.

WOMAN: Excuse me?

The man waves it off.

MAN: Nothing.

The woman gets up and walks away, then stops.

WOMAN: Are you coming?

The man thinks about it for a couple of seconds. She waits.

BLACK OUT:

LIGHTS UP

INT. WOMAN'S APARTMENT—NIGHT

The woman stands in front of her bed. Just off to the side of the stage is a faux fireplace with a huge stack of books resting on it. The man checks the place out.

MAN: You mind if I ask you a question?

WOMAN: Oh, no. We're starting over already?

MAN: Why did you invite me over here?

She thinks about it. And starts straightening things up a bit.

WOMAN: I don't know, really.

MAN: Not really the safest thing in the world to do.

WOMAN: You don't scare me.

MAN: Well, that's because I'm good-looking. It's very rare that criminals look as good as I do. But I still think you gotta pay attention, and keep in mind there's always a chance.

WOMAN: You know what I think?

MAN: Not even a little bit.

WOMAN: I think that you don't think very highly of yourself.

MAN: Maybe you're right.

WOMAN: I'm serious.

MAN: So am I.

WOMAN: That's why you sound the way you sound. I have a lot of information on the subject, you know. My books? Not romance novels, so you know. I'm very interested in the mind, and the way it works.

MAN: Me, too.

WOMAN: Look how much we have in common.

MAN: What else?

WOMAN: How am I supposed to know?

MAN: I don't know. You know everything else. About me anyway. What about you?

WOMAN: I'm from somewhere, I live here now. I have dreams I can fly, and I don't own a television.

MAN: That's deep enough.

WOMAN: What's your problem, anyway?

MAN: I have a lot of them.

WOMAN: I can see that.

MAN: You can see it because you can relate. I think that's in those books, too.

The woman thinks about it.

WOMAN: Maybe it is. Or maybe they are. Or maybe I didn't do so well in school and that's why I can't speak.

MAN: Where did you go to school?

WOMAN: I don't know.

MAN: That's funny.

WOMAN: You think that's funny?

MAN: No. That's why I said it and didn't laugh. When something's funny, I just laugh.

WOMAN: Then why say it?

MAN: Because I'm running out of things to say.

WOMAN: Would you like something to drink?

MAN: No.

WOMAN: Then what do you want to do?

MAN: Talk.

WOMAN: About what?

MAN: I do't know. How it is. How it was. What it's like now.

WOMAN: Are you retarded?

MAN: No. Are you?

WOMAN: Listen here, dummy. I speak English, okay? That's it. A little French, maybe, but that seems to be rusty as of late. You get what I'm saying here?

MAN: You ever spend time in France?

WOMAN: No.

MAN: Then why do you speak French?

WOMAN: I don't know.

MAN: Well, you have to know. Did you go to a French-speaking school? Did you have a Parisian nanny when you were a kid? I mean, come on!

WOMAN: What is your problem?

MAN: What is your problem? You mean to tell me you've never seen the Eiffel Tower?

The woman doesn't say anything.

WOMAN: All right, I'll tell you one thing, and that's it. Sit down.

The man sits.

WOMAN: You're a sad person.

MAN: Is that what you were going to tell me?

WOMAN: No.

MAN: So?

WOMAN: So, what?

MAN: You were saying?

WOMAN: What was I saying?

MAN: Something.

WOMAN: About?

MAN: One thing. You were going to tell me one thing. I'm interested. Do you have something to say or not?

WOMAN: I do. I have a lot to say. I'm just not sure where to start. I don't want to lose you.

MAN: I can keep up.

WOMAN: You married?

MAN: No, I'm not married.

WOMAN: Divorced?

MAN: Never married, close once, never divorced.

WOMAN: Now we're getting somewhere.

The man stands up.

MAN: Where? Where are we getting? Where are we going? You're like a talk box that doesn't say anything. Just spits out questions, and can't reply because of wiring or something.

WOMAN: Just sit down.

The man sits.

MAN: What?

WOMAN: Just tell me what could be so bad.

MAN: Are you serious?

WOMAN: Life is tough for you, you gotta go sit in the park and talk to pretty girls. You sit around and wait for someone to say, "Awww, what's the matter?" What? I'm just interested.

MAN: Where do you get off?

WOMAN: Right here. I get off right here. This is my last stop. Either you tell me what the hell is so bad or I'm gonna call the cops.

MAN: The cops?

WOMAN: Or whatever. I'm gonna ask you to leave.

The man stands up.

MAN: I can't do this anymore.

WOMAN: Well, it was nice to meet you...

MAN: Jack. My name is Jack. Say it.

WOMAN: Jack.

MAN: Say it again.

WOMAN: Is this gonna get kinky?

MAN: I don't know. You want it, too?

WOMAN: Well, you're not quite attractive yet, but you're getting warmer.

MAN: You find me to be stunning.

WOMAN: Where do you get this?

MAN: It's a fact.

WOMAN: Oh, yeah. What about me?

MAN: I think you are the prettiest woman I have ever seen in my life.

WOMAN: You don't mean that?

MAN: Yes, I do.

WOMAN: What about my dress?

MAN: Ugliest fucking dress I have ever seen in my life.

WOMAN: Well, at least I know you're honest.

MAN: Always. I am always honest. I've never lied to you... I will never lie to you.

WOMAN: Well, I'll never lie to you either. I may not speak to you again, but if I do, I won't lie.

MAN: That's not very nice.

WOMAN: Well, I dig honesty is the point. Big bonus with me.

MAN: Me, too.

WOMAN: Well, look at that. We sort of do have a lot in common.

MAN: I'm starting to think so, too.

WOMAN: So, were you gonna leave? We were just getting kinky. Where were we?

MAN: You were going to tell me something. I was thinking of leaving because of the ongoing problem we are experiencing here. It's your problem actually. The completion of a sentence is what you struggle with. Maybe you would like to sit down and try again.

WOMAN: You're funny.

MAN: I know! Thank you.

WOMAN: Can I ask you a question?

MAN: Only if I can ask you one, too.

WOMAN: You can ask all you want.

MAN: But will you answer me?

WOMAN: Depends on the question.

MAN: You can't even answer that one.

WOMAN: What do you want to know, Jack?

MAN: You remembered my name.

WOMAN: You only just told me.

MAN: Well, it's a funny thing, the memory.

WOMAN: Oh yeah? Why's that?

MAN: I don't know. I feel like you're able to remember the things you care to remember.

WOMAN: Not always.

MAN: That's true, maybe you just have to try harder.

WOMAN: I do.

MAN: Well, that's all anyone can ask, I guess.

WOMAN: I go to sleep having remembered my entire day.

MAN: What about when you wake up?

WOMAN: I don't know.

MAN: Maybe I'll ask you some questions now.

WOMAN: Okay.

MAN: Have you ever been in love?

WOMAN: That's so funny.

MAN: You're not laughing.

WOMAN: No, I mean it. Ironic, not funny. Is there an action for ironic?

MAN: Excuse me?

WOMAN: Funny haha. Ironic…?

MAN: Oh, right. I don't know.

WOMAN: Funny or ironic because that's what I was going to ask you.

MAN: Well, I asked you first.

WOMAN: I think you know my answer.

MAN: You don't know.

WOMAN: Or I can't remember.

MAN: Might have been just yesterday.

WOMAN: Who knows?

The man takes a few seconds.

MAN: Is that why you're so upset?

WOMAN: Who said I was upset?

MAN: You did. And it was today, so you should remember.

The woman seems deeply engaged for the first time.

WOMAN: You tell me about love and maybe I'll remember.

The man walks around the room for a while. The woman waits.

MAN: What do you want to know?

WOMAN: Whatever you can tell me, I guess.

MAN: I'll tell you what I can tell you.

WOMAN: Well, I can't ask for more than that.

MAN: For me. What it is for me. Maybe you can relate, maybe not. But we seem to have a lot in common.

WOMAN: Maybe we do, maybe we don't.

MAN: Love!

WOMAN: Love!

MAN: The most excruciating heart-wrenching torture I have ever had to deal with in my entire life and to tell you the truth, I don't wish it on anybody. But at the same time, I wouldn't give it up, not for a billion dollars.

WOMAN: You know what I think?

MAN: I have no clue what you think.

WOMAN: I think you should write that down and send it to Hallmark because it was really, really special.

MAN: Sorry.

WOMAN: If I wanted that, I could have just turned on the TV.

MAN: You don't have a TV.

WOMAN: For that very reason.

MAN: Oh, yeah. Then what do you got?

WOMAN: No way.

MAN: No way?

WOMAN: That's right, no way.

MAN: At least I have something.

WOMAN: You don't have shit.

MAN: I got more than you.

WOMAN: Is that what you think?

MAN: That's what I know.

WOMAN: Well, you're wrong, you don't know.

MAN: What? What don't I know?

WOMAN: Anything. Life, love, any of it.

MAN: Then tell me. Prove me wrong.

WOMAN: I killed myself for it. That enough?

MAN: You killed yourself or you tried to kill yourself?

WOMAN: Both.

MAN: No, you didn't.

WOMAN: Who the fuck are you? Yes I did.

MAN: You didn't do that.

WOMAN: Don't tell me what I didn't do.

MAN: Well, don't tell me what you think you did.

WOMAN: What do you know?

MAN: I know all kinds of shit.

WOMAN: Oh, yeah? Like what?

MAN: The sky is blue. Trees are trees. And you are most certainly not dead. You might be halfway there, maybe further even, but you are here. That is a fact.

WOMAN: You don't know where I am, and you don't know where I came from either.

MAN: Well, I'm not a fucking mind reader.

WOMAN: Forget it.

MAN: Forget what?

WOMAN: You're not worth it.

MAN: I'm not worth what?

WOMAN: My time, my energy, or my explanation. Love is this and love is that. You're a child. I tried to kill myself, I crashed. You don't know about anything. You're like an infant crawling around wondering what everything is like, and you hate it, so you make things up. You make up stories so that it doesn't all have to be about bottles and tall people.

MAN: What the fuck are you talking about?

WOMAN: You want to know something, you better tell me something. And if you write me another fucking Christmas card, I'm gonna throw up all over the floor.

MAN: You're so pathetic, you know that? What did you do? What the hell is wrong with you? You killed yourself? Bullshit. You didn't do shit. You don't know. And you don't want to know.

WOMAN: What don't I know?

MAN: You don't know anything. You can't remember, you're not sure.

WOMAN: I'm full of shit?

MAN: Yeah. Goddamn right you are. Maybe you're not worth it. Maybe that's it.

WOMAN: Get out.

MAN: No.

WOMAN: Get out.

MAN: I'd like to hit you.

WOMAN: Fine.

MAN: Bye.

The man moves for the door.

WOMAN: Bye… Jack!

The man stops at the door.

MAN: I'll see you.

WOMAN: I never want to see you again.

MAN: Okay.

The man exits.

The woman sits alone on stage and begins to cry.

BLACK OUT:

LIGHTS UP

INT. MAN'S APARTMENT—DAY

The man's apartment. The bed is on the opposite side of the stage. Almost no furniture. Some moving-boxes.

NOTE: This is a new day, both the man and the woman are wearing a new change of clothes.

The woman walks around the apartment.

The man packs some personal belongings into a box.

WOMAN: Looks like it's your lucky day, Jake.

MAN: Oh, yeah. Why's that?

WOMAN: I usually don't go home with men I meet at the park.

MAN: I see. What do you usually do? Take 'em to your place?

WOMAN: Absolutely not. I'm a very private person. I would never do that.

MAN: Right. And it's Jack, by the way.

She looks around and takes the place in.

WOMAN: Right. So, what are you, a Virgo, Jack?

MAN: Why do you ask me that?

WOMAN: I don't know. Just checking compatibility, I guess.

MAN: Really?

WOMAN: No. Not really. Looks like an operating room in here.

MAN: You believe in that stuff?

WOMAN: Operating? Sure, saves lives.

MAN: That's cute.

WOMAN: Hey, look, whatever works for you. Some people look for signs, some people take life for what it is.

MAN: Oh yeah? What do you do?

WOMAN: And some people like furniture, some people don't. Whatever floats your boat.

MAN: I'm moving.

WOMAN: Oh, yeah? Where are you going?

MAN: I'm not sure yet.

WOMAN: So mysterious.

MAN: Not really.

WOMAN: I'd ask, but I'm sure the answer's just way too complex. I love it when people are deep with me the very day that I've met them. It turns me on.

MAN: What does turn you on?

WOMAN: You do.

MAN: Really?

WOMAN: What do you think?

MAN: I think that you are an asshole.

WOMAN: Wow. What a gentlemen. Nice to have met you.

MAN: Yeah, well, I give up.

WOMAN: Don't got a lot of try in you, huh?

MAN: You have no idea.

WOMAN: I bet. Now I know why you're skipping town. You've probably been here for days upon days. Even weeks maybe.

MAN: I don't even know what to say to that.

WOMAN: You don't have a lot to say about much, do you?

MAN: Why are you like this? I have to know.

WOMAN: Well, I don't, okay?

MAN: Okay.

WOMAN: So, you really don't know where you're going?

MAN: I don't know, any suggestions?

WOMAN: Everywhere sucks.

MAN: I figured as much.

WOMAN: You might as well stay where you are.

MAN: I can't do that anymore.

WOMAN: Why not?

MAN: Because I'm starting to hate the park.

WOMAN: What the hell does that mean?

MAN: Nothing. Maybe it's a metaphor.

WOMAN: Maybe you're a metaphor.

MAN: Oh, yeah? What am I metaphor...for?

WOMAN: That's funny?

MAN: You actually laughed.

WOMAN: Well, that's what I do when things are funny.

MAN: That's funny.

WOMAN: You're not laughing.

MAN: Never mind.

WOMAN: Never mind what, weirdo?

MAN: Yesterday.

WOMAN: What was yesterday?

MAN: Fucking Tuesday.

WOMAN: What?

MAN: What did you do yesterday?

WOMAN: I don't remember.

MAN: Right.

The woman takes a beat. The man puts his head down.

WOMAN: You really don't know where you're going?

MAN: Not really.

WOMAN: But you're going?

MAN: Pretty sure.

WOMAN: Just giving up?

MAN: Maybe.

WOMAN: I guess I can understand that.

MAN: Tell me about it.

WOMAN: Yeah.

MAN: No, I mean, tell me about it. Literally tell me.

WOMAN: That might be a little deep, don't you think? I mean, we did just meet.

MAN: Right.

WOMAN: You know what I think?

MAN: No.

WOMAN: I think you must be pretty weak.

MAN: Really?

WOMAN: I mean that in the most constructive way possible.

MAN: Sure, I didn't take offense to it. I'm already finding the real meaning. The depth of it all. The bright side.

WOMAN: I mean, I suppose I understand being hurt, or having problems, but it's not like you just walk away from the bird house and forget how to fly. I mean if you're crazy, you're crazy, you know what I mean? Here, there, wherever. You're still a nutjob.

MAN: Well, I'm hardly a nutjob, but thank you.

WOMAN: Nutjob, broken-hearted, it's all the same stuff. It's a malfunction. A derailment. Something gone awry. I read a lot of books, for the record. On this subject, specifically, so I don't want you to think I don't know my business here, 'cause I do. See, we're all born with the same parts up there, but sometimes things don't go as planned. Train's supposed to stay on the track, but sometimes it doesn't, and when it doesn't, guess what, bad shit happens. You drive a car like an asshole and eventually the transmission stops working. All this to say, you got a delicate piece of work up there that's been twisted and turned, but running off to Costa Rica or some place isn't gonna help nothing. You might as well just chop your head off. At least that would be productive.

MAN: Well, I guess I choose the lesser of two evils.

WOMAN: What good is evil if it doesn't work.

MAN: So, what are you saying?

WOMAN: I say be a man.

MAN: You want me to stay?

WOMAN: I don't care what you do.

MAN: Well, that's why I'm leaving.

WOMAN: That doesn't make any sense.

MAN: Well, maybe I should read some more books.

WOMAN: Tell you the truth, that doesn't really help either. In my experience, you just gotta sit. People like to run. Are you a jogger, Jack?

MAN: Not yet, but I think I'm gonna give it a try, Sally.

The woman takes a long look at him.

WOMAN: Why?

MAN: 'Cause I can't do it anymore. I can't do the same thing every day and not have something different happen.

WOMAN: Try something different.

MAN: I've tried everything. Twice.

WOMAN: So, that's it?

MAN: I don't want it to be. But I don't know what else to do.

WOMAN: Tell somebody.

MAN: I do. Every day.

WOMAN: Well, give it one last shot. I bet you've never tried it with a stranger.

The man thinks about it.

MAN: Okay.

WOMAN: Great.

MAN: I hope you don't make fun of me.

WOMAN: I might, but who cares? This is for you. It's not about me.

The man takes a breath.

MAN: I pretty much spent the majority of my life making really bad decisions.

WOMAN: People do that.

MAN: Not neccessarily bad, just wrong.

WOMAN: Wrong, bad. Semantics.

MAN: The people I spent time with.

WOMAN: Women.

MAN: Hurting women. Not on purpose, just living in a place where I couldn't be hurt.

WOMAN: That's it?

MAN: No. Something happened.

WOMAN: What happened?

MAN: Things changed.

WOMAN: Great. What changed?

MAN: Everything. I got a chance to look at something different. Something like me, maybe. But different.

WOMAN: That's deep.

MAN: Deep and gone.

WOMAN: Oh, yeah? Well, where did that fly off to?

MAN: I don't know.

WOMAN: Is that where you're going?

MAN: I wish.

WOMAN: So, now what?

MAN: Life, I guess. Just every day. Walking around with nowhere to go. Driving for miles with no music. Thinking about nothing.

WOMAN: Sounds great.

MAN: Maybe it is. Empty, but at least alone and unaware.

WOMAN: Of what? Music? Destination? You talk in dots and dashes, you know that?

MAN: Well, that's life I guess. A bunch of dots and dashes.

WOMAN: So, where's the good part?

MAN: Right here. It's right here. If you could just open your eyes and see that it's standing right in front of you.

WOMAN: You?

MAN: And you.

WOMAN: Me?

MAN: That's right.

WOMAN: You're an idiot.

MAN: I know.

WOMAN: And you're a borderline nutjob as far as I'm concerned.

MAN: I don't think so. I think the definition of crazy is trying the same thing over and over and expecting a different result. I think giving up is what makes me sane.

WOMAN: I think checking into a facility would at least support a form of sanity for you. But you're fucked. At least partially, anyhow.

MAN: Not even partially. I have hope. Nothing worse than hope. It keeps you there. It doesn't let you surrender.

WOMAN: Apparently it lets you surrender just fine.

MAN: I have no choice.

WOMAN: You always have a choice.

MAN: Well, I can see what you chose. You chose death.

WOMAN: Wrong. I said you have a choice, I didn't say that I did.

MAN: I'm giving you a choice right now.

WOMAN: You're giving me a headache right now.

MAN: Well, at least you're listening.

WOMAN: What do you want?

MAN: I want what I had.

WOMAN: I still don't know what that is.

MAN: Sure you do. You want the same thing.

WOMAN: I want reality.

MAN: You got it.

WOMAN: What do you got?

MAN: Want. I have want. I have need and want. I have alone, I have empty, and I have lonely.

WOMAN: I have nausea.

MAN: I have to go.

WOMAN: Then go.

MAN: After you.

WOMAN: No, please.

MAN: I live here.

WOMAN: Not anymore you don't.

The man takes a few steps.

MAN: It doesn't have to be like this.

WOMAN: It most certainly does.

The woman takes a step toward the door.

MAN: Sally.

She stops.

WOMAN: What?

MAN: Where do you think she went?

WOMAN: She's a figment of your imagination.

MAN: Maybe she is.

WOMAN: Well, you can't have dreams, we both know that.

MAN: Maybe it's not a dream.

WOMAN: She's a dream.

MAN: I want her.

WOMAN: She's gone.

MAN: Then I want you?

WOMAN: Well, I'm not on the market.

MAN: Why is that?

WOMAN: 'Cause I'm not. I died a long time ago, buddy. You're too late
and I'm out the door.

MAN: Wait.

WOMAN: What?

MAN: Don't leave.

WOMAN: I'm leaving.

MAN: Don't leave. If you leave, I'm leaving, too, and I know you don't
want me to do that. I'll stay. I'll stay forever, just tell me what you
remember.

WOMAN: Remember what?

MAN: That you didn't try to kill yourself and that you're not dead.

WOMAN: Leave it alone, Jack.

MAN: it was an accident.

WOMAN: It was no accident, Jack. It was the end, and that's why I tried to kill myself.

MAN: NO! That's why you can't remember, because you had an accident. So if you can't remember, then just shut the fuck up and listen to me, 'cause I do.

WOMAN: I'm listening.

MAN: Say you had an accident.

WOMAN: Say I did.

MAN: No. Say it. Say the words. I had an accident.

WOMAN: This is silly.

MAN: Will you just play along?

WOMAN: I had an accident.

MAN: There was a horrible crash.

WOMAN: What kind?

MAN: No. Just say what I say.

WOMAN: There was a horrible crash.

MAN: But I loved you and you loved me and everything's okay now.

WOMAN: You need help.

MAN: No shit. So help me out here. Just say it, please.

WOMAN: It's over.

MAN: Fine. Then start over. Try again. If you would just say something, then it would exist. Maybe I'm crazy, maybe I am stupid, I'm most likely an asshole. But here I am and I love you. Who cares why? Who cares how it goes or how it happened. It just did. Why isn't that enough? Every fucking day with this shit. I can't take it anymore. Why can't you just stop? Move forward! Live. Be a human being and have something. So goddamned busy trying to get the past that you're missing the future. And I'm being dragged along. I don't want to do it anymore. I can't do it anymore. Take a fucking swing already because I've had it.

The woman takes a beat.

WOMAN: Why are you screaming?

The man falls down on his knees.

MAN: Please.

WOMAN: What?

MAN: Will you just love me. Please just love me.

The woman gets on the floor with him and takes his hands.

WOMAN: I'll love you.

MAN: You promise?

WOMAN: I do.

They embrace. Kiss. Touch.

BLACK OUT:

LIGHTS UP

INT. MAN'S APARTMENT—MORNING

The man lies alone in his bed sleeping. He wakes up, and immediately realizes he is alone.

He jumps out of bed.

MAN: Sally… Sally.

He opens the door searching for her.

MAN: Sally?

He finds a note pinned to the front door. He removes it and begins to read it.

The man starts to cry. He falls down onto the floor wailing and clutching the letter.

MAN: SALLY!

BLACK OUT:

LIGHTS UP

EXT. PARK—DAY

The woman sits alone on a bench staring straight out into the audience.

The man enters and notices her. He checks her out for a couple of seconds and then heads over to her. He stands in front of her.

The woman stares up at him.

WOMAN: Can I help you with something?
MAN: I don't know. Maybe. Can I ask you a couple of questions?
WOMAN: No. Go away.

The man waits a beat, then puts his head down and walks away.

He stops, looks back at her, and then out to the audience.

BLACK OUT:

THE END

The group theater of necessity, to fulfill their vision, had to eventually produce their own playwright. That playwright was Clifford Odets. I have always thought of Scott as Playhouse West's Clifford Odets. Both are distinguished by a very unique use of dialogue. Clifford's characters spoke like no one had ever spoken in plays before. Scott Caan's characters speak like no on has ever spoken in plays before.

His writing is thoroughly original, filled with a sly humor only Scott Caan could produce, and a kind of dialogue that I can only attempt to describe as street poetry. His plays speak to his moment in history. Like all good writers, he confines himself to only writing what he knows, and he knows a lot.

—Robert Carnegie

The following vignettes were written during the course of our production class. The idea was to write something similar to Minor Conversations, *but a more contemporary version. It begins with a couple meeting, and it ends with a couple splitting apart. The pieces were written in the style of vignettes rather than one-acts, simply because of the way I was writing at the time.*

Minor Conversations

A Collection of Vignettes

Minor Conversations *was originally produced by Darryl Clements for The Playhouse West Repertory Theater Company—artistic director, Robert Carnegie, at Playhouse West Studio One, North Hollywood, California, July 2014. It was directed by Val Lauren; stage management, lights, and sound design by Michael Miraula; additional crew, Kelly Russo.*

Below listed are the locations that the director chose to place all the vignettes. They may differ from the descriptions written in the original plays. They were all performed with nothing on a stage but a table and two chairs. The male role in the last vignette was cast with a woman. The cast was as follows:

The Room Before—A Waiting Room
JED..................Ross Gallo
TRISH..............Robyn Cohen

Wrong Side—A Living Room
SLOAN..............Mia Serafino
TED..................Danny Barclay

Clean It Up—A Locker Room
MAN..................Anton Narinsky
BUDDY...............Will McMahon

A Theory—A Restaurant
LUCY..................Keleigh Kremers
TINA....................Ariana Basseri

Cheating—A Kitchen
JUNE..................Mia Serafino
KASEY...............Joseph Pease

No More—A Restroom
CARRIE..............Ashley Osborne
DEB.....................Tera Conners

Right's Right—A Park
TONY...................Danny Barclay
JACK....................Jospeh Pease

The Last Conversation—A Café
KELLY..................Mia Serafino
SEAN...................Robyn Cohen

The Room Before

Minor Conversations—The Room Before

A WAITING ROOM

A MAN sits down in the waiting room. This is JED. After a few beats, a WOMAN walks in. She sits down, not acknowledging Jed. This is TRISH. Jed checks her out. But slick, so as not to get caught. She ignores him, but can feel his eyes. She pulls a book out of her purse and begins to read.

A few more silent beats. Then Jed leans in.

JED: Just waiting, huh?

She slowly picks up her head.

TRISH: Yeah.

Jed nods his head.

JED: Yeah.

She clearly wants to be left alone.

JED: You mind if I ask what for?

She thinks a bit.

TRISH: Yeah.

Jed shifts back in his seat.

JED: Okay. No problem. Don't want to be a pest. Just a question.

He waits. Leans in to her.

JED: Too big?
TRISH: Excuse me?

JED: The question. Too big? Is the question too big? Not in length, obviously. Not the statement itself, but rather the... You know? The weight. It's heavy. It's got some stuff to it. Yeah?

TRISH: Maybe, yes.

JED: Right. I get it. Believe you me, I understand. What are we doing? What's going on? What's it all about? I get it. It's a lot.

TRISH: Right.

JED: You ever think? I mean, not you personally. I mean yes, I'm asking you, but not you specifically. Like the general you. Us really. You ever think?

TRISH: Do I ever think what?

JED: This. This here. This is where we'd end up? Waiting. Just waiting.

TRISH: Yeah.

JED: Right?

TRISH: Yeah.

JED: Not a lot for words you, huh?

TRISH: Excuse me?

JED: You got a nice mouth. Should use it maybe.

TRISH: Who the hell are you?

JED: Hey, listen, lady. Don't go left with me. This is your fault. I'm being nice. I'm killing time. What are we doin'? I even complimented you. You want to be left alone? Fine. Not another word.

She is completely dumbfounded.

TRISH: What is your name?

He waits. Offers a hand.

JED: I'm Jed.

She takes it.

TRISH: Trish, Jed.

JED: That short?

TRISH: No. Just Trish.

JED: Nice.

TRISH: How about you, Jed. Waiting for something specific?

JED: Funny you should ask.

TRISH: Because we're here?

JED: Yeah.

TRISH: Well, that's why I ask.

JED: Just trying to figure it out, Trish.

TRISH: Yeah. Me, too.

JED: That's right.

TRISH: I didn't mean to… You know, be mean.

JED: You gotta be careful. I get it.

TRISH: Crazies everywhere.

JED: You don't gotta tell me. Just yesterday, I was waiting with this guy. About six feet tall. Big fella. Outta nowhere he starts screaming at the top of his lungs, "GET ME OUTTA HERE, GET ME OUTTA HERE, I CAN'T TAKE IT ANYMORE."

This really gets her attention.

TRISH: Really?

JED: I'm telling you. They pulled him out with a zapper.

She's confused.

JED: One of those cattle prods.

TRISH: Stop.

JED: I'm telling ya. You don't fit in, they want you out.

TRISH: Unreal.

JED: I know it. Forget the fact the guy was scaring people. I mean, sure, you gotta look out for yourself, and that's really the point here. But tools? Electric tools?

TRISH: Last week, I'm waiting with a few of my friends. Just minding our own, and right out of the blue, this big Chinese woman comes running down the steps with a rope and some pain pills.

JED: What'd they do?

TRISH: They tackled her. Tied her up with the rope and took the pills.

JED: Unbelievable.

TRISH: Who knows what she was up to?

JED: Maybe she needed the pills.

TRISH: Maybe she needed the pills. What? Was she too big? A rope's illegal? Since when?

JED: Not where I come from.

TRISH: Right?

A beat or two.

TRISH: Where is that?

JED: Where I come from?

TRISH: Yeah.

JED: All over.

TRISH: Yeah? Me, too.

JED: Nice to see you here.

TRISH: Yeah. You never know.

JED: That's it. You never know.

Trish nods her head. Then goes back to her book. Jed shifts around in his seat a bit.

JED: Never. Not once.

She looks up.

JED: I'm sorry.

TRISH: No. Go ahead.

JED: I just never thought that this would be it. I always figured myself for a do-er, you know?

TRISH: Yeah.

JED: Go out and get it. That was always the thing, and now here I am. Here we are.

TRISH: It's not so bad.

JED: That's personal.

TRISH: Maybe you should get up, then.

JED: Maybe you should, too.

TRISH: Now that's personal.

JED: Maybe we should get up together.

TRISH: Oh, really?

JED: You want to sit here today? You wanna do it tomorrow, too?

TRISH: I'm here. Aren't I?

JED: Yeah, but why? That's what I'm saying.

TRISH: With you?

JED: Why not me?

Trish thinks.

JED: Where are we going? What are we doing? If this is it till the end, then I'm ready to stop now. I mean, this is something else. Forget that. It's not even something to begin with.

TRISH: You want to know something?

JED: What the hell am I saying?

TRISH: Fine. You sit tight. You just relax. Maybe that's not the kind of person you are. To tell you the truth, I might not be either. But we're here. We're following the rules.

JED: Don't like those.

TRISH: Rules?

JED: That's right.

TRISH: Such a man.

JED: Please.

TRISH: It's true.

JED: I'm getting under your skin and you know it.

TRISH: Ha.

JED: You want to get out of here, don't you? Don't lie to me.

A moment.

TRISH: I don't know what I want.

JED: Yeah.

TRISH: Yeah.

JED: That's what we're doing.

TRISH: Just like everyone else.

Jed nods his head.

JED: I tried.

TRISH: Maybe try again.

JED: Now?

TRISH: No. Next time. If that happens, I mean. Today I'm not ready, but next time I might be.

JED: That's no good for me.

TRISH: Well, I'm sorry.

JED: So am I. If it happens, it happens.

TRISH: If it doesn't, it doesn't.

JED: It won't. I'm ready today. Tomorrow? You keep waiting. I'm gonna go now.

He stands up. Waits a bit.

TRISH: Wait. Would it be too late now?

Jed thinks on it.

JED: No. Right now would be just fine.

Trish stands up.

THE END

Wrong Side

Minor Conversations—Wrong Side

A BEDROOM

A MAN and a WOMAN lay in bed. TED and SLOAN. Both mid-thirties. Maybe she's a bit younger. The place is nice, but not too nice. It's where an artist and his gal sleep.

They might be sleeping. She might be, but he's definitely not. He looks around the bedroom. Side to side, he wants to get up, but not enough to actually get up. Something is certainly wrong. He slides up into a ninety-degree siting position.

Somehow Sloan wakes up. Maybe he moved around too much, made some noise.

She sits up in the bed next to him. Takes a few looks at him.

SLOAN: So?

He nods his head. Negative.

SLOAN: Bad?
TED: As opposed to good?
SLOAN: Scale of one to ten?

He thinks about it for a second or two.

TED: I don't know. Up there, though, for sure.
SLOAN: I'm sorry.
TED: Yeah.
SLOAN: Is there anything I can do?
TED: I don't know.
SLOAN: How bout a waffle?

He nods. Negative.

SLOAN: Blowjob?

He forces a smile.

SLOAN: (*Cont'd*) Let me know.

She gets up out of the bed and heads toward the bathroom. He just sits there staring at the walls.

TED: I'm sorry.

SLOAN: (*Off*) You don't have to be sorry to me.

TED: Who should I be sorry to? You have to live with it. You have to wake up next to it every day.

SLOAN: (*Off*) Not every day.

TED: Close enough. I mean, I suppose I could be sorry to myself but that's not really gonna get me anywhere, is it?

No response. He puts his head down into his hands.

TED: This is so stupid.

She comes out of the bathroom.

SLOAN: It's not stupid, it's the way you feel when you wake up.

She sits back down on the bed next to him.

SLOAN: (*Cont'd*) It's important. I suppose the most important moment of the day. Sort of sets you up for the rest of it, until you fall back asleep again.

Ted agrees.

SLOAN: Maybe you should try to fall back asleep again for a bit, see if anything changes.

TED: No. I'll never get out of bed. Then it's called depression. I think I'm just barely beating the diagnosis with the staying awake and feeling like shit most mornings. Slowly oozing out of bed, you know.

SLOAN: Okay. What do you think about?

TED: What do you mean?

SLOAN: When you wake up and feel this way. What are you thinking about?

TED: It varies. Nothing specific. I mean, sure, there are specifics within the specific moments, but just general bad shit. It's like smoking pot. You know you're watching TV, and you're trying to pay attention, but next thing you know, due to the reefer, you're off thinking about other shit. I mean, you're staring at the TV, sure, for all intents and purposes you're watching it, in theory. Reality? You're really off somewhere else thinking about other shit, bad shit in my case, but whatever. Stuff. Someone asks you where you were. Hey, snap out of it. What were you thinking? I don't know. I have no clue.

Sloan thinks about it. She may have an idea.

SLOAN: What did we watch last night?

Ted thinks about it.

TED: See, I have no idea.

SLOAN: Did something happen during the day?

TED: Yeah. The day.

She thinks for a bit.

SLOAN: Maybe you're smoking too much pot.

TED: No. See, look. I don't want to do this.

SLOAN: Do what? What don't you want to do?

TED: Reason. Solutions. Complete waste of time.

SLOAN: Well, that's what most people do.

TED: Fine. Then I don't want to be people. Sleep more, don't smoke pot? Think of fairies instead of dead people? As a matter of fact, I do remember what we were watching last night. Keith Richards.

SLOAN: The documentary.

TED: That's right. He's talking. I'm halfway listening due to the reefer, and all I can think about is that this guy's fucking old. I mean, he can barely speak. Now when I was younger, that's not what I thought. He was younger, too, but that's not the point. I used to watch the guy, and all I thought was what a badass he was. He must really enjoy being Keith Richards. I mean, what's not to like? I do whatever I want, I'm a genius, and I'm Keith fucking Richards. Now I watch the guy, and I'm thinking about how sad he must be. Yeah, he still plays. They do shows. Tours. I don't know. But he's gotta know it's all coming to a close at some point very soon in the future. I would imagine that's overwhelming. I imagine that takes a hold, and all the good times get smashed away into this other place, where all we're doing now is, aside from trying to figure out what state we're in because we're senile and done too many narcotics, but this state, this constant state of trying to piece it all together and come to terms with the depressing fact that it's almost fucking over. We're left just trying to remember the good, but we can't due to everything I just said. So what? Stop watching television because it makes me sad and puts me in touch with something, that in my right mind, I'm far too young to be in touch with. That's not right. We gotta watch TV. What the hell else do you do at night? Read? That could be potentially depressing as well.

She's speechless.

TED: I don't want any solutions. Please.

She gets up and heads back to the bathroom.

SLOAN: I was just trying to help.

TED: Don't do that.

She stops.

SLOAN: What am I doing?

TED: Don't be offended.

She just stares at him.

TED: Don't be offended. I know you're trying to help. We're both doing the same thing here. Don't be offended because I didn't like what you had to offer. That's not fair.

SLOAN: Okay. Then I'm going to take a shower.

TED: Right. A very specific type of shower that I'm asking you not to take.

SLOAN: It's a shower. Water and soap.

TED: I know what it takes to cleanse, okay?

SLOAN: Then what are you talking about?

TED: You're gonna shower, water and soap, but you're not gonna enjoy it. You're upset. This is a moment to start the day, and I'd rather you do it right.

SLOAN: Fine. Then that's what I'll do.

TED: I don't believe you. You're upset you can't help.

SLOAN: Well, I can't help that, can I?

TED: Well, I don't want to be responsible. Like I need that feeling on top of the one I woke up with.

She's getting fed up.

SLOAN: What do you want me to do?

TED: Take a shower and be happy.

SLOAN: Fine.

TED: Great.

She heads into the bathroom. He gets out of the bed and starts to dress.

TED: See this shit? All I did was wake up. You see what happens?

She comes back out of the bathroom.

SLOAN: What do you want me to do? You don't want solutions because… Because what? I missed it, but fine. For some reason, that's out. I can handle the not understanding things if we are gaining something else. Like some sort of peace. A change. A shift. But that doesn't happen because we're stuck with the fact that you are not happy that I might have some sort of human response to something that you've said. Did I take it personal? Sort of. Am I going to have a terrible washing experience? No, I'll be fine.

TED: I thought we were done with this part.

SLOAN: This part didn't exist, not until you reacted to my completely reasonable reaction. I'm just trying to help.

TED: Do you see this?

SLOAN: Yes, I do.

TED: Not that. This. This is what happens. I wake up and feel like killing people, you try to help. It doesn't work, then I'm upset that you're upset. Then you're upset that I'm upset. It's a cycle. It fucks up the whole day. This is life? What happened? I gotta watch TV. I gotta get high. I can't sleep in all day. This is a problem.

SLOAN: Right. One can't be solved, because solutions are out.

TED: You're still stuck on it.

SLOAN: Well, what are we talking about?

TED: Absolutely nothing and that's the fucking point.

SLOAN: No.

TED: No? What do you mean, no? What is that? No one asked a question. You're just saying no now, when you hear something you don't like?

SLOAN: Yes, that's it.

TED: Okay. No what?

SLOAN: No everything. Let's just get to it. Let's use logic and break up here. There's nothing to eliminate, as in what can be done before the act of waking up. So let's go from here. I'm not stuck on anything. I'm present, right now. You with me?

TED: I suppose.

SLOAN: You suppose? What did I say that you missed?

TED: I'm right here.

SLOAN: Good. Now tell me. How are the details of your life?

TED: What does that mean?

SLOAN: How are things? You like me?

TED: What kind of a stupid question is that?

SLOAN: It needs an answer. That kind.

TED: Of course I like you. I love you.

SLOAN: Great. You like this house?

TED: I bought the bitch, didn't I?

SLOAN: Great. Next. You like your job?

TED: Who the fuck likes their job?

SLOAN: Great, so that's out. You're two for two. I suppose the third was rhetorical. What else is there?

TED: I don't know.

SLOAN: Then stop waking up in a bad mood.

Ted thinks about it for a second. A bell goes off in his head.

TED: Oh my god, babe.

SLOAN: What?

TED: You did it! AMAZING. Everything is fantastic now. I'm sure to wake up feeling like a million bucks. We should have done the grand, overwhelming life assessment thing months ago. Do you like me and the house? Yes! Fantastic. Peachy all the way around. What the hell were we thinking this whole time?

She pause for a second or two to take in the hurt, brushes it off, then slowly heads back toward the bathroom.

TED: No.

She turns back.

SLOAN: No?

TED: You can't just walk out.

She points to the bathroom.

SLOAN: That's not out. It's in.

She points to the other door.

SLOAN: That's out.

Ted thinks about what she's implying and nods his head.

TED: You know, because maybe you don't understand what it is that I go through on a day-to-day, morning-to-morning basis, that maybe it might be a good idea for you to maybe leave it alone.

She takes it in. Almost finds a way to chuckle to herself due to how ridiculous the sentiment.

SLOAN: I'm afraid at some point, that's going to be a major problem.

TED: As opposed to the smooth sailing we're experiencing now?

SLOAN: Oh, it can get worse. Trust me.

TED: What is that? Impending doom this way cometh?

SLOAN: Absolutely. You think that by ignoring what you wake up with every day, it is going to somehow be solved?

TED: That's the thing, though. There is no solve. There's just this. It's mine, I admit, but it's here.

SLOAN: So what? Just wait and see what happens?

TED: That's life I suppose.

SLOAN: Not the one I want.

TED: That could be taken personally.

SLOAN: Good, I want it to be taken personally. Because what I don't want is to be part of a problem, mine or yours, that has no room for solutions. I love you, but I need a few things. Not a ton. Just some things. One of them has to be harmony. Not constant. Not everyday. Communication. Problem solving. Sparse little gems. They go such a long way. I feel this, you feel that, then I do this, then you do that. Isn't that nice? It's called functioning like humans. We need it. Without it we have problems that end. Period. And not well.

Ted thinks. Sloan watches him for a while. She gets a bit soft with him. Maybe leans in. A touch even.

SLOAN: Look, I know what I signed up for here. I'm not asking for normal. But it is getting worse. This thing, whatever it is that you've been waking up with lately, needs one of two things. To go away by itself, which I don't see happening, or, we figure it out together. I like that one. It does so many nice things at once.

He's stuck.

SLOAN: I'm going to wash now.

She exits, leaving him alone in the bedroom.

THE END

Clean It Up

Minor Conversations—Clean It Up

OUTSIDE

A MAN comes out of a room. Talks to his BUDDY who stands alone, deep in thought.

MAN: These people, man. I tell ya what.

BUDDY: You're telling me.

MAN: I'm telling you, I woke up with some kinda charge this morning. Some kinda something that's getting me worked up in some kinda way. These people.

BUDDY: Who we talking?

MAN: These people with all their crap. Their clothes and their tchotchkis. I hate a tchotchki more than anything. What do we need with this stuff?

BUDDY: I don't know.

MAN: No. You don't cause there ain't nothing to know. It's got no point is what I'm saying. All this stuff we hold onto as humans, I'm saying, it don't make or break nothin'. It ain't holdin' things together. There's no bridge.

BUDDY: I'm working on a potential handle of what you're getting away with here.

MAN: I'm sayin' what do we really need? Like really need, I'm sayin'? At the end of the day.

BUDDY: I get it.

MAN: I'm askin' you.

BUDDY: Me, personally?

MAN: Yes, you. That's what I'm askin'.

BUDDY: Few laughs. A warms spot when it's cold. Maybe some air when it's... You know.

MAN: Yes, I know, that's what I'm sayin'. We don't need all this extra. On top of the fact that it's crowding up the space, it's just a waste of energy even thinkin' about the stuff. Talkin' about it. Like right now. We could be doing something completely else, but here we are stuck.

BUDDY: Time.

MAN: Time. My time.

BUDDY: Our time.

MAN: Our goddamn time. What we got, and what we don't got enough of, that we sit here wasting.

BUDDY: No good.

MAN: Absolutely not. You got stuff to do?

BUDDY: Of course I got stuff.

MAN: I'm askin' you.

BUDDY: Specifically?

MAN: Yes or no. The point is there's things. Am I wrong?

BUDDY: No, you are not. We could eat, we could hunt, we could run around a bit. What do I know? Exercise! Be fit or be damned. We could be engaged, but no.

MAN: Waste of time.

BUDDY: That's exactly right.

MAN: And so I'm saying this…

BUDDY: Get rid of all this unnecessary crap. I see what you're saying.

MAN: Right. And stop wasting space, time, and energy. You see this. You see how many things solved with one wallop?

BUDDY: At the end of the day. Get rid of all of it. We don't need it, and we certainly don't need talking about it.

MAN: Clean sweep, my friend.

BUDDY: Good stuff.

THE END

A Theory

Minor Conversations—A Theory

A CAFE

Two women sit across from each other at a table. LUCY and TINA. Lucy is clearly on about something in her head. Tina plays with her phone.

LUCY: I have a theory.

Tina doesn't look up.

TINA: Okay.

LUCY: I'm thinking I'm not going to ask Charlie where he's been anymore.

TINA: What are you talking about?

LUCY: My father was a hunter.

TINA: That's funny.

LUCY: Why is that funny?

TINA: What do you mean, he was a hunter?

LUCY: He liked to hunt.

TINA: See? That's better. My father was a hunter sounds different than he liked to hunt.

A beat. Lucy continues with her thought.

LUCY: Anyway, my father liked to hunt.

Tina puts down her phone. She starts looking around.

LUCY: Everyone knew that's what he liked to do. He'd come home with a deer. A beaver. The occasional fox.

TINA: That's horrible.

LUCY: It's not so bad when you get used to it. I used to hate it too, but then after a while I just got used to it.

TINA: A fox?

LUCY: Yeah.

TINA: How do you kill a fox?

LUCY: With a pistol.

Tina makes a face.

LUCY: A rifle. Something. I don't know.

Tina looks around the room again.

LUCY: Anyway, that's not the point. What are you looking for?

TINA: A goddamned waiter. I ordered a lemonade. I'm dying for a lemonade.

Lucy waits.

TINA: Sorry. I'm edgy. I'm thirsty and I'm edgy.

She continues to look around.

LUCY: The man enjoyed hunting.

TINA: So barbaric.

LUCY: I agree, but that's what he liked to do, and like I said, you get used to it.

TINA: You from the woods?

LUCY: The woods?

TINA: I don't know. Deer and beaver? We went to high school together. We went to the mall. What do we know from hunting?

LUCY: We had a summer home.

TINA: I see.

LUCY: Spent a good amount of time.

TINA: Not for me. I prefer a desert. Or a tall building. I hate bugs.

LUCY: That's fine.

Tina looks around.

TINA: Where is this guy?

Lucy waits a bit.

LUCY: I'm thinking maybe about not asking Charlie any more questions.

TINA: He like to hunt?

LUCY: He's from Encino.

TINA: I'm really dying for a lemonade.

LUCY: My mother always wanted to know where he was. Not Charlie, my father. Here he is with a dead fox, and she's sitting there with her arms crossed asking, "Where have you been?" Now we're kids. I'm young, but not too young as to not understand the man with the dead fox or whatever was clearly in the woods. It's not complicated, and for the life of me, I can't put together how this woman could be standing there asking such a stupid question. But over the years, I'd find myself standing in the kitchen with my arms crossed, my dad walks in and I'm asking where he's been. He's got blood on his pants and there's a deer head strapped to the hood of his Buick. Not six months earlier, I'm sitting there thinking to myself, what a stupid question, next thing I know, I'm curious, too.

TINA: You knew where he was.

LUCY: Of course I did, and so did she. All along. She's asking because she didn't have anything better to do, and I'm sitting there, I mean, I had things to do, I could have been playing, but instead I start asking, too.

TINA: Then what happened?

LUCY: Nothing. He never answered and I'm pretty sure I know why. Drove my mother crazy. Even started to drive me crazy.

TINA: So, you're there. You know all of this, and you're going forward with the stupid question asking anyway?

LUCY: No. At this point, I have no clue. I started out knowing how silly it was, but somehow got lost. I mean, at first, I'm just a kid watching my mom thinking, "what an idiot", next thing I know, I'm living with a man asking stupid questions all the time.

TINA: But Charlie doesn't hunt.

LUCY: That's not the point.

TINA: Then what is?

LUCY: We don't fight. We don't have any problems. The only time we do is when I'm asking him where he's been.

TINA: But he doesn't hunt. Didn't he come home at three in the morning?

LUCY: Yes.

TINA: And what did you say?

LUCY: I asked him where he was.

TINA: And what did he say?

LUCY: He said he was at Tommy's.

TINA: Doing what? That guy's a piece of shit, by the way.

LUCY: Tommy?

TINA: Yes, Tommy, he's a pig.

LUCY: Tommy's okay.

TINA: He's an animal. But doing what? What did he say they were doing?

LUCY: Smoking, drinking, I don't know.

TINA: Well, you should know. What happened?

LUCY: I started to ask some more questions, he seemed to get annoyed, I left it alone.

TINA: Why did you do that? You can't do that. You left it alone? That's exactly what he wanted you to do. You gotta get in there. You want the truth, you gotta dig.

LUCY: He said he was telling the truth, that's why I left it alone.

TINA: No. You left it alone because you started thinking about foxes and dead beavers. This is something else. This is modern. This is city life. There's no woods. He's over at Tommy's doing who knows what, and here you are at home worried sick. Were you worried?

LUCY: Not really.

TINA: Why not?

LUCY: Because I assumed he was at Tommy's.

TINA: Then why'd you ask?

LUCY: That's what I'm saying.

TINA: And I'm saying you're wrong. You think we create problems by asking questions? Bullshit. It's the other way around. We solve things. That's what we do. And I'm not so sure about your dad, by the way. You can buy dead animals. I can get you a fox.

Lucy is spinning.

TINA: Don't get caught up here. Don't get it confused.

LUCY: I really am, though. Maybe things don't have to be so complicated.

TINA: Everyone has something to do. You feel something? You ask. It's that simple. Don't spend too much time thinking about it, because that's when you get lost. Trust me.

THE END

Cheating

Minor Conversations—Cheating

AN APARTMENT

A MAN follows a WOMAN into an apartment. Nice place. Some vintage stuff. Furniture. Couple hip posters. One of 'em's got good taste. This is CASEY and JUNE. Both adults, 30 to 40, maybe.

JUNE: That is the most ridiculous thing I have ever heard. I think in my entire life, maybe.

CASEY: You don't want to have this conversation. Trust me.

Casey drops his keys on a credenza near the front door and blows past June through the house toward a beer.

JUNE: Yes, I do. This is me wanting to have this conversation.

She stays close behind, dropping her purse on the floor. She steps toward him as he grabs a beer out of the fridge. She stands in front of him with her arms crossed.

JUNE: See?

Casey studies her.

CASEY: Okay.

JUNE: Okay. Go ahead.

CASEY: You sure, now? Because this is one of those things.

JUNE: No. Let's get it out. Let's do it. We've been together long enough.

Casey takes a sip of beer.

CASEY: Okay. Men shouldn't be jealous.

JUNE: You said that. Why? And for the record, I was not flirting.

CASEY: Yes, you were.

JUNE: I was not.

CASEY: The kid was cute. I get it. You were definitely flirting.

JUNE: I'm telling you.

CASEY: And I'm telling you I don't give a shit. You were flirting and you looked like you were having a good time. Cheers.

JUNE: I wasn't flirting.

CASEY: Let's go to bed?

JUNE: I'm not tired.

CASEY: Then let's fuck and you can think of the cute kid you were flirting with.

JUNE: You are disgusting.

CASEY: That was a joke. I draw the line there. That, I would not like.

JUNE: Good to know. You are a human being.

CASEY: Fine. Were you or were you not flirting with the teenager?

JUNE: He was not a teenager.

CASEY: Come on. Poor kid's been trying to grow that mustache all year.

JUNE: Casey?

CASEY: Yes or no, June? This is important. It has everything to do with what we shouldn't be discussing right now that you are insisting upon. It's about so much more than just this. Trust me. I don't like this part.

JUNE: What is this part, dear? You're so dramatic.

CASEY: Dramatic? No. Appropriate? Yes. I'm a man.

JUNE: You don't say.

CASEY: Careful. You see? It's starting already.

JUNE: Just speak.

CASEY: I don't give a shit that you were flirting with him and that doesn't sit well with you, does it?

She takes some time to think it through.

JUNE: Are you trying to trick me?

CASEY: Yes or no, June?

June thinks about it.

JUNE: Okay, yes. I was flirting with him.

Casey nods his head. He seems pissed.

JUNE: What, are you mad now?

CASEY: Yes. But not because you were flirting. All that only to get to the bottom of something. Forget the bottom. I mean, I knew it anyway, but it's general principle. How do you expect to get anywhere in a conversation based on facts when you can't even admit to something, that at the end of the day, doesn't even have a consequence? I mean, what the fuck? What a pain in the ass.

JUNE: Maybe I'm just saying it, agreeing with you, so that we can move forward. Did you ever think of that?

CASEY: No, I didn't think of that. You want to know why?

JUNE: Sure.

CASEY: Because it's not fucking true and we both know it. That's why I didn't think of it. And speaking about thinking, this goes back to the point I was trying not to make by not having this conversation in the first place. I'm not jealous.

JUNE: That's not the conversation I wanted to have in the first place, speaking of first place.

CASEY: Yes, you did. You just didn't know it, because you were too busy not using your brain and that's what this is ultimately about.

JUNE: You are so confusing it's driving me completely insane.

CASEY: That's because you are using the wrong parts. Don't feel bad, all women do it. You want to be original?

JUNE: Oh, this is going to be brilliant. I can feel it already.

CASEY: Feel. Yes. Feel. Feel your way through. It's doing wonders so far.

JUNE: What the fuck are you talking about?

CASEY: Use your head. That's what I'm talking about. The reason men shouldn't be jealous is because we are not driven by our emotions. We, for the most part, the evolved version of the group I'm speaking of, try to use logic. We see you flirt, we imagine you are having a good time, we know who you're going home with. We're men. We're supposed to be secure, and if we're not, one of two things is going on. One, we're with the wrong chick. Two, we're insecure. I don't have either of those problems. I don't give a shit who you flirt with.

JUNE: Good for you. I don't feel the same way.

CASEY: No shit. That's what I'm saying. I'm also saying that's okay. We're different. Not just two people who feel different things. As humans. Women can be jealous. Why? Because they are fueled by something else. A much greater power takes over and gets to use the brain as it pleases. They are called emotions, commonly mistaken for another body part, the heart. Like it has any other function aside from pumping blood.

JUNE: Oh, I see.

CASEY: I don't think you do.

JUNE: I'm an idiot?

CASEY: Did I say that?

JUNE: No. You said you use your brain and I clearly don't. Clearly, I'm jumping to conclusions.

CASEY: That's not it.

JUNE: Then find and define it, because I'm slowly becoming upset. We're moving from fun to not very quickly.

CASEY: This is not a slight. I love women. More importantly, I love you.

JUNE: Didn't need the first part of that sentence.

CASEY: Look. You see your guy flirting, you absolutely know he's capable of sleeping with the person he is flirting with and still coming home to you like it didn't happen. Women don't share that same mechanism.

JUNE: Oh my god.

CASEY: Relax, okay?

JUNE: Sorry, but no. I'm curious. Is this an example of a man using his brain? You can't possibly be making a point about... Something I've lost track of, but somehow, somewhere, something about women not using their heads, and then stand there with a penis saying the things you are saying... Are you stupid?

CASEY: Listen to me?

JUNE: I can't. It hurts my face.

CASEY: This is what I'm saying. The reason he doesn't... The reason he...

JUNE: Stop.

CASEY: What.

JUNE: Who's he?

CASEY: He. The man. I'm not here anymore. This is all hypothetical. The man has absolutely nothing to do with himself, he doesn't choose to not flirt or cheat because he doesn't want to, it's because he knows how horrible it would make you feel. Her feel.

JUNE: Okay. Let me just untangle your bullshit for a second. Basically, what you are saying is that when I see you flirting with someone, I can just assume you would like to sleep with them?

CASEY: I'm sorry. When did you ever see me flirting with anyone?

JUNE: Hypothetically.

CASEY: Hypothetically?

JUNE: Yes.

CASEY: Then abso-fucking-lutely. Why do you think I'm hypothetically flirting in the first place? Because I'm actually interested in what they're saying? No. I'm literally pretending that my goal is to sleep with them. I'm acting as if. It's like a game. And then at the end of the night, I go home to the person I love. You. The hypothetical you.

June is beside herself.

CASEY: Look, I'm being honest. I wouldn't do it. I would never cheat on you, but not because I don't think it's okay to do. You don't. Therefore, by the standard rules of relationships, and more imporantly maintaining the one I'm in, I don't. And would not. You win. Women, in general, win. Your point of view about the thing rules and we go along.

June is really stuck. She actually would like to kill him. Casey waits. June walks to the other side of the room and sits down on the couch.

CASEY: Are you upset?

JUNE: Upset? No. I'm just thinking. Trying real hard to use my brain. Tough for us, you know.

CASEY: June, please.

JUNE: No. You know you really only hear of men sounding that dumb. You don't imagine it actually happens. It's like a monster in the forest, or the tooth fairy, only instead of getting paid, you realize you're with a monkey.

CASEY: Would you stop?

JUNE: No. I'm completely thrown. You've either outsmarted me or yourself. One of the two.

CASEY: I said I didn't want to have this conversation.

JUNE: Now I know why. Because you sound like an asshole. Where in that constant, and highly-functional man brain, did you think I would accept all of this and not take it personally?

CASEY: I knew you'd take it personally and that's why I didn't want to get into it in the first place.

JUNE: You think women are just inherently jealous? No. There's a reason. It all starts somewhere. No one is born insecure.

CASEY: So it's my fault?

JUNE: No more or less than it's my fault cheating is unacceptable.

CASEY: Fine. Then we're both in the clear. Can we just stop? Why are we even doing this? That crusty old shmuck at the party made that one comment about cheating on his girlfriend and I agreed. So what?

JUNE: It was stupid, and you agreed, and that's why we're doing this. I need to know. I left it alone in the moment.

CASEY: No, you didn't. You stewed.

JUNE: Yes, I did. It was the best I could do. In the moment.

CASEY: You don't think it's a shame that he was tortured by his girlfriend all those years?

JUNE: That's not the point at all, but no, I don't. He cheated on her. He deserved it.

CASEY: Then she should have left him. Told him to kick rocks. But no, she stuck around just so she could tell him what an asshole he was, every day. It's terrible.

JUNE: Right. And also, for all we know, he could just be a shmuck. A shmuck pig who just decided to cheat on his girlfriend.

CASEY: Either way…

JUNE: He's a shmuck.

CASEY: No. He's a shmuck because… What are we even talking about anymore?

JUNE: I'm not sure. Why are we even having this conversation?

CASEY: Why? Is that a real question? Why are having this conversation? Because you insisted. That's why.

JUNE: Well, maybe I don't want to have it anymore.

CASEY: That's fine with me.

JUNE: But I, unfortunately, have no choice. I feel like it's something that needs to be discussed. I don't like that my boyfriend, whom I live with… We share space, we share a home and stuff. I don't like knowing that the person I'm with, and have been with for a good amount of time now, thinks it's okay that shmucky guys are out there cheating on their girlfriends and he thinks it's cool. You. Not him.

CASEY: Fine. Then let me clarify everything. I don't think it's cool. I didn't even say it was okay. I simply said that I understand. I understand what it might have meant to him. There is the difference. I'm not saying cheating is acceptable, but I'm only not saying it because of the way you feel. I'm saying I could do it, and it could mean absolutely nothing. Beyond nothing. To me, to us, even including the shmuck, unless we are discussing an ongoing affair which we are not, it's literally the equivalent of masturbating with someone else in the room. That's how we are. Men. We don't need love to fuck. We don't even need conversation. On the other hand, women, or the women I've cared to surround myself with, couldn't do that. Something's missing. You need love. We don't, and that's the point.

June stews. She looks like she's about to short out.

JUNE: We really should not have had this conversation.

CASEY: No shit.

She walks offstage.

THE END

No More

Minor Conversations—No More

A ROOM

Two LADIES stand or sit. Or both. DEB and CARRIE.

DEB: This is bullshit.

CARRIE: What is?

DEB: All of it. It's fucking bullshit. Tell me. I look like a cliché to you?

Carrie doesn't know quite how to answer.

DEB: I know. Stupid question, right?

CARRIE: Not necessarily.

DEB: Well, I'm not. I'm no specific way. Certainly not something regular. Who is? We're all special. Are we special?

CARRIE: I think so.

DEB: I'm not saying special like something ordinary out of the ordinary, that's not what I'm saying. No better or worse. I just don't want to be in a box. You wanna be in a box?

CARRIE: No. Certainly not.

DEB: You wanna be thrown into a pile with everyone else?

CARRIE: I don't.

DEB: Right. Well, neither do I. I'm me. I'm not someone else.

CARRIE: That's right.

DEB: Nobody is everybody. Am I right?

CARRIE: We're all very specific and different, that's correct. Here we are.

DEB: Do you drink?

CARRIE: I try not to.

DEB: What is that?

CARRIE: What is what?

DEB: Forget it.

CARRIE: I'm sorry.

DEB: Whatever. You either drink or you don't. Do it or don't. I'm saying in general. Nothing personal, I'm saying. Maybe I need a drink.

CARRIE: That's what I mean. I try not to need.

DEB: Oh, really? Is that right? So what? I'm a jerk because I need something? I'm going through something here. This guy smokes, that guy does something else. What's wrong with a drink?

CARRIE: There's nothing wrong with a drink. Why are you attacking me?

DEB: I have no choice. You're the only one here.

CARRIE: Fair enough.

DEB: You think I'm an animal?

Deb waits.

DEB: Do you?

CARRIE: I think you might be a little rough around the ends, but I don't know if I'd call you an animal.

Deb studies her.

DEB: What about you?

CARRIE: Me?

DEB: Yes, you. We just established no one else is here. You. What about you?

CARRIE: What about me, what?

DEB: I don't know. I'm sorry. I'm really, really sorry.

CARRIE: It's fine. Don't be.

DEB: No, I am. I'm so sorry. I'm really a mess. It's not you, it's obviously me. I don't know what to tell you. I'm just...

CARRIE: It's okay. You don't have to tell me anything. I get it. I mean, not it specifically, but we all have our things.

Carrie waits.

DEB: Yes, we do.

CARRIE: Our own specific things that have nothing to do with anybody else.

Deb checks her out. She's okay.

DEB: I'm Deb.
CARRIE: Hi Deb.

Deb waits.

DEB: You don't have a name?
CARRIE: No, I do.

Deb nods her head. She gets it.

DEB: Fuck you, lady.

THE END

Right's Right

Minor Conversations—Right's Right

A BASEMENT

Two men in a room. TONY, mid-thirties, JACK, mid-twenties.

They sit in silence for a few beats.

TONY: I don't want to give you bad advice.

JACK: I don't want bad advice.

TONY: I know that.

Another long beat of silence. Jack waits.

TONY: Not so much bad… Look, what's right is right. You're young. You're handsome. What the fuck?

JACK: I don't know.

TONY: I mean, what are you gonna do? You gonna marry this chick?

JACK: I don't know.

TONY: Well, I do. The answer is no. And even if you do, it's a long way away, so still. It doesn't matter.

JACK: That's the thing, though. What if it does?

TONY: Does what? Matter?

JACK: Yes.

TONY: But I'm telling you it don't.

JACK: Yeah, but you're also telling me I'm not gonna end up with her, which at the end of the day, just really ends up being a matter of, who knows, I mean so far as your opinion on things. I mean, I ask you for something and what you're telling me is based on what you think might not ever happen, and neither of us is sure if that's right or not? I mean… You see what I'm saying?

TONY: Unfortunately, yes, I do. But here's what. I'm saying what I'm saying from a place of I know what I'm talking about. Trust me. This ain't my first go here. You end up with her, fine, either way you're gonna ultimately end up doing what you gotta do, and that, at the end of the day, is what I'm saying.

Jack thinks about it.

TONY: Not so sure?

JACK: I mean, we're talking. That's what we're doing. Yes, I'm not so sure.

TONY: Okay. I can see you're confused and by all rights you should be. It's confusing shit. But it doesn't have to be. Let's keep it simple. You love this girl?

JACK: I do. I really do.

TONY: Okay. Then that's that. Nothing else to talk about.

Jack studies Tony for a beat.

JACK: What, are you testing me? I don't want to be tested.

TONY: And I don't want to give you bad advice, but I'm just trying to do the right thing here.

JACK: Then just do it. What's bad?

TONY: I don't know. I suppose you dancing around sleeping with this one and that one behind the back of someone you love could be considered or fall under the category of bad.

JACK: So, that's it. Bottom line.

TONY: No, just the opposite. That is exactly what I'm saying you should be doing at your age. I mean, not with everyone, you gotta be picky I suppose.

JACK: Well, it's not like I'm trying to break any records.

TONY: Exactly. That's it. We're not animals. You're not an animal.

JACK: Not at all.

TONY: But you gotta do what you gotta do. What are you gonna do? Say no? You got this six-foot redhead with bright green lasers looking at you like she ain't seen this side of handsome since the television and she's saying… What? I just need you to see what the inside of my place looks like. You being you. You say what? Sorry. I don't think so.

JACK: No. I know it. It's almost impossible. And I mean that for what it is. Not possible. Forget almost.

TONY: Okay. So then, what are we talking about? You're not gonna do that. Not because you don't want to but because things impossible are just that.

JACK: Okay. We're saying the same thing, but still.

TONY: It is what it is.

JACK: But, I mean, I love this girl.

TONY: Who doesn't. She's six-foot. The lasers. The legs. You're a human being.

JACK: Not her. She's great, too, and although a figment of both our imaginations…

TONY: It's not figment. You could find this girl, you look hard enough. Where are we? This ain't Omaha.

JACK: Right. I could love her too. Find her and love her. I get it and I agree. But this woman I got.

TONY: It's a real problem, I know.

JACK: She might be the greatest person I know.

TONY: As much as I envy you, at the same time I don't. You have any idea how many amazing people I did bad shit to?

JACK: I'm guessing a lot.

TONY: It's crazy. But out of where? What place did I do these things? No malice. Bad intentions. You think I was out there trying to do this shit? Hurt people? What am I?

JACK: You're a good dude.

TONY: Thank you, and so are you. This is me being real with you. I didn't want to hurt anyone's feelings and neither did you.

JACK: Especially not hers.

TONY: Right. So that's what I'm saying. Where? Out of what place did I do these horrible things?

JACK: Is this a question?

TONY: Yeah, but I got it. I was young. I was a kid. I was out there enjoying my life, preparing myself for the part where that all stops. You squander that and I can only imagine the regret. And therefore, here, me today, I have no regrets.

JACK: That's really good to hear.

TONY: It's really good to say, trust me.

JACK: But here's the thing. I feel guilty already.

TONY: Of course you do. You're in the now. Later you won't. But in the most right way possible. Not because you forget it and move on, thoughtless, but rather you grow up and realize you did what you did because you were where you were and you really had no choice.

Jack thinks.

TONY: I mean, we all have choices, right, but not really. I choose this, I choose that. Simple stuff? Fine. Apples over grapes? Fine. But this is something else.

JACK: It's still a choice. Just because it's tough doesn't make it something else.

TONY: I don't know. I'm not saying it's not worth looking at, but it's certainly not the same thing. You can't choose something not knowing what it's gonna taste like later. That's not a choice. It's gotta be something else. If you're really using your head, you gotta see then to make a choice now.

JACK: Right, but I don't have then, I have now. I don't have the future of when I'm looking back at the choices I made. I only have now, and now stings because it's all I got. Now.

TONY: Like I said, I don't envy you. I do and I don't.

Jack thinks.

TONY: Play the tape out. You're my age. You stayed with this girl who, by the way, I think is fantastic.

JACK: She really is though.

TONY: We got no beef there. I'm with you. A solid gem. One hundred percent.

JACK: She likes you, too.

TONY: We get on. I'm telling you, I really like this girl. I even like her for you, and that's not an always. Those two are not always next to each other. So what? You spend the next fifteen years gritting your teeth at all the opportunities. Then what? You think you look at this girl and say to yourself, "Boy, I'm glad I stuck it out? I'm glad I didn't have all those experiences I could have had because instead I got you?"

JACK: Sounds nice, yeah.

TONY: Right, so does flying to the moon, but I ain't going, and neither are you.

Jack waits.

TONY: Maybe you got a shot, but I certainly don't.

JACK: You're confusing me.

TONY: I'm confusing myself, let's go back. Yes, it sounds nice. Yes, people say it and mean it, but they started later than you and they aren't you. Like I said, you're from Wichita or some other place, fine. You get the prom queen, you keep her.

JACK: I'm actually from a little town close to Wichita.

TONY: Not anymore you're not. You're here now and not only are you ten years too young to be looking forward to saying you found the right one fifteen years back, it just ain't the case for you. Just my opinion, but I'm pretty sure I'm right.

JACK: Well, I could see myself saying those kinds of things.

TONY: Of course you could.

JACK: Well?

TONY: Fine. Get ready to say 'em. I think you're gonna want to kill someone at that point and it may very well be her, but that's my bad advice. Take it or leave it.

JACK: Look, I agree with you. I got no choice but to take it, but I'm really stuck here.

TONY: I know.

JACK: Okay, what about you?

TONY: As per what?

JACK: As per your girl. I've seen you two together. It's fantastic. Looks great. You telling me if you met her fifteen years ago…

TONY: Yes.

JACK: Yes, what. I haven't even finished yet.

TONY: You didn't need to. The answer is yes. I would have fucked it up. I already told you, I met plenty of people I could have been happy with, but life's a box of watches, buddy. You gotta have a nice watch to have a good time. You know what I mean?

JACK: What?

TONY: Timing.

JACK: Timing?

224 • SCOTT CAAN

TONY: That is correct.

JACK: Yeah, well, it's also very hard to swallow.

TONY: So are big vitamins. Welcome to being a handsome grown-up.

JACK: Okay. Okay. Let me just gather here for a beat. Just so I'm clear. You're saying that if I stay faithful to this woman, who I do dearly love, I'm gonna have more regret there than I would having not been true however many years down the line? Is that the thing? I mean, is that the pitch here?

TONY: I suppose that's part of it, yes.

JACK: Well, what's the other part?

Tony thinks some more.

TONY: The other part I suppose would be you do the right thing and just break up with the poor girl because of where you are in life, but that's an entirely different conversation, and one that has a lot to do with heartache, on your part I mean, and I'm not nearly good enough a guy to suggest that you put yourself through something like that.

JACK: No. That I can't do. You're right.

TONY: Right. So then no other parts. We're done. I stand correct... And corrected.

THE END

The Last Conversation

Minor Conversations—The Last Conversation

A COFFEE SHOP

A diner. Maybe a home. No, a diner, that's better. SEAN and KELLY sit at a table. He's almost forty. She's on her way.

KELLY: This is it.

SEAN: What do you mean?

KELLY: This. Right here. This is it.

SEAN: You said that. What's it mean?

KELLY: I don't want to do it anymore.

Sean shifts in his seat a bit.

KELLY: I can't do it anymore is what I'm saying.

Sean thinks about it. Maybe a bit of sadness, but he pushes it down.

SEAN: Okay.

She waits. Is there more?

KELLY: Wow.

SEAN: You don't really leave a lot of room.

KELLY: If that's how you see it.

SEAN: Me?

KELLY: Yes, you.

Sean takes a beat. Watches her.

SEAN: Is this what you imagined?

KELLY: No.

SEAN: I mean today. Now. We take turns being tough.

KELLY: Is that what we're doing?

SEAN: You tell me. I just got here.

KELLY: You just got here? What does that mean?

SEAN: It means I just got here. I sat down. You've been thinking, I can only imagine. So what? You tell me. I'm just here.

KELLY: We're both just here, Sean.

SEAN: No. I'm just here. You don't want to do it anymore. In fact, you can't. I'm just here. You? Something else. Something completely else.

Kelly just stares at him, frozen.

SEAN: What happened?

She looks for the words.

KELLY: It's just…

SEAN: What? It's just what?

KELLY: Everything.

SEAN: No. It's not everything. That's too easy. Everything is everything. This. What is this? This here.

KELLY: Please don't.

SEAN: Please don't what?

KELLY: Tell me. You're too good. I can't win.

SEAN: Well, who knows, maybe there's a reason for that.

KELLY: See.

SEAN: No. I don't see. See what? What am I looking for?

KELLY: You're looking at me. You're too quick. You're so sharp. You got all the right things to say and I can't win. So that's it. That's everything. I surrender.

SEAN: No, you don't.

KELLY: I don't.

SEAN: You don't surrender, you give up. There's a difference, you know.

KELLY: Well, I don't know the difference.

SEAN: Sure you do.

KELLY: What do you want?

SEAN: Me?

KELLY: Who am I speaking with?

SEAN: It's what you want. I don't want. I'm just here. You asking me what I want? I didn't want anything. I didn't know I was going to be in that position. In fact, I'm not. At all. What do I want? No. What do you want?

KELLY: Is that really a question?

SEAN: I don't know.

KELLY: Right.

SEAN: Right what? You want to know something? Ask me. Or tell me. You want something, say so. You can't do it anymore? Nothing I can do about that. Unless there is.

KELLY: So, it is a question. That's all. Don't make me seem crazy for not being sure. What am I? New?

SEAN: Look it…

KELLY: No.

SEAN: No?

KELLY: Yes, no. You look it. You pay attention. You show up and be here and listen to me. Don't talk me out of my way. I know what I'm doing and then you get going and I end up with no clue.

SEAN: Well, I don't know what to say to that.

KELLY: Think of something.

Sean stands up.

SEAN: See, this is something. It's really something else. You say something to me, something that doesn't have much to go on. It's a period. This is this, it's the way it is and there ain't nothing else, but then you keep going. You want to blame me? I confuse you? Maybe you confuse yourself. If there's something to talk about, I'll talk, but I'm stuck trying to figure that out. There either is or there isn't. You get what I'm saying.

KELLY: Nobody gets what you're saying and that's the problem. It's you. It's always you. It's whatever you're dealing with and if the rest of us want to play along, then we get an invite to the puzzle. It's not about us. We're not even here. Unless we really want to be. Unless we decide to throw everything else away and stick. And that's not easy to do, but we do it.

SEAN: But not anymore?

KELLY: I can't. And that's what I'm saying.

SEAN: So, what's the question?

KELLY: I guess there isn't one.

SEAN: How 'bout an answer? You got that one?

KELLY: Maybe.

SEAN: Well, here I am. I'm right here. Willing to be right here. Right now. Right here.

KELLY: Are you sure?

SEAN: How can I be sure of anything? There's nothing being presented to join. Speak.

KELLY: I need something else.

SEAN: That I can't help you with.

KELLY: From you.

SEAN: Try me.

Kelly takes a deep breath.

KELLY: I just want to be with the part of you that doesn't think. That doesn't write me down. Doesn't take notes. I'll help you figure out everything, but it needs to be together. I can't be on the end of it all. I need to be with you. I can't be artwork anymore. I can't be the problems being solved or the loser of minor conversations. I just want you. The bad parts are fine, but I can't and won't be part of the problem anymore because I know I'm not. And it's taken me a really long time to realize that.

SEAN: I don't know what I'm supposed to do.

KELLY: Yes, you do. You've been doing the opposite for all your life. It's easy. Just do the opposite now.

SEAN: How?

KELLY: Just stop.

SEAN: Stop what?

KELLY: All of it. Forget the detail. Let's just go. Together. Me and you.

SEAN: You and I?

KELLY: Both of us. Everything doesn't have to be funny. It doesn't have to be entertaining. Just stop. That's all I'm asking.

Sean thinks about it.

SEAN: It's just me though.

Kelly nods her head.

KELLY: No, it's not. If it was just you, I would have left a long time ago.

SEAN: Well, I think it's me.

KELLY: I think you're wrong.

SEAN: Then that's a problem.

KELLY: I know, so let's fix it.

Sean takes his time.

SEAN: I don't want to, though. That's the problem. I don't want to fix something that I like.

KELLY: You like it? How can that be?

SEAN: I don't know, but it is. You're not wrong, maybe it's just not for you, but if I start changing things, things that I don't know why but I just like, trying to make other things smooth, that's no good. We gotta do what we know how to do. Be what we are. Maybe I could change that, but I don't want to. All the things that make us crooked are the same things that keep us straight.

Sean kisses her on the forehead.

SEAN: I see, but I'm sorry. I really am.

He just stands there looking at her. It's over.

THE END

I wrote the first two scenes of Word Faithful *about ten years ago. I was going through a pretty bad breakup, and couldn't seem to get the girl off my mind. Having never finished the play, I realize now I must have met someone new because, in my experience, you never really get over love until you find a good replacement. In some cases I suppose that doesn't work either because, I believe, the person you find has to be "better" than the one you left or that left you. There is no elegant way to put it. That's just how it is. For me. If that new person doesn't make you forget, she never will. Obviously the word "better" is way too simple. But, like I said, for me, it's really that simple. I can't explain it, but I know what it means.*

Ten years later, inspired by some of the young actors in the production class, I decided to pick the play back up and finally finished it. Between the director, myself, and the final cast, we chopped away at the old, played with the new, and ultimately came up with what exists now.

Word Faithful

Word Faithful *was originally produced by Val Lauren and Joel Slabo for The Playhouse West Repertory Theater Company—artistic director, Robert Carnegie, at Playhouse West Studio One, North Hollywood, California, August 2014. It was directed by Kathleen Randazzo; set design by Shana Borromeo; stage management, lights, and sound design by Michael Miraula; crew chief, Sebastian Velmont; stage crew: Arturo Encinas, Devon Goodman, and Garner Jerrett. The cast was as follows:*

SAMANTHA.................*Mia Serafino*
JAKE................................*Danny Barclay*
BRIAN.............................*Jim Nieb*

Word Faithful

ACT ONE • SCENE ONE

The lights and music come up over a very fresh and newly decorated studio apartment. It looks perfect. Picture frames rest on a mantle. A bed with crisp, white sheets. A beautiful floral arrangement rests on a counter top. A couch with meticulously arranged pillows, and a couple of modern chairs surrounding a coffee table. A few lit candles sit dead center on the coffee table.

Stepping out of the bathroom walks the lovely and graceful SAMANTHA. Wearing a pair of tight blue jeans and white tank top, she checks herself out in the full-length mirror. She likes what she sees.

A knock at the door. She takes an extra beat and a long look at herself before heading for the door. She opens the door. Standing in the doorway is JAKE. Handsome and well-built. Casually, but not carelessly, dressed.

They look at each other for a few beats and then embrace in a long hug. But not too long. Samantha breaks out of the hug.

SAMANTHA: Hi.

JAKE: Hey, love.

SAMANTHA: How are you?

JAKE: I'm excellent.

SAMANTHA: Well, that's good.

JAKE: Yeah. How about you?

SAMANTHA: I'm excellent, as well.

JAKE: Well, you look excellent.

Samantha takes a beat. She looks at Jake. He looks good too, but she keeps her thoughts to herself.

SAMANTHA: Thank you.

JAKE: And look at this place.

Jake walks in and takes a look.

SAMANTHA: You like it?

JAKE: Yes, I do. Congratulations.

SAMANTHA: I escaped.

JAKE: This place is great. I'm proud of you.

SAMANTHA: Shut up… But thank you.

Jake walks over to the pictures. He spots a wedding picture.

JAKE: Your sister got married?

SAMANTHA: Yes, she did.

JAKE: That's scary.

SAMANTHA: Tell me about it.

JAKE: That's scary.

They laugh a bit. They stare at each other for a while. Jake starts to look at the rest of the pictures.

JAKE: Desmond got married.

SAMANTHA: I heard.

JAKE: How scary is that?

SAMANTHA: I guess that's what happens.

JAKE: What happens?

SAMANTHA: People get married.

JAKE: People, yes. Desmond, no. Not to mention, your little sister. She eloped.

SAMANTHA: Two years.

JAKE: I know. How weird is that? Has it really been two years?

SAMANTHA: Two years that she was with her husband before they got married.

JAKE: Right. I know. Still, certain people, you never think.

Jake points to a picture. A close-up shot of a man's face.

SAMANTHA: Brian.

JAKE: Brian. That's Brian. He's cute.

SAMANTHA: I think so.

JAKE: I think so, too. You happy?

SAMANTHA: I am.

JAKE: Good.

SAMANTHA: You?

JAKE: Excellent.

SAMANTHA: Great. You want a drink?

JAKE: Sure. Beer or water, or whatever.

SAMANTHA: I have both.

JAKE: Surprise me.

Samantha walks offstage.

Jake checks out the apartment. He takes his coat off and catches himself in the full-length mirror. He takes a step closer.

Samantha walks out with a couple of beers.

SAMANTHA: How do you look?

JAKE: I bet almost as good as you did when you were checking yourself out before I got here.

SAMANTHA: I'm a mess.

JAKE: Yeah, you look it.

She hands him a beer and waves at the room.

SAMANTHA: So, what do you think? Sit down.

They sit.

JAKE: I think it's fantastic. It's you. You look great. Your place looks great. I'm happy you're happy. Tell me about John.

SAMANTHA: Brian.

JAKE: Brian.

SAMANTHA: Tell me about Kelly.

JAKE: Kim.

SAMANTHA: Kim.

JAKE: She's great.

SAMANTHA: Well, look, everything is great. It's excellent, it's fantastic.

JAKE: What does Brian do?

SAMANTHA: He trains horses.

JAKE: Shut up.

SAMANTHA: He does.

JAKE: So, you guys don't spend a lot of time together?

SAMANTHA: What does that mean?

JAKE: You hate horses.

SAMANTHA: I do not hate horses.

JAKE: I took you horseback riding.

SAMANTHA: And I said I hated it.

JAKE: That's where I got the idea.

SAMANTHA: Well, you shouldn't jump to conclusions.

JAKE: Conclusions? That's not a conclusion. If you were sneezing by the horse and I accused you of being allergic, that would be a conclusion. You said, "I hate horses."

SAMANTHA: Well, we should have tried again. I might have liked it the second time.

JAKE: Okay.

SAMANTHA: What, that's crazy?

JAKE: A little bit, yeah.

SAMANTHA: Well, there you go.

JAKE: There I go. What does that mean?

SAMANTHA: I like horses now.

JAKE: Great. We should go horseback riding.

SAMANTHA: Great. I'll get us a tee-time. So tell me about... It's Kim, right?

JAKE: Kim, yes. What do you want to know?

SAMANTHA: Tell me everything.

JAKE: I already did.

SAMANTHA: We spoke on the phone for five minutes.

JAKE: Is that what you want to do? You want to talk about Kim, Samantha?

SAMANTHA: I hate hearing my name come out of your mouth. Especially when it's next to Kim's.

JAKE: What do I call you, then? Baby, honey?

SAMANTHA: That's not what I was saying.

JAKE: I'm not saying you were. Not that I wouldn't feel comfortable doing that.

SAMANTHA: Well, I would.

JAKE: I figured that.

SAMANTHA: What's that supposed to mean?

JAKE: Just what I said. I assumed that would make you uncomfortable so, out of respect, I refrained from doing so.

SAMANTHA: You called me love when you walked in.

JAKE: You're lovely, what do you want?

Samantha takes a beat.

SAMANTHA: Look, I just wanted you to see my new place.

JAKE: And that's what I wanted to do.

SAMANTHA: But if it's gonna be weird…

JAKE: All right, stop. Would you? Let's just be human here. Tell me about Johnny.

SAMANTHA: His name is Brian.

JAKE: I know. I know his name is Brian.

SAMANTHA: I'm happy. Very happy. Things are different. Good.

She takes a moment. Jake waits.

SAMANTHA: I went to this… You're gonna make fun of me.

JAKE: I would never do that.

SAMANTHA: Sure you would.

JAKE: Not now I wouldn't. Like, right this second. I might warm up in a bit.

SAMANTHA: I don't care anyway. I went to a seminar.

JAKE: Seminar. What kind of a seminar?

SAMANTHA: Like a… Like a life seminar.

JAKE: Like a Johnny Robbins seminar.

SAMANTHA: What's with you and Johnny?

JAKE: Brian, Tony, Johnny. You went to a seminar.

SAMANTHA: Not a motivational seminar. A filter.

JAKE: A filter?

SAMANTHA: Let's just call it something I needed that I went and got.

JAKE: Okay.

SAMANTHA: I needed something different. I paid six hundred and forty-seven dollars to listen to these people speak for three days straight.

JAKE: Sounds like a hoot.

SAMANTHA: Don't.

JAKE: I'm not making fun. Hey, I pay that a week just for a couple hours of therapy.

SAMANTHA: Yeah, well, you're rich.

JAKE: No, I'm just really fucked up.

SAMANTHA: Whatever. The point is, things are different for me now, and I'm happy. It worked, is what I'm saying. You could save yourself some money. Whatever works for you though, right?

Jake seems uneasy all of a sudden. He shifts around in his seat.

JAKE: Right. Whatever works.

Jake shifts again.

JAKE: It's really good to see you.

She studies him, sense something's up.

SAMANTHA: What is that?

JAKE: I don't know.

SAMANTHA: Spit it out, Jake.

JAKE: I don't know. I got things. We all have things.

SAMANTHA: What kind of things, Jake?

JAKE: I don't know.

SAMANTHA: Yes, you do. Just like I know this routine. You know. You know what's going on. You're like a broken record for ten minutes. I don't know, I don't know, I don't know. So dramatic. Then, sooner or later, it all comes out. Like it was written. So skip the bullshit. Get to the point already.

Jake sits back and gives her a look.

JAKE: When did you start cursing?

SAMANTHA: I don't know.

JAKE: Well, you said bullshit.

SAMANTHA: I remember.

JAKE: Well, what is that? Does Brian curse? Does he pee on the toilet seat and make you pay for dinner?

SAMANTHA: Brian is fantastic.

JAKE: Right. Great and fantastic. Everything is great.

Jake starts to move around a bit. A little uncomfortable all of a sudden.

SAMANTHA: Fine. You don't want to talk? Then don't talk.

JAKE: That's not it. I want to talk. What do you think? You think I just came here to see your new place? I want to talk.

SAMANTHA: Well, it's a shame you're not here right now.

JAKE: Well, how the hell am I supposed to know? I don't know what's going on with you. I haven't seen you in two years. You don't just do that. You don't just walk in and get into it all right away. What do I know? Things aren't so simple. You've got a Brian, I've got a Kim.

SAMANTHA: What does that have to do with anything?

JAKE: It has everything to do with everything. It's a whole deal. It's a whole thing. Look, I don't know what they do down at the seminar, but out here, we think before we do things. You call me out of the blue. Come see my new place. I don't know what that means.

SAMANTHA: It means what it is.

JAKE: Does it?

SAMANTHA: Yes. What's wrong with that?

JAKE: It's insanity. Who does that?

SAMANTHA: I lived in a dump for five years. Three of which we were together. I haven't seen you in almost two years. I've come a long way, and I wanted you to see.

JAKE: Yeah, but for what? And out of where?

SAMANTHA: For visual experience. Here! What the hell is wrong with you?

JAKE: Don't play dumb with me.

SAMANTHA: Okay. Game over. You want to go round and round like this, I don't have time for it.

JAKE: You gotta be somewhere?

SAMANTHA: No.

JAKE: Where's Brian?

SAMANTHA: He's at the ranch.

JAKE: That's funny.

SAMANTHA: What's funny?

JAKE: So mysterious. At the ranch. I mean, who says that? It's not like we live in Kansas. It's rare you hear something like that here in Los Angeles. Can you imagine if you asked me where my girlfriend was, and I said she's out back hanging the whites? She's getting some water down by the well. Can I have another beer?

Samantha takes a beat.

SAMANTHA: Sure.

JAKE: Thanks.

She gets up and heads for the back.

Jake stands up and walks over by the mantle. He picks up the picture of Brian.

JAKE: Faggot.

He puts the picture back and then settles back down into the couch.

He scratches his head.

JAKE: What the fuck is going on here?

Samantha returns with another couple of beers.

Jake pops open one of the beers and takes a long swig. He stares at her.

SAMANTHA: What? What are you looking at?

JAKE: Just looking.

SAMANTHA: Well, stop it.

JAKE: Why did you call me?

SAMANTHA: What?

Jake checks her out.

JAKE: I mean, I know why I would have called you. But I didn't. And believe me, there were a lot of times I really wanted to, but out of respect, I didn't.

SAMANTHA: I wanted you to see…

JAKE: Your new place. I know. Why else? You got me here, I see it, it's lovely. What do you want me to talk about? You want to hear about my life? You want to hear about what's wrong with me?

SAMANTHA: Oh, that again. Thanks, but I'll pass. Forget it. I was just trying to help.

JAKE: No, let me help. I want to help you.

SAMANTHA: Help me with what, Jake?

JAKE: Whatever it is that you're trying to accomplish.

SAMANTHA: And what is that?

JAKE: I think the more you hear about me, the better you're going to feel about you. I can only assume that deep down we feel the same way. About each other, I mean. Fuck assumption. I'm right, but if you can find a way to feel just slightly better than me…

SAMANTHA: That is beyond stupid.

JAKE: Is it?

SAMANTHA: No, I was kidding. It's brilliant.

JAKE: You have purpose. Clearly. I'm here. You want to help me? No. I'll help you. Let's get on with it.

SAMANTHA: Jake.

Jake stands up.

JAKE: Nope, nope, nope. Let's talk about the lovely and amazing Kim.

SAMANTHA: If that's what you want to do.

JAKE: Do? Let's talk about that. What do I want you to do? That's a really good question, because I want to drive my car into a tree, that's what I want to do. But two things. One, I'm not driving right now, and two, I'm way too scared of the impact.

Samantha waits.

JAKE: She drives me crazy. She's adorable and sweet. And just about every time she opens her mouth, I want to close it with a left hook. How's that? The therapy's working though, cause I'm able to just smile. Thanks for breakfast, hon. There's eggshells in this here scramble, dear. Next time this happens, I'm gonna have to kill you. Okay? We clear, dear? NO MORE FUCKING EGG SHELLS, HONEY. AND IF THE BACON IS ANY MORE BURNT, I'M GONNA SMASH YOUR KNEE CAPS WITH THE FRYING PAN. But I'm doing great. Couldn't be better, I got a great girl. I got a fantastic lady. Cooks, cleans, and smiles. PERFECT. But here's the thing. I can't control my fucking brain. I turn the lights on, I make the stereo play, I'm able to manipulate and control a three thousand fucking pound car, and I don't even own it. It's a fucking lease. But I own this.

Jake points to his head.

JAKE: This is mine, but I can't seem to control it. I'm just out there looking for a tree. Driving around looking for a tree, arguing with myself. That's fun. I argue with myself. Like I got two people. What do you want to do, George? Stay? I don't know, Frank, maybe we should go. Fucking kill yourself. I got it all, babe. I really do. Things could not be any better. The normality is intense. Let me tell you. What do you think?

Samantha takes a second.

SAMANTHA: Sounds to me like you're not being stimulated.

JAKE: Ya think?

SAMANTHA: Get out.

JAKE: Of here?

SAMANTHA: If you keep screaming and acting like a lunatic, then yes, you'll have to leave. But no, your relationship. Get out of your relationship.

JAKE: I can't even get out of my own way.

SAMANTHA: You're not twenty years old, Jake. You're not even thirty. This stops being cute at thirty.

JAKE: No shit.

SAMANTHA: How old is she?

JAKE: That's not the point.

SAMANTHA: Fine.

JAKE: How old is Brian?

SAMANTHA: That's really not the point. But he's thirty-seven.

JAKE: Thirty-seven?

SAMANTHA: Yes. He's thirty-seven.

JAKE: Thirty-seven? No wonder he works on a ranch. He's forty.

SAMANTHA: How old is she?

JAKE: Nineteen.

SAMANTHA: Nineteen.

JAKE: Yes, nineteen. That's not the point.

SAMANTHA: Nineteen?

JAKE: Why did you call me?

SAMANTHA: Because I wanted to see you. And I wanted you to see me.

JAKE: Why?

SAMANTHA: Because I've changed.

JAKE: Bullshit.

SAMANTHA: Now you can leave.

Samantha walks over to the door and opens it.

SAMANTHA: Get out.

JAKE: I'm miserable without you.

Jake walks over to Samantha.

SAMANTHA: Get out.

Jake slams the door shut.

JAKE: When the phone rang and it was you, I felt like I could breathe for the first time in two years. I even started to write again. How's that?

SAMANTHA: Stop.

JAKE: Been drawing a blank for two years. Nothing. Absolutely nothing. Just felt my pulse again. Coincidence? I doubt it. But whatever.

SAMANTHA: Please, Jake.

JAKE: You inspire me. I feel empty without you.

SAMANTHA: Yeah, well, I don't need you, and I don't want you.

JAKE: Do you mean that?

Samantha turns away.

SAMANTHA: Yes.

JAKE: I'm right here. What are you looking at?

She looks back at him.

JAKE: Now, say it again. Truth be told, I probably deserve it, but hey, I'm only human. I mean, I tried. We both tried. You don't need me? You don't want me?

Samantha looks away.

JAKE: Tell me this isn't what you wanted. But, please, with a straight face. At least give me that.

Jake has her cornered.

SAMANTHA: You're sick.

JAKE: So are you. Now tell me I'm wrong. Tell me you didn't have this idea in your head and now you're watching it backfire.

SAMANTHA: You're wrong.

JAKE: Don't lie to me. You wanted to smile and send me on my way. Send me away a fucking wreck, and you know it. Here you go. I love you and I still miss you every day. Now tell me to get out.

Samantha doesn't say a word. Jake slams his hand on the door.

JAKE: Tell me to get out.

SAMANTHA: Get out.

JAKE: Mean it, and I swear to God, I'm gone.

SAMANTHA: I don't want this.

JAKE: What do you want?

SAMANTHA: I just wanted you to see me.

JAKE: I love you.

SAMANTHA: Get out.

JAKE: Mean it.

SAMANTHA: I love you.

JAKE: I love you, too.

SAMANTHA: Get out.

Jake puts his hand on her face, pulls her close, and then kisses her hard on the mouth. They go at it tearing into each other.

LIGHTS OUT

ACT ONE • SCENE TWO

Samantha sleeps soundly in Jake's arms. Jake slowly sneaks out of the bed trying not to wake her up. He slides off the bed and quietly puts his jeans on. He grabs the rest of his things and tiptoes for the door.

SAMANTHA: Where are you going?

He's caught.

JAKE: What?

SAMANTHA: What? What does that mean?

JAKE: What?

SAMANTHA: Anybody who says what can hear, Jake. Where are you going?

Jake is speechless.

SAMANTHA: What are you doing? Tell me you started smoking or you need air or something non-traumatizing. What are you doing?

JAKE: I gotta go.

SAMANTHA: Are you coming back?

JAKE: Tonight?

SAMANTHA: Oh my god. You're kidding me now, right? You are. Tell me I'm correct that you're kidding right now.

JAKE: What do you mean? Kidding about what? Kidding how?

SAMANTHA: I'm gonna freak out right now.

JAKE: Please, don't do that.

SAMANTHA: Then tell me what you are doing and have it make sense. Have it not be something terrible. Say something nice.

Jake is stumped.

SAMANTHA: Put down your shoes and say something nice to me, Jake, or I'm going to short.

JAKE: Don't do that.

SAMANTHA: I'm gonna do it. I'm right there, I swear to God. I can feel it. It's starting to happen.

Jake searches for the words and then suddenly blurts it out.

JAKE: Desmond.

SAMANTHA: Desmond?

JAKE: Desmond. I can't get into the details because that would be breaking a promise that I made and that's not something I want to do, but you're going to have to trust me when I say Desmond.

SAMANTHA: Desmond?

JAKE: Yes.

SAMANTHA: Well, why didn't you say that? Where are you going, Jake? Desmond, Samantha! Everything would have been clear. Are you fucking retarded, Jake?

JAKE: I'm not going to talk to you if you keep cursing at me. What is that you've picked up? It's unacceptable. It's like ranch dialogue or something.

SAMANTHA: Don't you dare. Don't say ranch. Don't say anything. Just talk.

JAKE: Why are you freaking out? Why are you freaking out? My friend is having an issue with his wife and he needs me to help him. He called me. He needs me, I'm a good friend. So I'm going.

SAMANTHA: Oh my god.

JAKE: What. Oh my god?

Samantha gets out of bed and throws a robe on. She stars to pace. She pulls the robe up over her head and begins to hyperventilate.

SAMANTHA: Please do not let this be happening.

JAKE: Things happen. Things are happening. Marriage is tough and they're going through a thing.

SAMANTHA: Please get me something.

JAKE: Like a water?

SAMANTHA: Something.

Jake steps offstage.

Samantha paces a bit more and then sits down on the couch.

She does a calming breathing exercise and then begins to recite a mantra.

SAMANTHA: Six, five, four, three, two, one. Seven, five, four, three, two, one. Five, four, three, six, seven. Negative, negative, negative, positive. Okay. Shit!

Jake comes back out with a glass of water. He sits down next to her and gives her the glass.

She takes the water and starts to drink.

JAKE: Kitchen's nice.

SAMANTHA: Please talk to me right now.

Jake leans back.

SAMANTHA: Please tell me what is going on. And if you say the word Desmond within your explanation, I am going to throw this glass of water at you, and then punch you in the face.

Jake thinks about it.

JAKE: You want to know what's going on?

SAMANTHA: Please?

JAKE: I'm going to tell you.

SAMANTHA: That would be nice.

JAKE: Are you calm?

SAMANTHA: Given the circumstances, very.

JAKE: Great. See that? If you could just stop spinning for a second, you could see.

SAMANTHA: See what?

JAKE: That nothing bad is going on here. Nothing evil. I'm just going to help a friend. That's all.

SAMANTHA: Who are you going to help?

JAKE: Desmond.

Samantha splashes Jake in the face with the water and hits him square in the jaw with her left hand.

Jake covers his face.

JAKE: What the hell is the matter with you?

Samantha gets up and starts to pace again.

Jake sits there dumbfounded.

SAMANTHA: You deserved that on so many different levels. I can't even put it all together right now. You upset me to a place where I can't even think. Thinking hurts. The layers are so thick. The dysfunction. This is a Cobb salad of dysfunction, Jake.

JAKE: You do not punch me in the face.

SAMANTHA: I should kick you in the face. I should rip your eyes out with my fingernails. You have got the most extreme amount of nerve. I can't stand it. I arrest you. I'm making a citizen's arrest before you murder me because I can't take it anymore. How dare you.

Samantha breaks down.

Jake walks over to her.

JAKE: Baby.

SAMANTHA: Don't you call me baby. Don't you ever call me that. I haven't even begun figuring out the mess you've put me in and already there's this. Like looking forward to the morning wasn't bad enough. Piecing it together. The anticipation of that alone was torture, but I can't even get there. You won't allow me to get there.

JAKE: Hold on a second. One thing at a time.

SAMANTHA: What am I? Some moron? Some blonde cocktail waitress? Am I a pole dancer, Jake?

JAKE: What are you talking about?

SAMANTHA: What do you take me for?

JAKE: I don't take you for anything. Now just slow down, and one thing at a time. I'm here. You're here. We're both here. Let's just chill out and be here for a second. Okay?

Samantha takes a deep breath.

JAKE: Here we go. All right, the thing about Desmond was bullshit.

SAMANTHA: You are such an asshole.

JAKE: Oh, big deal. Like you didn't know that was bullshit.

SAMANTHA: Why did you do that?

JAKE: 'Cause you were starting to freak out and I didn't know what to say.

SAMANTHA: So you lied.

JAKE: You know I don't know. We do a lot of things. It's not like you people come with booklets. Half of the time we don't know what to say. Good intentions. Bad intentions. We're just stuck most of the time. We just sit there trying to think of what to do, and sometimes we just lie. We're stuck. You know?

SAMANTHA: We? You people? What is this? Just stop now. You're digging further. The object is to get out of the hole. The exit is this way, Jake. You're going the wrong way.

JAKE: Just relax, okay?

SAMANTHA: No. You will not talk your way out of your own way. You did this. You will take responsibility for your actions and you will speak up for them.

JAKE: Where are we right now? What is this, group? Is it my turn yet?

SAMANTHA: Yes, it is.

JAKE: Good. I'll keep my speak short and precise. I will not take blame.

SAMANTHA: Why not?

JAKE: 'Cause I did it already. I spent two years doing that. Going over it and over it and over it. What did I do? How did it all get so messed up. My fault. I did it. I love her and how did I destroy it so bad. Then all of a sudden, I realized, I didn't do anything. It wasn't me. It was us. We tried. I tried. Our whole relationship was who's fault is it. Well, you know what? It wasn't mine, and I don't blame you, so go figure.

SAMANTHA: Just tell me. Why and where did you think you were going?

JAKE: I don't think I have to answer that.

SAMANTHA: Think again.

JAKE: I don't.

SAMANTHA: Please, Jake. I swear to God nothing bad can happen if you just tell me something. Be honest with me. Talk to me. Talk to me like you care about me, and there is no harm that can come. I'm begging you. I just need to know. Why were you sneaking out of here.

Jake takes a long beat and a breath.

JAKE: Because I woke up and I had no clue what was going to happen. I had no idea about how to feel or what to do. I was scared. And something about the sun being up and walking out of here and saying goodbye to you was terrifying. And I didn't know what to say.

SAMANTHA: What do you mean, saying goodbye to me?

JAKE: I don't know. Or saying "see you later." Or whatever was gonna happen.

SAMANTHA: So what? You just wanted to leave it for me. You just wanted to let me have it. I might have rolled over and thrown up tomorrow had you been gone. And what? That would have been okay with you.

JAKE: I didn't think about that.

SAMANTHA: Of course not. Why would you have thought about that?

JAKE: It just happened. It was fast. The thoughts ran so fast, and next thing I know, I was getting dressed.

SAMANTHA: And tiptoeing.

JAKE: And jogging. What difference does it make? I just didn't want to have this.

SAMANTHA: And what is this?

Jake just stares at her.

SAMANTHA: Say something, please.

JAKE: What do you want me to say?

SAMANTHA: Say that you have purpose. That you know what you're doing. Say that you didn't come here to disassemble me. Humiliate me. Rip me apart and then walk.

JAKE: See? That I can't deal with.

Jake turns to leave.

SAMANTHA: I don't want you to go.

JAKE: Why?

SAMANTHA: I don't know.

JAKE: Well, that is unacceptable.

SAMANTHA: For the three years we were together, I could not stand up. I couldn't move. It's taken me almost that long away from you to find myself. And here I am. I've done too much to have made a decision like the one we made last night and not have it be right. I can't accept that. I can't accept it to be false.

JAKE: That's it?

SAMANTHA: That's right.

JAKE: That's cheap.

SAMANTHA: I will kill you.

JAKE: What about reality?

SAMANTHA: This is my reality.

JAKE: Well, there's other people here right now. Some are at home, some are in this room, and some of them are at a ranch.

SAMANTHA: I already know your relationship's over and mine's a phone call away.

Jake is shocked.

JAKE: You are really sick.

SAMANTHA: Sick enough to work this out.

JAKE: Out of what though? Out of fear that you made the wrong move? That's no good for me. I need more than that. I mean, don't you?

SAMANTHA: I choose right. Right now, I'd rather be right and miserable than happy and wrong. I don't want to be happy, I want to be right. Okay?

JAKE: No. It's not okay. That's the worst proposal I have ever heard in my life. Let alone the dementia. Do you hear yourself?

SAMANTHA: Yes, I do, and I stand by it.

JAKE: Well, I disagree. I want to be happy. That's what everything is. All this pain and all this and all this shit. What's the goal? Happy, if you ask me. We all go through this hell. We're born into it. We live it for what seems like forever so that one day we can be happy. Mistakes are okay, misery is not. I mean, what are we doing here? I'll take wrong a million times over if I can end up smiling.

SAMANTHA: That's all fine and I'm not looking for misery.

JAKE: That's all fine? Is that what you just said? That's all fine? My expression of the meaning of this torturous existence and that's all fine?

SAMANTHA: I'm saying that things happen for a reason. There were no plans. There was nothing I wanted, but this happend, and I love you.

JAKE: Well, I love you, too.

SAMANTHA: So, we can figure this out.

JAKE: Not right this second we can't. Not on this. On this alone.

SAMANTHA: Then what were you doing? Why did you do this?

JAKE: I don't accept that. As a question I deny. No plans. You just said it.

Jake stands up.

SAMANTHA: Please don't leave.

JAKE: Why? So you can be right?

Samantha takes a second to think.

SAMANTHA: Yes.

Jake steps over to Samantha and tries to give her a hug.

Samantha backs away.

SAMANTHA: Don't.

Jake stares at her for a few seconds, then heads for the door. He walks out and doesn't look back.

Samantha stands alone onstage and starts to cry. Maybe she screams.

SAMANTHA: Okay. I don't want to be right, I want to be happy.

Lights fade as music slowly creeps up.

ACT TWO • SCENE ONE

Music fades up as the lights slowly come up.

Samantha is packing up her apartment. The place is a shell of what it used to look like. Boxes everywhere, and all decorations now gone. What's left of the furniture is now pushed to the side.

The phone rings. Samantha grabs it.

SAMANTHA: Hello... Hey... I'm fine, what are you doing? Okay, perfect. The truck's coming later, but we can move all the small stuff now. Okay, babe... I'll see you in a bit... Love you, too.

She hangs up the phone and then starts moving a couple packed suitcases over by the door.

A knock at the door.

She quickly opens the door.

SAMANTHA: That was quick.

Jake stands on the other side of the door wearing a suit and tie.

She stares at him for a few seconds.

SAMANTHA: No.

She tries to shut the door in his face. Jake catches it and walks in.

JAKE: No, what? I haven't even said anything yet.

SAMANTHA: Just generally, no. No to you. You have to leave.

Samantha walks to the other side of the stage.

JAKE: Well, I'm not going to do that.

SAMANTHA: Yes, you are.

JAKE: I want to talk to you.

SAMANTHA: Too late. You have to go. I don't want to know anything. I don't want to hear anything. No. I just want you to leave.

Jake looks around and sees the suitcases.

JAKE: Where are you going?

SAMANTHA: What if I kill you?

JAKE: What's with the boxes?

SAMANTHA: Okay, you have five minutes. I swear to God, that's all I have for you. Not a second more. I refuse to interact. I will listen for five minutes, and then you have to leave. Deal?

JAKE: No. That's not really going to work for me.

SAMANTHA: It's going to have to.

JAKE: What the hell is going on?

SAMANTHA: That's a trick question and you know it. Too much to say, certainly in five minute's time. I'll call you. Get out.

JAKE: Not until you tell me what's going on.

SAMANTHA: What are you doing here?

Samantha breaks down. She curls into the couch and begins to sob.

SAMANTHA: Why are you here? What do you want and what are you doing? What is this? What kind of a world is this?

Jake comes over and sits next to her.

JAKE: Babe.

SAMANTHA: I hate you so much.

JAKE: I'm sorry.

SAMANTHA: For what?

JAKE: For leaving the other night. For not speaking. For being unsure. Being scared. All of it.

SAMANTHA: What are you doing?

JAKE: I'm telling you how I feel. For once and for all. The truth. Reality. Everything.

SAMANTHA: I don't want to hear it.

JAKE: Yes you do. You know you do.

SAMANTHA: Don't tell me what I know. I know nothing.

JAKE: I love you.

SAMANTHA: I'll kill you.

JAKE: Just listen to me.

Samantha jumps up.

SAMANTHA: We already did this part, Jake. We did it and then you left. I was there, and now I'm gone. It's too late. It's too late and now I know.

JAKE: You know what?

SAMANTHA: The other night was a mistake. I wanted to believe it to be more than that, and I believed it was, but it wasn't. It was a mistake. A glitch. Just a hiccup. That's all it was.

JAKE: That's bullshit.

SAMANTHA: Fuck you. You blew it.

JAKE: Just listen to me.

SAMANTHA: I won't.

JAKE: Then watch me.

SAMANTHA: Watch you what?

Jake gets down on one knee and produces a box.

SAMANTHA: Oh my god.

JAKE: I want you to marry me.

Samantha backs up.

SAMANTHA: What are you doing?

JAKE: I'm asking you to marry me. I'm saying that I'm better with you and you are better with me. I apologize that it took me so long. But three days is not so bad.

SAMANTHA: This is illegal.

JAKE: No, it's not.

Samantha steps over to Jake and snatches the box out of his hand.

She walks over to the other side of the room and peeks into the box.

SAMANTHA: There's nothing in here.

JAKE: There will be.

SAMANTHA: How?

JAKE: I'm going to get a ring. You can even help me pick it out. I just didn't have time to get it. All this happened so fast.

She looks at the box again.

SAMANTHA: How this? This, I mean? Who does this? How do you do this? How do you justify a ring-less box?

JAKE: I just told you.

SAMANTHA: This is so perfect. This is who you are. This perfectly symbolizes your existence to me. An empty box.

JAKE: Please don't make this ugly.

SAMANTHA: Oh, it's ugly, Jake. It's the ugliest thing I have ever seen. It's putrid and grotesque.

JAKE: Slow down.

SAMANTHA: No, you speed up. Speed up that washed-out head and get a clue. Who does this?

JAKE: This is not quite the reaction I was expecting.

SAMANTHA: That's cause you are an idiot. I forgot. I forgot what it was like being around a crazy person. I can't believe how easily I almost slipped. The power of crazy.

JAKE: Stop saying crazy.

SAMANTHA: But it's true. You are. And what's so scary and terrible is how close to that I must be. Well, you know what? I'm with a human being now, Jake. And I like it.

JAKE: Oh, what, Brad? Ranch Brad?

SAMANTHA: HIS NAME IS BRIAN.

JAKE: So, what?

SAMANTHA: You want to know where I'm going, Jake? I'm going to the ranch.

JAKE: That's just great.

SAMANTHA: Brad is on his way here right now. Brian! His name is Brian. And you better leave.

JAKE: Really?

SAMANTHA: That's right.

JAKE: And is he going to beat me up when he gets here?

SAMANTHA: He might.

JAKE: That should be good.

SAMANTHA: I'm moving in with him.

JAKE: Really?

SAMANTHA: Yes.

JAKE: And when did we decide this?

SAMANTHA: It's something he's been wanting and with your help, I decided it was the right thing to do.

JAKE: What about your place here?

SAMANTHA: It's dirty here. I need to start over.

JAKE: Dirty, huh?

SAMANTHA: You should leave. I'm not joking.

JAKE: I'm petrified.

SAMANTHA: Okay.

JAKE: Let me ask you this.

SAMANTHA: GET OUT.

JAKE: Not a chance.

SAMANTHA: Please don't do this to me.

JAKE: Does he know?

SAMANTHA: Yes.

JAKE: You told him.

SAMANTHA: Yes.

JAKE: Are you sure?

SAMANTHA: Please leave?

JAKE: Answer the question?

SAMANTHA: Yes, he knows, I swear to God. I told him, now leave.

BRIAN: (*O.S.*) Hey darlin'.

A knock at the door.

SAMANTHA: He doesn't know, please don't say anything, I swear to God I was going to tell him.

Jake sits down on the couch.

SAMANTHA: Get off the couch.

JAKE: Get the door.

SAMANTHA: I hate you.

JAKE: Don't say that.

Samantha moves for the door.

SAMANTHA: Be quiet.

Samantha talks to Brian through the door.

SAMANTHA: Babe, I don't feel so good.

BRIAN: (*O.S.*) Well, open the door and I'll make you feel better.

JAKE: If you really loved him, you'd let him in.

SAMANTHA: Shut up.

BRIAN: (*O.S.*) Samantha.

SAMANTHA: Yeah.

BRIAN: (*O.S.*) Come on, open up.

SAMANTHA: No. I can't. Can you just come back in a little?

JAKE: Brutal. Slightly evil and brutal.

SAMANTHA: I learned it from you, now shut up.

BRIAN: (*O.S.*) What?

SAMANTHA: Nothing babe. I just feel really sick.

JAKE: Don't call him babe.

BRIAN: (*O.S.*) Come on, love, open up.

JAKE: Love? That I can't deal with. BEAT IT, SHITTY. TAKE A HINT ALREADY.

Jake turns to Samantha.

Silence.

JAKE: Sorry.

Samantha sits down on the couch. So mortified, she just sits there with her mouth wide open.

Then more silence. They wait for a response.

After what feels like an hour...

BRIAN: (O.S.) Samantha.

SAMANTHA: I can't let you in here right now.

BRIAN: (O.S.) Okay. But who's that in there with you, hon?

Jake holds up a finger. Silencing Samantha. He stands up.

Samantha is frozen and horrified, not really sure what to do. Jake steps over to the door.

Jake projects toward the door.

JAKE: Hey, there.

BRIAN: (O.S.) Hello.

JAKE: My name is Jake.

BRIAN: (O.S.) Hey, Jake. Everything okay in there?

JAKE: That all depends, Brad.

BRIAN: (O.S.) Okay, but the name is Brian.

JAKE: I know that, Brian.

Jake and Samantha share a look.

BRIAN: (O.S.) Okay, well, what's going on, Jake?

A long beat.

JAKE: I love your girlfriend.

Samantha's head drops into her hands.

BRIAN: (O.S.) Yeah?

JAKE: Yeah.

A long beat.

BRIAN: (O.S.) I understand.

JAKE: You do?

BRIAN: (O.S.) Sure. I love her, too.

JAKE: Well, that's a problem, Brian.

BRIAN: (O.S.) Why's that, Jake?

Jake turns to Samantha and whispers.

JAKE: Not so bright, huh?

Samantha nods her head disapprovingly.

JAKE: It's a problem, Brian, because when two people love the same gal, it usually ends in a fight.

BRIAN: (O.S.) Yeah, I can see that. I suppose you got a point.

Jake waits.

JAKE: Well, is that something you'd be interested in?

BRIAN: (O.S.) I suppose. If it's necessary.

JAKE: Well, that's what I'm saying. Given the circumstances here, I think it is. Or is gonna be. Necessary.

BRIAN: (O.S.) Right. Then yeah. Fine.

Jake is taken aback.

JAKE: You seem very calm.

BRIAN: (O.S.) Yeah.

JAKE: Are you a large man?

BRIAN: (O.S.) Decent-sized.

264 • SCOTT CAAN

Samantha stands up. Jake motions for her to stay put. His confidence is fading.

JAKE: I'm gonna open this door, Brian.

BRIAN: (*O.S.*) Okay.

JAKE: But I want you to know something.

BRIAN: (*O.S.*) Shoot.

Jake looks at Samantha.

JAKE: I've made some mistakes in my life. I've acted in a way that I'm not proud of.

BRIAN: (*O.S.*) That's okay, man. We're only human.

JAKE: Thank you, Brian. I'm trying, that's really my point here.

BRIAN: (*O.S.*) All anyone can ask.

Jake is really thrown. He shakes it off and turns to Samantha, but he projects toward the door.

JAKE: I love Samantha very much, and I know I've let her down. More than once.

Samantha drops her head. Completely helpless.

JAKE: We've tried several times to make things work, but for one reason or another, things turned… Well, they just turned, I guess. But it never goes away. This feeling. What I have for her, it never goes away and that's why I'm here. I really have no idea what's going to happen, I'm not really sure how she feels. I have an idea, a hope, really, but I've made such a mess of things that at times it's hard to tell, certainly now.

BRIAN: (*O.S.*) Well, I know she's not feeling very well, but she's sitting right there. Why don't you ask her?

Jake turns back to Samantha. She gives him the finger.

JAKE: Now's not the time, I think.

BRIAN: (*O.S.*) Fair enough.

JAKE: Back to you and I. I'm gonna open this door, and I want you to know I don't care how big you are. We're gonna fight for the… I don't know what to say. I suppose we're just gonna fight. But before we do, I want you to know I don't care what happens. I mean, I care and everything, I just mean I'm not concerned with my well-being. What I do care about is the woman sitting in front of me and I aim to prove that by opening this door. I've tried using my words, and that just seems to get jumbled, so maybe this can be something else. I don't know what I'm really trying to say here.

BRIAN: (*O.S.*) I think maybe you're just stalling.

JAKE: That could be true.

BRIAN: (*O.S.*) I mean, for all you know, I could be capable of killing you.

JAKE: Right. Are you?

BRIAN: (*O.S.*) I guess we'll know soon enough.

JAKE: Right.

Jake continues to stall.

JAKE: You have any weapons?

BRIAN: (*O.S.*) Just my two fists.

JAKE: You consider those weapons?

No reply.

Jake walks over to Samantha and kisses her on the forehead.

JAKE: I love you. Whatever happens. I love you and always will.

Samantha just stares up at him, no reply.

JAKE: I'm not being dramatic. I don't mean whatever happens with the fight, just in general. I love you.

Jake moves over to the door, takes a deep breath, and slowly opens it. He backs away a bit.

BRIAN slowly steps into the apartment. He is not intimidating, to say the least. Almost the exact opposite of intimidating.

Brian looks at Samantha, takes the room in, checks Jake out.

Jake is all of a sudden very relaxed.

BRIAN: Samantha, you okay?

SAMANTHA: I'm really sorry.

BRIAN: As long as you're okay.

He looks over to Jake.

BRIAN: Jake.

JAKE: Brian.

Brian notices the box. Points.

BRIAN: What's in the box?

Samantha looks down and realizes she is still clutching the ring box.

SAMANTHA: Oh, nothing.

BRIAN: You can tell me.

SAMANTHA: No, nothing. There is literally nothing in the box.

JAKE: For now.

Brian and Samantha both turn to Jake. After a few beats...

BRIAN: So?

JAKE: I'll fight you if that's what she wants me to do.

SAMANTHA: Shut up, Jake.

JAKE: We're not gonna fight.

BRIAN: No, I guess not.

Brian turns back to Samantha. Takes a few seconds to think everything through.

BRIAN: You love him?

Samantha takes her time, but nods her head yes.

BRIAN: You want to be with him?

Again, she takes her time, but shakes her head no.

BRIAN: You love me?

She nods her head yes.

BRIAN: You want to be with me?

She takes a beat, and then nods yes.

Jake watches. He's crushed.

After what feels like forever, Jake moves over to Samantha and puts out his hand.

She hands him the empty box.

Jake takes it. He leans forward, grabs Samantha, kisses her forehead, and then moves for the door.

JAKE: Lucky man, Brian. Nice to meet you.

BRIAN: You, too.

And Jake exits.

A bit of silence.

SAMANTHA: I'm so sorry.

BRIAN: Things happen.

SAMANTHA: No. Things happen, sure, but they're not supposed to. Not like this. Not to you.

BRIAN: Why not to me?

SAMANTHA: Because you're good?

BRIAN: What about you?

SAMANTHA: I'm not good. Not like you are.

BRIAN: I don't think that's true.

Samantha takes her time.

SAMANTHA: I slept with him.

BRIAN: I figured that.

SAMANTHA: Recently.

This catches him off guard.

BRIAN: That I did not... How recently?

SAMANTHA: The other day when I called you and told you I was ready...
I slept with him. A few hours before I made that call. To you.

BRIAN: The one where you said we could try...

SAMANTHA: Sharing space. Yes.

Brian has to sit down. He is floored.

BRIAN: Wow.

Samantha starts to speak. Brian puts up a finger.

BRIAN: Hold on. Just wait. I'm processing.

SAMANTHA: Okay.

Brian thinks about it some more.

BRIAN: Okay.

SAMANTHA: Okay what?

BRIAN: I'm done with the processing. Why would you do that?

She starts to speak.

BRIAN: Wait.

She waits.

BRIAN: I'm thinking here. Pluses, minuses, ups, downs. I mean, part of me
is thinking that it must have not been that good of a time. Had it been,
I can't imagine, just moments after, feeling the need to all of a sudden
want to live with someone else. So that's good, maybe you tried it and
it felt horrible and all you could think of was me. I guess that's a plus,
for me, I mean. Is that what we're talking about here?

SAMANTHA: No.

BRIAN: I didn't think so.

A moment.

BRIAN: One more question and I promise I will stop.

SAMANTHA: You can ask me anything you want.

BRIAN: I don't want to overdo it. You've clearly been through a lot.

SAMANTHA: Why are you being so nice to me?

BRIAN: Because I'm in love with you. Okay? I'm sitting here trying to give you good reasons, in my own head, not that you're even offering them, I'm trying to make them up, just so that I can figure out a way to move forward, forget about it, and help you finish packing. I just want it to never have happened.

SAMANTHA: It did, though.

BRIAN: I got that. I've been pushing the visions out of my head since you said it. Processing? That was me doing the aforementioned.

SAMANTHA: You're very cute.

BRIAN: Fuck!

SAMANTHA: What?

BRIAN: I knew it. I knew when I met you something like this was going to happen.

SAMANTHA: What do you mean?

BRIAN: You think I'm able to get a hold of girls like you? Pretty girls who have jobs, go to seminars, and are into self-help? Sure, I ride horses. So what? Horses smell like shit.

SAMANTHA: I like horses.

BRIAN: No you don't. Nobody likes horses. I like horses, and that's my point.

SAMANTHA: That doesn't make any sense.

BRIAN: Look at this. I'm so pathetic. You're consoling me.

SAMANTHA: No, I'm not.

BRIAN: Why did you say yes, or nod yes, when I asked you if you wanted to be with me? Why?

She thinks about it.

SAMANTHA: The same reason I called you after I slept with Jake. The same reason I went to seminars, because that's what I want.

BRIAN: Then can we forget about this whole thing?

SAMANTHA: I don't know.

BRIAN: That was a rhetorical question. No we cannot, and that's the point. You don't belong with me and I don't belong with you.

SAMANTHA: That's not true.

Brian thinks about it.

BRIAN: You know, if I was intentionally being manipulative here, it would be working.

SAMANTHA: I don't want to be with him.

BRIAN: Why not?

Samantha thinks about it.

BRIAN: Don't answer that. I don't care. A: because I don't believe you; and B: because... Forget B. A cancels B. I don't believe you. Better question, do you want to be with me? And if the thinking about it in any way has anything to do with that guy, then I already know the answer.

Samantha thinks about it.

BRIAN: Say something.

SAMANTHA: I love you. I really do. I mean that. I'm not letting you down easy. That's not what I'm doing, because I will finish gathering my things, and I will move in with you today and I will mean it, because the truth is it's everything I should want. But I'm so in love with that guy that I can't even see straight. Seminars, moving, being hypnotized, nothing works. I hate him so much, but not as much as I love him. I wish I could help it, but I can't.

Brian takes it all in. Then after a few long beats, he slowly moves over to her, kisses her forehead, and moves for the door. He looks back one last time and then exits.

Samantha starts to cry. Again.

LIGHTS OUT

ACT THREE • SCENE ONE

A few months later.

Lights back up on Samantha's apartment. Now fully furnished, again. A bit different than before. Less decoration, a bit less perfect. More lived in.

A knock at the door.

Samantha steps out from the bathroom, takes a look at herself in the mirror, takes a deep breath, and then moves for the door. Opens it.

Jake stands outside. They look at each other for a few beats.

SAMANTHA: Come in.

He steps into the apartment. Checks the place out.

JAKE: Looks nice in here.

SAMANTHA: Thank you.

JAKE: Different, but the same, I guess. I don't know. Is something different?

SAMANTHA: I don't know. Just lived in, I suppose.

JAKE: It's nice. More you.

SAMANTHA: You want something?

This throws him off.

JAKE: Excuse me?

SAMANTHA: To drink.

JAKE: Oh, no. I'm good, thank you.

A bit of silence.

SAMANTHA: How you been?

JAKE: Good. You?

SAMANTHA: Good.

JAKE: Good.

272 • SCOTT CAAN

SAMANTHA: You writing?

JAKE: I am. Have been. It's good.

SAMANTHA: Good.

Another uncomfortable silence.

SAMANTHA: Well, it was good to see you.

JAKE: Wow.

SAMANTHA: I'm kidding, but seriously.

JAKE: What?

SAMANTHA: You called me this time.

JAKE: Yes, I did.

SAMANTHA: Well?

JAKE: Well? Jesus. I just got here.

SAMANTHA: I offered you a drink.

JAKE: I'm not thirsty, so what, I have to leave?

SAMANTHA: Jake.

JAKE: What? You look good.

SAMANTHA: Don't start.

JAKE: Don't start, finish, I got no chance here.

SAMANTHA: Chance at what?

JAKE: I wanted to see you.

SAMANTHA: I got that.

JAKE: Well, how are you?

SAMANTHA: We did that already. I'm good. So are you.

JAKE: Why are you being like this?

SAMANTHA: How should I be?

JAKE: Can we start over?

SAMANTHA: No.

JAKE: No?

SAMANTHA: No, on so many levels, no. That is the answer. We cannot start over.

JAKE: This is going amazing.

SAMANTHA: Going? What's going?

JAKE: Nothing's going. So literal. I'm just here.

SAMANTHA: Then tell me something?

JAKE: What do you want me to tell you?

SAMANTHA: I don't want me to tell you anything.

JAKE: I haven't seen you in six months.

SAMANTHA: I certainly don't need you telling me things like that. This I know. I'm good with time. Six months, pleasantries, pleasantries, let's go.

JAKE: Where are we going?

SAMANTHA: Nowhere if you don't say something. I'm getting old. Literally and metaphorically. It's good to see you too, you look great, what do you want?

Jake is shocked.

SAMANTHA: I mean it. I am happy to see you. Truly, but that's about it. You called me, you wanted to see me, here I am. If that's it, then great, I'll see you next time. If not, let's go. We are way beyond, and if not, should be, beyond the bullshit.

Jake is really thrown. He takes his time.

JAKE: I don't know where to start.

SAMANTHA: Okay. I'll help you. Why did you call? It's been a while. Why all of a sudden?

Jake starts to put something together.

SAMANTHA: Let me help you some more. Skip anything that doesn't get directly to the point. And or is not factual.

JAKE: Is this seminar shit?

SAMANTHA: Not even close. No more seminar shit. No more therapy shit. I did take some Peyote, and that was helpful, but just for a couple of days. Anyway. This is Samantha shit.

JAKE: It's new.

SAMANTHA: This is not. This right here. You. Please.

JAKE: Okay.

SAMANTHA: Okay?

JAKE: I said okay. Can I breathe?

SAMANTHA: I'd rather you just speak.

Jake gets it.

SAMANTHA: Of course, you can do both at the same time.

He smiles. She smiles back. A small bit of relief.

JAKE: I waited to call you because I didn't know what was going to happen with whatsisname.

Samantha nods her head.

JAKE: I know his name.

SAMANTHA: I know that.

JAKE: I didn't want to do any more damage than I had already done, and if things were going to work out and you were going to be happy, then I didn't want to disrupt that.

Samantha waits for more.

JAKE: Can I have some credit for that?

SAMANTHA: You already did. It was silent.

JAKE: Thank you.

She forces a smile.

JAKE: So, I gave it some time, called you, and rather than ask questions over the phone, I assumed, seeing as your number had not changed, that you did not move, and that you were still here. I was relieved.

Samantha makes a face.

JAKE: You said facts. Truth. I was relieved. I wanted to see you. Here I am.

Samantha nods.

JAKE: I'm sorry things didn't work out with you and Ranch Brian.

She nods again.

JAKE: I don't really mean that.

SAMANTHA: Why not?

JAKE: Because I love you, I don't ever want to be without you again, and I really think we should get married. Start over right now.

Jake produces the ring box.

Samantha takes it in, then walks to the other side of the room.

SAMANTHA: All of a sudden.

JAKE: What do you mean? This is so far beyond all of a sudden.

SAMANTHA: Not to me it's not. I didn't know what you were doing for the last six months.

JAKE: I just told you.

SAMANTHA: What happened to Kim?

JAKE: She went back to high school. Was that a real question?

SAMANTHA: Why now?

JAKE: What?

SAMANTHA: What's different? Why now? For three years you were never ready, two years after that you couldn't even spend the night. Why now? What's so different?

JAKE: Nothing is different and that's the point. Because what we have is never going away, and that is something I know for a fact. You don't feel the same way, I'll listen, but I'll call you a liar when you're done.

SAMANTHA: That doesn't really leave me with any options.

JAKE: Also my point.

SAMANTHA: So you've just made up our minds then?

JAKE: There's nothing to be made up. That's just the way it is. Is it perfect? No. Will it ever be? No chance. But it's what we got and we're stuck with it. We can fight it for another couple of years and come to this conclusion, or we can just get started.

SAMANTHA: Oh my god.

JAKE: Oh my god, what?

SAMANTHA: To begin with, I can hardly stand the romance. Do you realize we are negotiating our potential partnership? This is not the way it goes. Not to mention, it's as if you're presenting a jail sentence that we both have no choice but to serve.

JAKE: Do you love me?

SAMANTHA: Of course I love you, you idiot.

He gets on a knee.

JAKE: Just take the fucking box, would ya?

She just looks at him, in shock.

JAKE: Life is edgy. I didn't know that when we met. I was young and I didn't know shit. If I knew what I know now, I would have asked you to marry me the day I met you.

Samantha takes a step closer.

JAKE: I'm sorry. I'm sorry for so many things. I'm sorry for being stupid, I'm sorry for not treating you the way you deserved to be treated. And I'm really sorry you had to watch your little sister get married before you. I know that sucked. Fuck. Even Desmond got married. I think you are the greatest woman on the planet, and even if I didn't, I'd still be on my knees right now. We belong together, we got no choice. You want me to be romantic, I'll give it a shot, but the truth is we're stuck with each other. Marry me.

He pushes the box out toward her.

Samantha slowly reaches out for the box, takes it, and opens it.

She is beyond horrified.

SAMANTHA: Are you fucking kidding me?

JAKE: No.

SAMANTHA: It's still empty.

JAKE: I know that.

SAMANTHA: Are you the stupidest person in the world?

JAKE: Is that a rhetorical question?

SAMANTHA: Yes. I know the answer.

JAKE: I asked around.

SAMANTHA: You what?

JAKE: Desmond's wife, some other people, I was even going to ask your sister, but I didn't want to ruin the surprise.

SAMANTHA: What surprise? The surprise of an empty box. That's not a surprise. It's the exact opposite. I'm surprised at what an idiot you are, but there is no tangible surprise here.

JAKE: But everyone I spoke to agreed that any normal woman would want to be a part of picking out her wedding ring.

SAMANTHA: Do I look normal to you? We're not normal. Nothing is normal. How do you justify a ring-less box? Twice?

JAKE: I just told you how.

SAMANTHA: Get out.

JAKE: What?

Samantha is serious, and all of a sudden very upset.

SAMANTHA: I mean it. You have no idea how much this means to me. Negatively speaking.

JAKE: Don't get upset.

SAMANTHA: Too late. You literally just fucked up for the last time.

JAKE: Don't swear.

SAMANTHA: Fuck you, don't curse! Do you have any idea the volumes in which this speaks?

JAKE: No.

SAMANTHA: It says everything. For you to come here, again, with an empty box, says so much more than any of that bullshit you just said to me.

JAKE: It wasn't bullshit.

SAMANTHA: No, it wasn't. But it is now. Just like that. Don't you see? Words. Thoughts. Ideas in your head, but nothing's tangible. A ring means something. I don't even care if it's nice. You could have tied a rock to a piece of metal, at least it would have been real. At least I could have seen it, touched it, anything but just hearing it. All you have are words, but guess what? Your words are no good here anymore. All they are is a representation of how poorly we communicate. Words. Yours and mine, but they are no longer good here.

JAKE: Everything I said?

SAMANTHA: What about it?

JAKE: Doesn't mean anything?

SAMANTHA: Not without a ring it doesn't.

JAKE: You're telling me that if I showed up here with a ring, said all the things that I said, felt the way I feel, all we've been through, the way you feel, all of it, it would have made a difference?

SAMANTHA: All the difference in the world, and the fact that you don't see that is just more proof that I'm right.

JAKE: No, I see it, and I agree. I just needed to be sure.

Jake pulls a beautiful diamond ring out of his pocket and presents it to her.

Samantha is beyond shocked. She stares at the ring, and then back at him.

SAMANTHA: You're so stupid.

JAKE: Fine, but you're stuck with me now.

Samantha steps forward and then slowly puts out her hand.

Jake slides the ring onto her finger.

SAMANTHA: What if it doesn't work?

JAKE: Then we'll move on and think about each other for the rest of our lives.

SAMANTHA: That's no good.

JAKE: I agree.

Jake stands up. Moves in and kisses her.

SAMANTHA: God, I hate you.

Jake smiles.

LIGHTS OUT

THE END

I was living in Hawaii. I was pretty much losing my mind. I missed home, my friends, my family, and on a daily basis was doing work that I was not proud of. It's funny, looking back now, on what a great opportunity I was blessed with. But sometimes it's just hard to see what's right in front of you. Especially when you are constantly looking so far ahead. As an actor, you try to always stay in the moment, but I suppose that doesn't always translate to life.

Val and I had decided to start our production class and I wanted new material for the students to work on, so I began to write. With no story in mind, I just started with a speech. Never in my life did I just sit down and write without at least some idea of where I was heading. This speech, which was really an extended version of a theater joke I had heard, inspired me to move forward and write a play called The Performance of Heartbreak.

Every minute of free time I had, I would sit down and just write these characters. Characters that all shared, and went on jags about, one idea or another that was going on in my head at the time. They were all looking for meaning. What are we doing here? What is the point of it all? Even the people in this play that seemed to have figured it out, at one point would realize they knew nothing. There were no rules and no structure being followed. The characters just lived through the play as I wrote them. That was really the exercise. Just to write and see what happened.

When I finished the first draft, I was so excited I'm pretty sure I didn't even do a spell check before sending it off to my agent in New York. The email heading read simply, "My new play, it's genius." A few days later, he called me. After some bullshit pleasantries, we got into it. I want to preface what I'm about to say with the fact that he was not wrong. I mean, sure he was, but technically speaking, no. He didn't get it. It's not a play, he said. Maybe if you present it as a night of scenes, he said. It needs an ending, or a beginning, both, and maybe a story. I can't send this out, he said. I wanted to kill him, but I was 2,500 miles of ocean and an equal amount of land away. I hung up the phone and at first decided I would put the play up, hopefully get some decent reviews, demand he send it to my publisher, and then fire him. Then immediately I realized what the point of writing it in the first place actually was. It was simply for students to work on and play with. It was also an experiment for me.

Rather than flying halfway across the globe to burn my agent's house down and then trying to force this play somewhere it maybe didn't belong, I instead decided to continue writing in the exact same way. For the remainder of my time in

Hawaii that year, I continued to write without any expectations. No preconceived ideas of where the plays were going and pretty much zero clue of how they would end. Again, just letting the characters write the story as it went on. I wrote an epilogue—called An Epilogue—*to* The Performance of Hearbreak, *then* Day In Life, *where the only connection to the original piece was the style and head space from which it was written.*

I thoroughly enjoyed the time and further enjoyed watching students pick these plays apart, break them down, and give them life—life that I wasn't even sure existed. I mentioned in my first essay, some of these plays might never be put up in their entirety. Specifically, I meant these. Again, that's not why they were written. The characters go on and on, sometimes in circles. The stories themselves lack structure, but they are honest. As a whole, there is certainly a beginning, middle, and end, but not in the traditional sense. Additionally, there's a reality in this collection, but if presented in its entirety—I mean all three of these plays together—it might not work, and/or drive the audience completely crazy. What it may lack in storytelling structure is, hopefully, made up for with truth.

I tried very hard to leave them alone and avoided too much editing. What exists is pretty much what I wrote and never looked back. I once heard that real writing happens in the rewriting. Not with these. Again, there is obviously a danger in writing this way. It's lazy at the end of the day. It turns out to be more of an exercise in therapy rather than storytelling, but maybe that was the point. Adjusting it or trying to turn it into something else would be a disservice. Some of my favorite stuff is in here and I think it's worth being printed as is. For actors, my hope is that they can find sections to have fun with and learn from. For readers? Something to understand, enjoy, and hopefully relate to.

The Performance of Heartbreak

The Performance of Heartbreak

SCENE ONE

THE STAGE

A young-looking thirty-five-year-old man glides across the stage. This is GIOVANNI.

MARTY, same age, pays attention. Or tries.

GIOVANNI: So, this kid, right? He's this actor. A real AC-TOR! High hopes and aspirations. A real thespian. So what's he doing? Funny you should ask. He's moping around the south side of Philadelphia doing shit. This guy. Here he is. Boom! The phone rings. Now keep in mind, this kid's been at it for a while. But here is still. The rent in New York, his sister's baby daddy drama, and his mom don't like him so far anyway. Anyhow... He's got a dumpy studio on the south side, and the rent's a mess... He's a fucking bum for all intents, so you can imagine the excitement of this call.

Marty just looks at him.

GIOVANNI: Got it. Hold on. The phone rings, right?

Marty nods.

GIOVANNI: Right. So he mopes over. Ain't nothing shaking but the leaves on the trees, right?

Marty nods.

GIOVANNI: Wrong! It's this cat's agent! Apple to the cheesesteak through the wire. Talk at me. I mean, he ain't heard a word since the last time he ain't heard shit, so needless to say my dude's got a little jump in his hump, right?

Marty nods.

GIOVANNI: So, here we go... Word is, and keep in mind that there's zero chance this cat's booker is taking him for a spin in the wind. I mean, no way… He'd kill the kid with a prank like this, at this point anyway… Break his already broken heart to bits… So, as a preface, this ain't no joke. So boom. Here's what. You got the part.

Marty lights up.

GIOVANNI: That's right. He steps right into a moonwalk halfway across the floor plan and back. And I'm talking six feet and back across. Bitch is bouncing off the walls. Literally. This is not a large space. And at this point, he don't even know what's what. He might have booked a tampon commercial, at this point we don't know. But then he settles. And mind you, he don't give a shit what it is. Tampon or Teflon, the bitch is in.

Marty smiles.

GIOVANNI: Right? So here's the news. Broadway, bitch! His dude might have even said those very words, he was so excited for his funky ass. And please believe this is one of those well-to-do, Barney's shopping motherfuckers too. He thinks who is he, this agent, who gets weekly mani-pedis talking about "Broadway, bitch!" He don't talk like that is my point.

Marty smiles.

GIOVANNI: Right? So turns out some kid caught a case. Been rehearsing for nine weeks and ate too much sushi… Whale poison. Mercury… Something. The point is… He dropped out and now our boy here gets the call. Period piece about Romans and gods and war and shit, I don't know. Medium-sized part, maybe even on the small side, but this is Broadway… There are no small parts, only small people. That's word on the street, anyway. So our kid's bouncing off the walls again. Holy shit, right?

Marty smiles.

GIOVANNI: I mean, he's been deep in the dump house. He's got the rent in one hand, his sister's baby in the other and a white towel wrapped around his neck that he's getting ready to wrap the baby in and throw the whole shit off the balcony. Not literally, I mean I don't want you to get the wrong idea, he's a good dude and would never throw a child out the window, or even a towel. He wouldn't even litter, is my point.

That's what a good dude our boy is. But metaphorically speaking...
He was about to give the fuck up.

Marty nods.

GIOVANNI: So! Here's the skin and bones and the bad news. The show
open at eight o'clock and you got the first line of the play. You say
some other shit too, but the first line is this and it reads as so. "Hark, I
hear the cannons roar."

Marty frowns.

GIOVANNI: I know. He's looking at his watch, which is broken for the
record, just to add insult, the poor bitch has to ask what time it is.

Marty nods.

GIOVANNI: Anyway... Boom. He's out the door. Numbers bouncing
around his head and hark I hear the cannons roar. Train to New York,
two hours, cab to the theater, twenty, thirty, give or take... If it ain't
bad enough he's pressed for time, he's also trying to figure out if he
has enough dough to make the trip. And all the while, "Hark, I hear
the cannons roar."

Marty looks like he has something to say.

GIOVANNI: Can I just tell the story, please?

Marty nods.

GIOVANNI: He's good. He's got just enough and he makes it on the train.

Marty smiles.

GIOVANNI: All antsy and shit. I'll get to it, just relax... So he makes the
train and now it starts. I mean, he's been racing since he picked up
the jack and hasn't had a chance to settle into his role. I mean, let's
refer back to where this all started. I mean, he is an AC-TOR. A real
thesp! He studied blood, sweat, and tears for this his whole life. Here's
his moment, foget the setup, forget the fact that he's running late for
the biggest moment of his life... The roots. The truth. The moment
we've, at the very least, he's been waiting for.... So, it begins. "Hark, I

hear the cannons roar… No, no, no… Hark, I hear the cannons roar… No. Hark, I hear the cannons roar…" I mean this silly bitch spends the next two and a half hours of his life pumping back and forth down the aisles of this fast train saying this line every which way to Sunday. "Hark, I hear the cannons roar." People on the train telling him to shut the fuck up. Some kid from the Bronx that was visiting his brother in some cuckoo's nest coming back from Baltimore slapped him in the mouth for saying the shit too much… Our dude's stressed, to say the least. And he's been slapped. MAYBE MORE THAN ONCE. But he's focused. "Hark, I hear the cannons roar." Up, down, and all around.

Marty checks his watch.

GIOVANNI: Good to have a watch that works. Unfortunately, his does not. And ain't this a bitch, he asks the kid from the Bronx what time it is. Turns out, he too has a nonfunctioning watch, so our boy gets slapped yet again.

Marty shakes his head.

GIOVANNI: Right? So he's off the train and into the city. Now what he did not factor in, nor did he have time to do so, was the fact that he'd be stepping out of Grand Central right about the time when getting a cab was less likely to happen then… Insert bad joke. I don't know, I'm on a tear here. Cut to… You like how I'm getting all cinematic with the shit?

Marty smiles.

GIOVANNI: Right? Cut to our boy doing nine-O, booking up the street screaming at the top of his lung. "HARK I HEAR THE CANNONS ROAR. HARK I HEAR THE CANNONS ROAR." This is New York City, so he's blending wonderfully… It's like a chorus line, homeless dudes start screaming the shit too. Which starts to give our boy some more ideas. So now he's mocking them mocking him, the whole thing's a mess… Leave alone the fact he's sweating, cramping, and about to be late for his Broadway debut… But he makes it. "Hark I hear the cannons roar." Still practicing his line like a whackjob over and over again as they rush him backstage and toss a big red cape over his head… Hark I hear the cannons roar. He can't stop, it's like he's obsessed… People now at this point know not to fuck with him, because he's an actor and that's protocol around these parts… 'Cause from the cape thrower to the nose powderer, they don't say shit while he's harking, they just get him all set and point.

Marty's at the edge of his seat.

GIOVANNI: So, this is it, the moment he's been waiting for his entire life. Six hundred people waiting. Curtains, playbills, popcorn... Maybe not popcorn, I don't know... But here he is. Music up. One last time in his head... "Hark I hear the cannons roar." He's got it! They give him a big sword and shove him out to the center of the stage, and KABLOOOOOOOM! An explosion echoes through the whole theater, and he goes, "WHAT THE FUCK WAS THAT?"

M: It's a joke.

GIOVANNI: True story, babe. I am a true blue kind of a guy. And there is a point.

LIGHTS OUT

SCENE TWO

A SMALL COFFEE SHOP

A man in a perfectly tailored suit, TERRANCE, sits at a booth. He checks his watch... A few beats... Reads from a newspaper, sips his coffee, then puts his paper down and checks his watch again.

LAYLA storms in. She's a hot mess, but gorgeous. She sits next to Terrance.

LAYLA: I'm so sorry, Terrance. I love you.

TERRANCE: You look a mess.

LAYLA: Thanks.

TERRANCE: I love you, too.

LAYLA: Sorry, I'm late.

TERRANCE: Timing is everything.

LAYLA: Should I start over? Walk back in and we can start over?

TERRANCE: That would be highly unproductive, considering.

LAYLA: I said I was sorry.

TERRANCE: And I said it was fine. I love you with all my heart. Why do you look like shit?

LAYLA: I'm really a mess.

TERRANCE: I see.

LAYLA: How was your flight?

TERRANCE: Horrid.

LAYLA: I'm sorry.

TERRANCE: It's really traveling all together. I mean, what's a good flight? Have you ever heard of a grand experience on an airplane? It's really, generally, an epic tragedy altogether. The humans, the sweat, and the bare feet. What's to like?

LAYLA: Did you always speak this way?

TERRANCE: No. I used to have a terrible accent. I was broke and I sounded like a grease ball from New Jersey. Things change and here we are. You?

LAYLA: Your sister good?

TERRANCE: She's excellent.

LAYLA: The kid?

TERRANCE: He's waiting in the car.

Layla makes a face.

TERRANCE: That was a joke. He still goes to school. It's nine in the morning and he's seven years old. What is this? I mean, what's the problem?

LAYLA: What?

TERRANCE: This. This thing you are doing?

LAYLA: What am I doing?

TERRANCE: It's a mechanism or something. Some sort of defence or setup or something else. What's the problem? All these questions I feel, and I could be wrong, and of course doubt it, but I get the feeling you are asking me to either avoid, which would not be like you, or more likely, setting me up for some sort of a rant. About you.

She stares at him. Dumbfounded.

TERRANCE: Don't give me that look, please. Yes, I am your agent but you are also a dear friend. In both cases, we encourage narcissim. So please.

LAYLA: I really care about you.

TERRANCE: I appreciate that.

LAYLA: And your sister.

TERRANCE: She appreciates it, I'm sure.

LAYLA: And I love, love, love little Joey.

TERRANCE: Jake.

LAYLA: Little Jake.

TERRANCE: This is Hollywood. I'm sure he'll change it when he gets old enough, does it really matter?

LAYLA: I really love that kid, and I'm ready to babysit always.

TERRANCE: Do you want me to throw up?

LAYLA: I'd really rather you not.

TERRANCE: Then, please.

Layla starts to cry.

TERRANCE: Oh, Jesus.

LAYLA: I'm cursed.

TERRANCE: Stop it. What happened?

LAYLA: Oh my god, I don't even know where to begin. It doesn't even matter. It just is what it is, and that's that. I can't. No more. I literally can't do it anymore. I mean, I just can't accept the beating that is my life. I mean, what are we even doing? We all end up hurt, we are all destined for it one way or another, so what really is the point? And don't say it's just that. 'Cause I can't accept that either. That old line of bullshit is out. Get in there and hurt because that's where the stuff really is. Life! Well I don't want it. I can't be a part of it anymore.

TERRANCE: What happened?

LAYLA: I hope he dies.

TERRANCE: Me, too.

LAYLA: I'm just going to be one of those old people, and you know what? I don't care. I accept it. I plan on booking every single thing you send my way and there hasn't been enough. I'm sorry, but it's the new me talking.

TERRANCE: Okay.

LAYLA: I want to work and I want to work... Most importantly, I refuse to care. About anything. You know what makes a really good outlaw?

TERRANCE: Excuse me?

LAYLA: A biker or a mob guy, like an Italian?

TERRANCE: What are you saying?

LAYLA: Aren't you Italian?

TERRANCE: I am.

LAYLA: Well, then, you should know this stuff?

TERRANCE: I'm sorry.

LAYLA: I'm all over the place, but you see what I'm saying?

TERRANCE: I don't.

LAYLA: The Hell's Angels.

TERRANCE: What about them?

LAYLA: Or the mob. Did I offend you?

TERRANCE: Not yet.

LAYLA: Well, I don't meant to, or the Italians for that matter, but it's relevant. I think. To what I'm saying, it is. These people, and they don't have to be Italian or ride motorbikes, but the lifestyle is what I'm saying. This kind of person. They have chosen a life of crime, and what makes them so amazing at what they do, they know their destiny. I know I'm scattered, but I can read and I did. So these guys, what makes them so great is their approach. They don't go around selling drugs and killing people thinking, "I'm not going to jail, I'm going to be the one that gets away with it." No! They know what's going to happen, it's just a matter of when. You see what that can do? You have any idea how powerful that can be? Fear is irrelevant. It doesn't exist. There is nothing to be let down from, because there was no expectation to begin with. That just makes them good at what they do. For all intents and purposes, their job. The ones that think otherwise? Can you imagine the rude awakening. No wonder they end up snitching on each other. I want to be a badass and that's the new me. I inevitably know what is going to happen, therefore I surrender.

Terrance takes a sip of his coffee.

LAYLA: Thank you.

TERRANCE: No, I'm glad I could help.

LAYLA: All right. Now, let's get me a job. I'm tready.

TERRANCE: Did you say tready?

LAYLA: Ready. I meant ready.

Lights up on the other side of the stage.

GIOVANNI holds a spoon. MARTY stares at it. He looks very depressed.

They sit at a table.

GIOVANNI: What is this?

MARTY: What?

GIOVANNI: Don't what me. I asked you a question. Not to mention, it's a simple question. Just answer it. Now what is this?

292 • SCOTT CAAN

Marty begrudingly plays along.

MARTY: It's a spoon.

GIOVANNI: Right. That's exactly right. Now is it a special spoon?

Marty starts to speak.

GIOVANNI: Wait. Is it a spoon with qualities that I would have trouble finding in other spoons?

MARTY: What?

GIOVANNI: Stop saying what and answer my questions. They're simple. This is not math. It's easy. You asked for my help, didn't you?

MARTY: Yeah, but…

GIOVANNI: Don't but me, either. I was sleeping, was I not?

MARTY: Yes.

GIOVANNI: Yes is right. And I don't mind, is what I'm saying. That's not the point. But, I was sleeping. You call and say what?

Marty thinks… Giovanni waves him on.

MARTY: Help me.

GIOVANNI: Right. So, here I am. Here we are. And I am going to do just that. Help you. That I guarantee, but you gotta do what I tell you to do, and more importantly you gotta answer my very simple questions… Now, can I trust that you will be able to do that?

MARTY: Yes.

GIOVANNI: Great.

He holds up the spoon.

GIOVANNI: Now, what the fuck is this?

MARTY: It's a spoon.

GIOVANNI: Very good. Now, you seen ones like it?

Marty thinks.

GIOVANNI: Don't think, it's really easy. You seen ones like it?

MARTY: Sure.

GIOVANNI: Sure? Don't placate me, buddy. I'm not here for the fucking pancakes. Yes or no?

MARTY: Yes, I have seen one like it?

GIOVANNI: One what?

MARTY: Spoon.

GIOVANNI: Spoons, others like it. Plural, as in many spoons. Yes?

MARTY: Yes?

GIOVANNI: Good. Now, even though I know, we know, that this is what it is.

He holds the spoon.

GIOVANNI: I still, for some reason or another, am able to hold this up really high in the air, literally and metaphorically speaking, and have high hopes for this here spoon.

Marty looks confused.

GIOVANNI: You're confused, I know. That's okay. Just stick with me here, and it will all slowly start to breach. Or unfold or whatever.

He holds up the spoon.

GIOVANNI: This. This is the greatest spoon of all time. This is a special spoon, there is no other spoon like it. What is this?

MARTY: It's a spoon.

GIOVANNI: Good. This is the only spoon I will ever hold in my hand to the end of time. What is this?

MARTY: Spoon.

GIOVANNI: You're doing great, and here is the important part. This spoon loves me.

Marty waits.

Giovanni picks up another spoon.

GIOVANNI: This one love you any more than this one?

MARTY: No.

GIOVANNI: Exactly. They're fucking spoons and that's that. They are everywhere and anyone who tells you different is selling forks. You see what I'm saying here, Marty?

MARTY: I do.

GIOVANNI: Good. How do you feel?

MARTY: Like shit.

GIOVANNI: Well, that's okay, because I'm only getting started.

LIGHTS OUT

SCENE THREE

A ROOM

Marty sits on a bed wearing a tuxedo. The bow tie is opened and the top two buttons on his shirt, as well.

He speaks into a cell phone.

MARTY: No… No… I said I'm not sure… Okay, listen to me so you can understand what I'm saying to you. I have one scene to do now, then I have a break. I'm not exactly sure how long that break is going to be, then I have to come back for one last scene and then I am done for the night… What are you asking me?

Marty waits.

MARTY: Okay, listen to me. I have one more scene to do here, then I have a break, then I have another scene to do. No, that is not what I said. That is…not… Are you listening?

Marty puts the phone down by his side. After a few beats, he puts it back up to his ear.

MARTY: Are you still…? STOP! LISTEN TO ME! I HAVE ONE MORE SCENE TO DO… Well, then why do you keep making me repeat myself? What is it that you want? I'm sure we can accommodate you… We! The proverbial we. We as in I… Next time I will… I'm not really sure what that means, so to tell you the truth, I'm also not sure why I said it. Maybe I heard it in a movie once. I really don't know.

He's getting fed up.

MARTY: Listen to me. We are having a communication problem here. I can fix it, if you let me, but you have to let me, and right now you are not. You know what I am doing, and at this point I can only hope and pray that's accurate… How could you not? Okay, here we go. I am not sure how long the break is… How can I answer that having told you what I just told you. What is it that you desire? That's all. Simply. What is it?

Marty waits.

MARTY: Well, would you like to come here now? I can arrange that? Okay, I can personally come and get you on the aforementioned break... Like I said, I'm not sure, but I'm taking a wild guess that it will be enough time for me to come and get you.

He waits.

MARTY: No... Then why did we just go through the options of you coming here?

Again.

MARTY: Please, just spit it out... I'm begging you. I love you so much but I'm begging you to stop torturing me. What is it?

Marty listens and then pops up out of the bed.

MARTY: Absolutely not... No! The answer is no! Because you are thirteen years old, Sam... Well, I hate saying it, but unfortunately it is a fact, and it is precisely the reason why the answer is no.

Marty waits.

MARTY: Who told you that? Really? Well, you tell your mother...

Marty stops himself.

MARTY: Hold on a second.

Marty puts the phone down, takes a few breaths, chants some mumbo jumbo, and then puts the phone back to his ear.

MARTY: Tell Enrique thank you, but your father just doesn't think it is a good idea, and tell your mother to please call me when she gets a chance. I love you and if you change your mind, call me and I will arrange for us to spend some time this evening.

Marty waits. He looks up, defeated.

MARTY: I have a scene, then a break, then another scene... I'm not sure.

SCENE FOUR

A SMALL BAR

Giovanni sits with a very pretty blonde girl named LUCY.

GIOVANNI: It's this guy, right.

Lucy just stares at him.

GIOVANNI: If I begin to bore you at any point, please let me know. That is not my intention. I have intentions is what I'm saying and to bore you is definitely not one of them, but suffice to say, I have some things on my mind.

LUCY: I'll let you know.

GIOVANNI: You need another drink?

LUCY: I'm good.

GIOVANNI: You want something, you just let me know.

She smiles.

GIOVANNI: What?

LUCY: I'm smiling.

GIOVANNI: I can see that, and it's lovely. I was just making sure.

LUCY: It was to say I follow and I am happy right where I am.

GIOVANNI: That was my guess but you can never be too sure.

LUCY: I like the way you talk.

GIOVANNI: And I like the way you look. Especially when you smile.

Lucy smiles again.

GIOVANNI: Nice. So this guy. My buddy. Marty. Great guy. I'd say the best in the west.

LUCY: Wait.

GIOVANNI: Already?

LUCY: Just a quick question.

GIOVANNI: Go ahead.

LUCY: Your intentions? What are they?

GIOVANNI: Say again.

LUCY: You said that you did in fact have intentions, aside from boring me, which you are not, and at first I figured they were general, and then I started to think that maybe they weren't, but then I realized that it might be something that would take some time to explain, and I ultimately didn't want to interrupt you, but at the same time, I was curious and I didn't want it to just fade away and be forgotten, on my part, I mean. So now I've said it, and I surely will not forget, so at a later time. Sorry, continue.

GIOVANNI: You were thinking all that in that little space there.

She seems offended.

LUCY: What little space?

GIOVANNI: Huh?

Lucy points to her head.

LUCY: This space here?

GIOVANNI: Absolutely one hundred percent not what I meant. That would, in fact, be the exact opposite of what I meant. I was commenting on what little time there was to have that sort of in-depth inner dialogue in such a small space of time. Actually implying what a big space that must be. Just the opposite. You are a clever girl or must be is what I was saying, Lucy.

She smiles.

LUCY: Thank you, Giovanni. And I like your name, too. Giovanni.

GIOVANNI: I like everything at this point. Isn't that great?

LUCY: Yes, it is.

GIOVANNI: Also the way in which two new friends are able to communicate. You see the ease in which we were able to sift or move through a potential misunderstanding. Grown up, relaxed, and simple. I like that, too, is what I'm saying.

LUCY: I agree.

GIOVANNI: These kids today. Holy shit, did I just say that?

LUCY: You did.

GIOVANNI: But it's the truth. Never thought the words would come out of my mouth. Hearing it from one day to the next, half my life, and all the while thinking I will never say such a thing and look at where we are.

Lucy smiles.

GIOVANNI: Excellent smile.

She smiles again.

GIOVANNI: Here's the point, though. You good on that drink?

Smile.

GIOVANNI: Smile's starting to sink in. Like one of those things you can ask someone to do for three to six months just to make someone happy.

LUCY: What about after that?

GIOVANNI: Three to six months?

LUCY: Yeah.

GIOVANNI: Half years at a time, please. We just met two weeks ago, it's chilly outside, your smile just got us summer, give me a break.

LUCY: You are excellent.

GIOVANNI: Thank you. Now here's what I was saying.

LUCY: I'm all ears.

GIOVANNI: Excellent.

LUCY: At least till June.

GIOVANNI: Where have you been all my life, I love this girl.

LUCY: July?

GIOVANNI: August, September, November! I'm in. Holy smokes. My intentions are slowly shifting.

LUCY: To?

GIOVANNI: Three, four, five, I'm on a roll.

LUCY: Yes, you are. Please, continue.

GIOVANNI: Okay. This is becoming very difficult but in the most fantastic way imaginable. Jesus Christ, I wanna drag you outta here like a caveman all of a sudden, but gently.

LUCY: Either way will do.

GIOVANNI: Check, please! I can't take it anymore.

LUCY: Control yourself. There is so much to say.

GIOVANNI: Yes, there is, and yes you are right. Control. Here we go. Kids today!

LUCY: Yes.

GIOVANNI: Along with lack of control, communication! I mean, what's the problem? I'll tell you what the problem is. We, not we, they, got their head glued to the cell phones and the pads and all the other things. All this modern talk and punching buttons has got us all amiss. Here we are, talking it out like grown ups, getting to know each other, and it's not going to end up a big mess just on the count of one of us maybe saying the wrong thing, because here we are like adults ready to sift it through.

LUCY: Very modern.

GIOVANNI: Yes. Wait, no.

LUCY: I see what you are saying, but the very progression, the evolution that has brought us to a healthy communication is the very same progression and evolution that has brought us to punching buttons and getting confused.

GIOVANNI: You know what, you are right.

LUCY: I know. Sort of a double-edged sword. The good and the bad, I guess.

GIOVANNI: I like you plenty.

LUCY: You seem okay.

GIOVANNI: Okay? A bad movie's okay. I'm great.

LUCY: Yes, you are.

GIOVANNI: I appreciate the compliment.

LUCY: I'm sure you do.

GIOVANNI: This is going great.

LUCY: I agree.

GIOVANNI: Are you bored?

LUCY: Not a little bit.

GIOVANNI: That drink?

LUCY: Still working.

GIOVANNI: I'm getting really close to caveman time, but I do want to say something here before we go.

LUCY: I see.

GIOVANNI: And there is the intention shift right there.

LUCY: Okay.

GIOVANNI: I mean no disresepct, but I'm very honest.

LUCY: Just seems a little confident.

GIOVANNI: I agree, but here's what, and I'm ready to have that talk now if you'd like. I intended to come here and have a few drinks, tell you about my friend Marty, maybe a kiss on the cheek, and that's that.

LUCY: Things have changed?

GIOVANNI: You bet your ass.

LUCY: That's fair.

GIOVANNI: Thank you.

LUCY: Tell me about your friend and then I have a proposition.

GIOVANNI: Okay, I will do my best, but I will have to admit, that unlike you, one who can keep their mind moving in several different directions while holding a singular conversation, an exceptional talent, I do not have such a talent. So, yes, I will try my best to tell you what I wanted to tell you before changing my mind, my intentions I mean, without obsessing, thinking, and ultimately ot being able to concentrate on what it is you are going to tell me when I finish.

She smiles.

GIOVANNI: God, I love that.

LUCY: You just do your best. Who knows, maybe you won't like what I have to say.

GIOVANNI: That doesn't make it any easier.

LUCY: I have faith in you.

GIOVANNI: I appreciate that.

LUCY: And I have faith in very few people.

GIOVANNI: More in common.

LUCY: Go ahead.

GIOVANNI: Marty.

LUCY: Yes.

GIOVANNI: Love him. He's the best.

LUCY: You said...

GIOVANNI: And I mean it. Was just saying this a couple nights ago, to someone who I'm not very close to. I add that, my feelings about the guy, not Marty, the guy I don't care too much for, not that I don't care for him, we're just not close, the other guy.

LUCY: Got it.

GIOVANNI: Explain that to me, I'm lost.

LUCY: I have faith.

GIOVANNI: Okay. I was talking about how friends in life, good friends, are so rare. When you're a kid, you got thirty of them. He's my best this, he's my best that. But they all fade away. Drugs, jail, wives, divorces, this one's broke and I'm tired of picking up the bill. They all fade away. But you got one, one like Marty that you'd take a bullet for and you know that he'd do the same? It's rare.

LUCY: Very.

GIOVANNI: Exactly. That's what I was saying. And that's Marty. I love him. Not even a friend. He's my blood. Not literally, but I'm an only child, in my own mind anyway, I mean, I got six brothers, but who knows where they are.

Lucy looks confused.

GIOVANNI: Don't be confused, it doesn't matter. But I dig that look just like the smile. Or like last summer, as they say.

She smiles.

GIOVANNI: Nope, the smile wins. Anyway, this kid is the best, but boy is he turned around behind love, the idea of finding, keeping, and in this case, losing. And I don't know what to do. I've tried everything. Grandma's hands, hard in the paint, I've even tried both at the same time. He don't listen, and what's worse is I'm starting to think he likes it, or at the very least, is so used to it, that he lives in it by way of habit. Can't find a way out or maybe doesn't even want to. Childhood, mom and dad, I'm not really sure. You got someone you really love?

LUCY: A few people?

GIOVANNI: I mean, really, though, like you'd take the hit if you had to?

LUCY: I know the feeling.

GIOVANNI: Okay, so you know. He's going through it, so I might as well be, too. I mean, I'm not waking up with the guy, so he's clearly got it worse than me, but I feel it, like on a regular basis. I don't know what to do.

LUCY: He seen a therapist?

GIOVANNI: He's seen all of them.

LUCY: Gotta keep pushing.

GIOVANNI: I guess, but where do you stop?

LUCY: You don't. That's the thing. You ever seen those things they put the dogs in with the wheels? The ones missing a leg or something? It's heartbreaking. Little guy's got a strap around his chest, wheel's moving one hundred miles an hour trying to keep up with the rest of his body. He's just running his little heart out. And he appears to be smiling too. He's never going to get his leg back, but somehow he learned how to run and smile. At first he probably was falling all over the place and couldn't figure it out. Not today! Now keeping in mind he's missing the frontal lobe of his brain, that we as humans have, apes have it, too, but that's not the point. He's not sitting around remembering the good old days when he would take off into a four-legged sprint is what I'm saying, but somehow he's figured out how to run with what he's got. Marty will, too.

GIOVANNI: You're something else.

LUCY: You want to hear what I was going to say?

GIOVANNI: At this point it doesn't matter, unless of course you were going to tell me you think I'm too tall or too short and this isn't going to work, and then yes, I would not like that and it would matter.

LUCY: I think your height is just fine.

GIOVANNI: Excellent.

LUCY: You can pick me up like a caveman, but I assure you, I like your company too much to allow anything more to happen than a good movie on your couch, with a lot of hugging and kissing.

GIOVANNI: My intentions exactly.

LIGHTS OUT

SCENE FIVE

THE COFFEE SHOP

Marty paces back and forth. Giovanni listens.

MARTY: Am I insane? I mean, is it me? Is it me? I'm asking you.

GIOVANNI: Is what you?

MARTY: I can't take it anymore.

GIOVANNI: That is certainly not true. You know it's really amazing what we as humans can actually take. Our true threshold. We just assume and imagine it's a lot less than it actually is. But that's not the case. You are going to be okay is what I'm saying.

MARTY: I don't know.

GIOVANNI: I do.

MARTY: I mean, what the hell is the matter with her?

GIOVANNI: There is a lot the matter with her and that is my exact point.

MARTY: But this. This is something else. This goes way beyond the two of us. Not you and I.

GIOVANNI: I understand that.

MARTY: Right?

GIOVANNI: No. I understand what you are saying. Who you are referring to when you say us, but I have to respectfully disagree.

MARTY: Why would you do that?

GIOVANNI: Because I, unfortunately, care about you and to not speak the truth would be a disservice... Hold on a second, we're getting all screwed up here. Here's what I'm saying.

MARTY: She's got some fucking nerve.

GIOVANNI: That I agree with, but to say one doesn't have to do with the other is just bullshit and you know it. You don't, then we have some talking to do, and if then you still don't, we got trouble.

MARTY: Oh, we got trouble. We have major trouble right his second... Where were you last night anyway? I was sick! Couldn't even breathe. Pacing around like a nutjob.

GIOVANNI: I met an excellent lady.

MARTY: I bet you did.

GIOVANNI: Really keen chick.

MARTY: I bet.

GIOVANNI: They are around.

MARTY: Not now.

GIOVANNI: This lady specifically had some head on her shoulders, really clever, and a fox, too. I personally don't see a future, but that's not the point.

MARTY: How do you do it?

GIOVANNI: That's the thing. I just do it. That's your problem, too. You imagine it. Or maybe you don't even do that and that's the problem. Thinking your way into not doing it or anything remotely close to what it should be.

MARTY: What are you saying?

GIOVANNI: It should be simple is what I'm saying.

MARTY: Where do you even come up with something like that? What the hell does it even mean. Where do you get the balls to say something like that to me. I mean, who the fuck do you think you are?

GIOVANNI: Okay, now you're coming apart.

MARTY: I'm not coming anything. This is it. I mean, where do you live, and in what world is it that people like you exist?

GIOVANNI: I'm right here.

MARTY: Apparently. You and all the fantastic, brilliant, easy-to-meet foxes of the world that you find so easy to discard.

GIOVANNI: I'm a gentleman.

MARTY: I don't mean it like that. You're a prince. I'm talking about this fantasy world where it all unfolds into your lap while the rest of us are pulling the hair out of our heads. You misplace more shit than I can ever afford.

GIOVANNI: Now you're getting goofy.

MARTY: No shit.

GIOVANNI: Here's what I'm saying... Would you just stop for a second?

MARTY: I'm sorry.

GIOVANNI: I love ya, it's fine.

MARTY: You know it's just…

GIOVANNI: Stop.

MARTY: It's envy, that's all it is.

GIOVANNI: Stop I said.

MARTY: I'm sorry.

GIOVANNI: Zip it, would you?

MARTY: Go ahead.

GIOVANNI: I'm all backward.

They stare at each other for a few beats.

GIOVANNI: This guy.

MARTY: Enrique? Yuck! What kind of a name is Enrique? I mean, who does that to a child?

GIOVANNI: The Spanish, I believe.

MARTY: I'm going to be sick.

GIOVANNI: Stop. So this guy's seeing your ex. The mother of your only child, I understand. Who knows what it is. Maybe they're friends.

MARTY: Do me a fucking favor, would you? Friends?

GIOVANNI: I'm just talking here, okay? Take it down for a second. So the relationship, whatever it is…

Marty waits.

MARTY: Yes?

GIOVANNI: Forget that. Your son.

MARTY: Yes.

GIOVANNI: What's the issue?

MARTY: Are you kidding me?

GIOVANNI: You got me all mixed up here, I'm confused.

MARTY: This guy rides a motorcycle of all things. I mean, who even does that anymore? We've evolved from two wheels. Have we learned nothing?

GIOVANNI: That's another thing altogether.

MARTY: God, I can't take it.

GIOVANNI: Yes, you can, you just have to listen.

MARTY: How could she allow this?

GIOVANNI: That's it right there. That's what I'm saying.

MARTY: Or better yet, how could she think I would? She couldn't. She has to know what I would say.

GIOVANNI: That right there. That, too.

MARTY: So, to even put me in a conversation to have the conversation! He's thirteen years old, no fucking way. Yeah, sure. He can ride on the back of your new boyfriend's motorcycle. No problem. Helmet? No! Who needs one of those. Probably just die if they go down anyway, so might as well have your hair blowing free. Get in the wind. Fuck it! Can you imagine this shit?

GIOVANNI: You're doing a great job here and I'm proud of you?

MARTY: What are you saying to me? Jesus Christ!

GIOVANNI: It's what you are saying to me. She knows what you're going to say before you do, and further, she knows it's completely unacceptable. But what does she accomplish? And what's more? It's all relative. She knows you're gonna snap behind this shit. She knows you're gonna hear about a bike and some Spaniard named Enrique. And worst of all, now your kid's involved and in danger. In more ways than one. She's doing it on purpose, all of it. It's an act. She's on stage, and it's the greatest thing you've ever seen. A real prime time performance. She's got you right where she wants you but it's all bullshit. You see?

MARTY: You're saying she wants me back?

GIOVANNI: No, you fucking jerk, she's an asshole. That's was I'm saying. Christ!

MARTY: You see how sick I am?

GIOVANNI: Yes, I most certainly do, but we're going to get through this, you and I. That I can promise. She's no good. That's the point and we gotta move on. I know you loved her, but she's a putz. We all make mistakes, but to keep making the same ones is illegal or not right or just flat-out insane. You can't do it, is all.

MARTY: I'm trying.

GIOVANNI: I know.

MARTY: I really am.

GIOVANNI: I know you are. We're gonna find what we're looking for.

MARTY: I hope so.

GIOVANNI: At the very least, the compass. We'll start with that.

LIGHTS OUT

SCENE SIX

THE BAR

Terrance and Layla sit at the bar. They tip glasses.

TERRANCE: Congratulations. You deserve it!

LAYLA: I knew it. What did I say?

TERRANCE: You are literally on fire.

LAYLA: Focus! Me. I was, still am, but that's the thing.

TERRANCE: I'm very proud and looking forward to the money.

LAYLA: Boy, did I need it.

TERRANCE: Future monies.

Layla raises her glass.

LAYLA: To future monies.

Terrance raises.

TERRANCE: To the future.

LAYLA: To work and working and working relationships and none of any other kind because who cares.

TERRANCE: Something like that.

LAYLA: Okay, now, tell me everything. Because when you're done, I have something very important to ask you.

Terrance waits.

LAYLA: I will not forget.

Terrance seems confused.

LAYLA: What I was going to ask you. What I am STILL going to ask you.

TERRANCE: Well, why don't you just ask?

LAYLA: Because first I need more compliments. And that's why I said I would not forget. I don't want this to be all about me, and I wanted you to know that… Not all about me, but me first.

She smiles a big smile.

TERRANCE: Obviously.

LAYLA: So?

TERRANCE: You had the part when you walked in.

LAYLA: Yes.

TERRANCE: You lit up the room.

LAYLA: More.

TERRANCE: It's weird. I'm anticipating what you are going to ask me, but at the same time, doing what I'm supposed to be doing. But I'm literally just trying to get through it quickly so we can move on.

LAYLA: That's life, isn't it.

TERRANCE: I guess so.

LAYLA: One more.

TERRANCE: You got the part and you start Monday. What the hell else is there, really? You are beautiful. I love you.

LAYLA: Perfect. Perfect. Perfect!

Layla soaks in the compliments. A few sighs and then some silence.

TERRANCE: Did we forget?

LAYLA: Ah! No.

Layla leans in.

LAYLA: I don't want to offend you.

TERRANCE: Very hard to do, but I don't want to be offended either.

LAYLA: Well, that's the point. You shouldn't be by what I'm about to say.

TERRANCE: Okay.

LAYLA: Or ask.

TERRANCE: Shoot.

Layla looks disgusted all of a sudden.

LAYLA: Please don't say that to me.

TERRANCE: I'm sorry. What did I say?

LAYLA: Hawaii.

TERRANCE: Excuse me?

LAYLA: I did this movie just out of high school, years before we met, and don't ask me how many. I'm sure you could find out if you really wanted to... I'm thirty-five years old, there I said it. I'm being quiet because I really don't want to offend and you never know who could be listening. This is Los Angeles and we always need keep that in mind. Anyway. Hawaii! What a place! What a fucking dump, and I'm sorry, but what a bunch of dopes. I mean, the nerve of us even calling the place America. It's not. I don't know what it is, but it certainly is not this. Us. I mean, half of the place looks like Detroit which I heard we are no longer claiming, and the other half is wet and belongs somewhere in South America. We should actually give it to them... As a gift. They wouldn't even have to change anything, just add a prefix.

Terrance raises his finger.

TERRANCE: Where is this going?

LAYLA: I'll come back around, I promise. Anyway, needless to say, I was excited as a young girl to go to this place. This Hawaii. The truth is they don't tell the truth. I mean, this is not Disneyland by any stretch. They being the people that tell the lies of aloha and mahalo. It's bullshit. The place sucks is what I'm getting at. And if the bad food wasn't bad enough... I mean, the idea of not being able to get one cuisine right and then opting to just fuck them all up and blend them together, you see the type of people we are dealing with.

TERRANCE: I do. Keep whispering.

LAYLA: So, if the aforementioned has not painted the picture I am trying to paint here... The people on this island, I mean! They have very few words and what's worse is they don't even use them with any sort of narrative or structure. I'm talking about sentences literally starting and ending with the word "shoot," or "shoots," and that's what you said. I was moved, backward, many years backward, and there is the rant.

TERRANCE: I meant it metaphorically.

LAYLA: Oh, so do they. But all the while not even knowing what a metaphor is.

TERRANCE: You know, I gotta say, I had the opposite experience. Enjoyed the food, people were nice, lovely place if you ask me.

LAYLA: I didn't.

TERRANCE: Perspective is all. Head space. Maybe you should try again.

LAYLA: Don't.

TERRANCE: Okay, I won't. If you don't ask me what you are planning on asking me, I'm going to call the casting director and tell him you are not available.

She leans in and focuses on Terrance.

LAYLA: What is your purpose?

TERRANCE: Excuse me?

LAYLA: I love you with all of my heart. I have been on a kick and I'm enjoying it. What is your purpose? What do you do? When you go home, what do you do?

TERRANCE: I take care of a nine-year-old boy.

LAYLA: I love that kid.

TERRANCE: Me, too.

LAYLA: What else?

TERRANCE: I lead people to believe that you are the best actress on the planet.

LAYLA: Why?

TERRANCE: Because it's true?

LAYLA: Cute.

TERRANCE: What are you getting at?

LAYLA: I feel that for the first time in my life, I have gotten a hold on myself. I have reached a plateau. Not one that I plan on falling from, but a good place. A real place. A place of purpose.

TERRANCE: Yes.

LAYLA: And now I want to help the ones I love. You.

TERRANCE: I don't need any help, but thank you.

314 • SCOTT CAAN

LAYLA: That doesn't work for me.

TERRANCE: I'm sorry.

LAYLA: Don't be sorry, let me help you.

TERRANCE: You don't help me, I help you.

LAYLA: That's not fair.

TERRANCE: That is also life. Trust me, this I know.

Layla looks confused.

TERRANCE: I'll tell you what's happening right now if you care to know.

LAYLA: I do.

TERRANCE: Rarely do two people serve the same purpose in one another's life. When they do, it's called a relationship. Another reason why they are so difficult.

LAYLA: Tell me about it.

TERRANCE: I am. That's what you are missing and that is what you want.

LAYLA: Wait a minute.

TERRANCE: I don't have a minute. I'm an agent.

LAYLA: Don't do this to me.

TERRANCE: I'm doing nothing.

LAYLA: Yes, you are.

TERRANCE: It is what it is.

LAYLA: Right. Now I know your purpose. To depress me.

TERRANCE: No. I'm a teacher. Think of me as God. Imagine the world, your world, a pie chart. And all the little pieces make you whole. Right now you have a few working splendidly, but because the others have been put away, your pie feels heavy on one side, but tremendously weak on the other. Think of this pie like you would a motor. If you have an explosion with no moving parts, what are you left with?

Layla thinks about it.

LAYLA: A one-way ticket to Detroit?

TERRANCE: Correct. You might as well be in Hawaii.

LAYLA: I hate you.

TERRANCE: Don't hate me. You just happen to be a part of my pie, but I unfortunately am not a part of yours.

LAYLA: Can we not?

TERRANCE: Yes. We can not. I love you, this will come up later, I'm sure. For now, let's enjoy what we have.

LAYLA: What do we have?

TERRANCE: You have a job and I have a nine-year-old that recently started calling me Dad. Let's talk tomorrow.

LAYLA: I took a cab because I planned on getting very drunk.

TERRANCE: I'll take you home, sugar.

They exit as Giovanni and Marty enter.

GIOVANNI: I just need you to relax, okay?

MARTY: I'm trying.

They find a seat and settle in.

GIOVANNI: That is not true. I know your try. It has a look. This is something else. And if by some chance I'm wrong, I stand corrected, and also ask, if you could, please try harder. We're just gonna have some laughs. Why not? It's what people do. Even here in Hollywood, I imagine.

They sit.

MARTY: So this Lucy…

GIOVANNI: Whoa, whoa, wait. What?

MARTY: I didn't say anything yet.

GIOVANNI: Yes, you did. You said Lucy. This Lucy you said, I just heard it.

MARTY: I wasn't done. I hadn't even started yet.

GIOVANNI: Well, that's why I stopped you, because her name is not Lucy; it is Tracy. Similar, but not good enough. It won't pass is what I'm saying.

MARTY: Tracy?

GIOVANNI: Yes.

MARTY: What happened to Lucy?

GIOVANNI: Obviously nothing worth discussing, certainly not at this point. These girls are to shortly arrive here, and this, I can only imagine, is not a fantastic opener. The other girl whose name we have confused with yours. She's gone and never to return. Good enough?

MARTY: Fine. Tracy's friend.

GIOVANNI: Excellent choice.

MARTY: That's all I was saying before.

GIOVANNI: Well, here we are now.

MARTY: Dominique.

GIOVANNI: Yes.

MARTY: I got that right?

GIOVANNI: The more important of the two for all intents. For you anyway. You got the right one is what I'm saying.

MARTY: I don't like the name. I'm just saying that before we go on.

GIOVANNI: What?

MARTY: Too many syllables.

GIOVANNI: What the fuck are you talking about?

MARTY: Too many syllables. I don't like it. Maybe it's not a problem, or maybe it is and it's just a little one. In any case, you have got to stack the deck and that is what I'm saying.

GIOVANNI: What are you saying?

MARTY: Stack the deck.

GIOVANNI: What are we doing?

MARTY: I was seeing this guy a while back and that's what he said. I don't see him anymore so maybe that's relevant, too, but I don't know. It is. It's like dating young girls. It's fifty-fifty at the word go, right? I mean, you meet someone you like, you got a fifty-fifty shot of things going well at best. But when you date young girls, you're stacking the deck badly, giving yourself shit odds, shittier than if you were dating, or looking to date, regular-aged grown-ups. I don't want to do that. So this is what I'm saying. It's the same thing with a name. Bad odds on top of something that doesn't have great odds to begin with is no good.

GIOVANNI: You were paying a guy and he told you this.

MARTY: The age thing, yes, the name thing I added. I think it's the same basic idea, and her name has too many syllabes.

GIOVANNI: What about my name?

MARTY: We play baseball and drink beers. I don't have to like your name.

GIOVANNI: Are you saying you don't, Marty, which by the way is a very boring name?

MARTY: I'm not...

GIOVANNI: Giovanni is original and it says something. Something special. What the fuck does Marty say? Nice to meet you, I'm an accountant, I can't fuck, and I wear white briefs.

Long pause.

GIOVANNI: I'm sorry. I didn't mean that.

MARTY: I just don't like girls with long syllable names.

GIOVANNI: Well, it's only three, so relax. Four? Okay, I get it. Four is a dealbreaker, fine. Three's okay, though. Is that fair? Can three be okay, please?

MARTY: I suppose.

GIOVANNI: Dom-A-Nique. It's good.

MARTY: I guess. I said I guess.

GIOVANNI: Please don't do this, if you're gonna do this, we might as well go somewhere else and say we got lost.

Marty stands.

GIOVANNI: Please sit down and don't do this.

MARTY: I'm sorry. If you can imagine, I'm slightly nervous here. I have been with the same woman for almost half of my adult life. Kelly and I...

Giovanni puts his head down.

MARTY: What?

GIOVANNI: You said we were not gonna do this.

MARTY: I'm making a point.

GIOVANNI: I don't want to hear it, and unfortunately I didn't want it to come to this, but you leave me no choice. I have to be quick here, so listen.

MARTY: What's the rush?

GIOVANNI: These people are coming here, these girls. What's the rush? Tracy being one of them who I like very much and she is very mean to me, so I want things to be nice.

MARTY: Wait a minute.

GIOVANNI: I don't have a minute.

MARTY: What the hell are we doing? I don't like this girl's name, the other one is mean to you, what are we doing here?

GIOVANNI: You have no idea what you are talking about, and therefore have to be led. That alone is grounds for no opinion. You not having one, I mean. About anything! So that's out. And this woman, Tracy, and I'm going to say her name over and over again to make another point, but I will get to that in a second...

He pauses, losing his train of thought.

GIOVANNI: What the fuck? You see what you are doing here?

MARTY: This woman?

GIOVANNI: Tracy.

MARTY: Being mean to you.

GIOVANNI: Yes, is precisely why I like her, another thing you will soon learn and understand when you start properly searching the world for women again. Here we are. Tracy, Tracy, Tracy! I say that repeatedly, so you don't slip and say the name Lucy. I see why one would jump to conclusions, but no. That's not why. I say it to refer back to what the hell I was trying to say in the first place. Your ex. Not whatshername. Your ex. I'm still making a point.

MARTY: Oh, good.

GIOVANNI: It's over, not just the relationship, but her name. We are dealing with science here, and I need you to play along. I learned this from a very wise man a very long time ago, his name was Vincent, if you must know, but I assure you it is not relevant. You don't say her name, you don't bring her up, you don't even think about her for ninety days. That's it. Someone who hasn't seen you for a while, he's not hip to current events, says how's whatshername? You say fuck off! Or I don't want to talk about that. Whatever you choose, that part is up to you. But the ninety days is nonnegotiable. I don't know why ninety and not some other number, maybe it's because of childbirth and the number nine, I'm not really sure, but I know it works. You do this, you follow through with this plan, and I promise you, you will feel better, and not only that, it will be over and you will have moved on. Now that is it and we start now.

MARTY: Okay, great. Can I just say one more thing about it, before we start?

GIOVANNI: You see this shit?

MARTY: I think it's important.

GIOVANNI: Fine.

MARTY: We have a child, one that we share custody of. I believe, and I could be wrong, doubt it but who knows, it might be a bit of a hard one to accomplish and or follow through with. Am I wrong?

Giovanni thinks.

MARTY: Am I wrong?

GIOVANNI: No, you are not. I will call Vincent first thing Monday morning. I'm sure there is a clause or an alternative blueprint with these very case-sensitive specifics. I mean, you can't be the only one who has ever been in this position, and this is fucking science, so don't worry.

MARTY: Okay. I feel better knowing that, thank you.

GIOVANNI: Christ, we need a drink.

MARTY: I'm fine.

GIOVANNI: I'm all worked up.

MARTY: I'm sorry.

GIOVANNI: I understand, please don't think I don't.

MARTY: I don't think you do.

GIOVANNI: Well, you are wrong.

MARTY: Destined for failure and loneliness. The feeling. You get that one often?

GIOVANNI: Not really?

MARTY: See? They wrote me off of the show, by the way. And what's more, I don't give a shit. Ain't that just the coolest?

Two gorgeous GIRLS walk into the bar. Giovanni springs up.

GIOVANNI: Hey.

He hugs Tracy.

GIOVANNI: Marty, this is the lovely Tracy, and the very talented Dominique.

DOMINIQUA: Dominiqua.

GIOVANNI: What?

DOMINIQUA: It's actually Dom-In-Iq-Ua? Not Dominique.

LIGHTS OUT

SCENE SEVEN

THE STAGE

Marty moves across the stage talking to a WOMAN sitting in a chair with her back to the audience.

MARTY: So, what are we talking about? A defeated man, really. A man with questions, mistakes, a man tortured by fear and the possibility of the unknown. But yet here he is, standing at the edge of the stage with his whole life ahead of him. His past and what he has been through just behind him on the other side of the curtain, and what lies beyond the audience, the lights, and through the doors out onto the streets that lead to the rest of the world... He hears a loud explosion... Hark! I hear the cannons roar.

WOMAN: Great, we'll let you know.

MARTY: I have another version of that I could do if you'd like to see something different.

WOMAN: No, really, it's fine. We'll let you know.

Marty waits, takes a bow, and heads offstage.

SCENE EIGHT

THE COFFEE SHOP

Marty walks in to find Giovanni with his head down, sitting at the table.

MARTY: You okay?

GIOVANNI: I really don't think so. You seem up.

MARTY: I feel up.

GIOVANNI: That's very good, I'm happy for you.

MARTY: What's the matter?

GIOVANNI: There's a lot of things that are the matter, in fact, if you are truly up, which by the look on your face, that I haven't seen in a very long time, is accurate, by my…

Giovanni seems frozen.

GIOVANNI: What's the word when you are getting something off of someone else?

MARTY: A read?

GIOVANNI: Reading? Read. Reading… No, that's not it. Whatever, from what I'm reading from you… That's not it.

MARTY: It's fine.

GIOVANNI: That's the point, it's not fine, and that's what I'm saying. You gotta get out of here is what I'm saying, because I'm in no mood to handle the mood you seem to be in, by way of reading you, and I don't want to be the one to crash down upon that. I don't need that guilt right now on top of everything else. You dig?

MARTY: I can handle it.

GIOVANNI: What's going on with you?

MARTY: With me?

GIOVANNI: What are we doing here? Is there a third party I'm not seeing? Yes, you.

MARTY: I'm good.

GIOVANNI: You're good?

MARTY: I'm really good.

GIOVANNI: Well, tell me everything quickly, so we can get it out of the way, cause we need to talk, or we don't and you should just leave now. I'm saying this from a place of love. I'm really going the wrong way here. You see what I'm saying?

MARTY: I do.

GIOVANNI: So, tell me.

MARTY: Ninety days.

GIOVANNI: Huh?

MARTY: Ninety days and I feel great. Although a variation on what you suggested, what Vincent suggested rather, and I'm feeling great. My son is great, we just had a blast of a weekend and I am feeling excellent.

GIOVANNI: You get a job?

MARTY: That I did not, but that, and this is something I feel, will come.

GIOVANNI: You got a broad?

MARTY: Same answer, but my son is excellent, and whatshername has truly become whatshername and she can dance with every Spaniard this side of Texas for all I care.

GIOVANNI: I am truly happy for you.

MARTY: Thank you.

GIOVANNI: You good?

MARTY: I am.

GIOVANNI: Mary Newton's mother just passed.

MARTY: Mary?

GIOVANNI: Newton, my ex. The blonde with the legs.

MARTY: I remember.

GIOVANNI: Calls me last night and tells me her mom passed. Just right out of the blue.

MARTY: Oh my god, is she okay?

GIOVANNI: I just told you she's dead. No, she's not okay, by any stretch.

MARTY: Mary!

GIOVANNI: Oh. No, she's a fucking mess.

MARTY: Horrible.

GIOVANNI: I agree.

MARTY: That's life.

GIOVANNI: No, it's not. It's death. Why do people say that when people die? That's life? It's not. It's the polar fucking opposite of life. It's death.

MARTY: It's a part of life.

GIOVANNI: And the exact opposite at the same time. Never say that again.

MARTY: Okay.

GIOVANNI: I'll tell you what life is… Life is moving forward and making people smile, or that's what mine has been anyway, but now I'm starting to think, and this unfortunately has nothing to do with the lovely-legged Mary Newton's mother, God rest her soul, but forget that. I'm not even talking about her, nor does she have anything to do with what the hell we're dealing with here.

MARTY: You need some water?

GIOVANNI: No, I don't need water, I need a bridge to get over the water, pal, because truth be told, quiet as kept, I'm slipping into the river here.

MARTY: What's the problem?

GIOVANNI: I'm done. I can't do it anymore. Something is changing. I've been playing a role for the last thirty-something years that all of a sudden I just don't fit for the part anymore, and nothing happened. It just is what it is. Mary's mother, whatshername, this one, that one. IT JUST IS!

MARTY: You're having a moment.

GIOVANNI: That indeed I am.

MARTY: It will pass.

GIOVANNI: Not this one. I got off the phone last night, tok a hit of some weed to try and relax, and when I woke up, I was anything but. This is serious.

MARTY: Did you dream?

GIOVANNI: Like a monster, but I can't remember shit… Actually scratch that. Remembering is all I have and that's what I've come to. All I got is, look back, and a bunch of "you remember that?" What the hell am I doing? I'm having a thing here and I need you to help me.

MARTY: I'm right here, and that's what I want to do.

GIOVANNI: I gotta search, we gotta search. We gotta do better than the people that came before us and all I'm doing is chasing broccoli. You understand?

MARTY: What happened?

GIOVANNI: The good old days, that's what happened. That's all I got. Remember when we used to have a blast? It was a blast, wasn't it?

MARTY: Wasn't it?

GIOVANNI: All of it. It all seems so great looking back. Remember having fun? Remember when we were wild and free and we killed that policeman together?

Marty doesn't reply.

GIOVANNI: Well?

MARTY: What policeman?

GIOVANNI: Exactly. It might as well have never happened.

MARTY: It didn't.

GIOVANNI: That's my point. It might as well have and that's what I'm saying. It doesn't matter what really happened if I ain't got nothing up front.

MARTY: Wait a minute.

GIOVANNI: I don't know if I got it to wait.

MARTY: You're happy.

GIOVANNI: I'm a clown.

MARTY: You're the best.

GIOVANNI: I will be, but not right now. I got to get out there and find out what the hell I'm doing. You? You've been doing it. You think it all comes so easy, because it has. You've been in the shit, and that's why you walk in here like you did today. You earned it. I got myself spread all over the place cause I just don't know where to land. The struggle's the road to the fruit, and I need to get into it, or something like that.

Marty takes a beat.

MARTY: Are you okay?

GIOVANNI: I think that I am.

MARTY: We're gonna be fine.

GIOVANNI: Tell me why?

MARTY: I can't tell you why, I can only tell you that it's so because it has to be. You got this thing, this thing that everybody in the world wishes they had. You serve a purpose in people's lives and to say that it's been a waste of time is a waste of time. Half the shit I been through in my life, I don't get through it without you.

GIOVANNI: Okay, what about me?

MARTY: Maybe it's my turn? And to be honest, I'm looking forward to it.

GIOVANNI: Okay.

MARTY: What do you need?

GIOVANNI: I don't know.

MARTY: That's okay, too.

GIOVANNI: I think I might have some fears, but that's not to say that I am scared of anything.

MARTY: It's okay if you are.

GIOVANNI: Okay, that's good.

MARTY: Tell me.

GIOVANNI: What is this?

MARTY: You don't like it?

GIOVANNI: I don't like anything right now.

MARTY: This is funny.

GIOVANNI: No it's not. It's an entire mess of a group of many bunched together things, but funny is not one of them. Or rather an adjective to explain it. Any of it.

MARTY: This is good.

GIOVANNI: Who the fuck do you think you are?

MARTY: Tell me what you are afraid of.

GIOVANNI: This is just too weird.

MARTY: For my sake.

Giovanni thinks about it.

GIOVANNI: That's good. That I can do. Very strategic. I like your style.

MARTY: I learned from the best.

GIOVANNI: Don't push.

MARTY: Sorry.

GIOVANNI: Okay. For your sake. Speaking my mind for the sake of helping you. This I can do. Okay. I met this gal a few weeks ago… No, forget that.

Giovanni is trying to put it together.

MARTY: Take your time.

GIOVANNI: Shut up.

MARTY: Sorry.

GIOVANNI: Please. I'm trying to help you out here.

MARTY: I appreciate that.

GIOVANNI: Any gal. Remember Tracy?

MARTY: I do.

GIOVANNI: How about Lucy?

MARTY: I might get confused if you throw too many names out there.

GIOVANNI: Me, too. Hold on. Don't matter. No names. This one's right, this one's wrong, I like the wrong one and the right one makes me sick. Or at the very least, bored.

MARTY: Why do you think that is?

GIOVANNI: I don't know, my mother was an asshole.

MARTY: Right.

GIOVANNI: But I know that.

MARTY: That's good. So you know that, then what are you afraid of?

GIOVANNI: Who said I was afraid of anything?

MARTY: You did, like three minutes ago.

GIOVANNI: Right. I'm working here.

MARTY: I see that and I'm proud.

GIOVANNI: All right with the bullshit.

MARTY: Stay focused.

GIOVANNI: Okay. What if it don't work?

MARTY: It probably won't.

GIOVANNI: What?

MARTY: Odds are it doesn't. Wait, what are we talking about? This or the girl?

GIOVANNI: What girl?

MARTY: No girl. What are we talking about?

GIOVANNI: Some fucking help you are.

MARTY: What if what doesn't work?

GIOVANNI: Lucy. This one, that one. Any of 'em. The right one.

MARTY: That's what I'm saying, it usually doesn't. But you move on until it does. I learned that from you.

GIOVANNI: I was just saying it so you would move on, not because I thought it was true. Or thought it was false. What are you saying? Forget what I say or said. You're making a mess here.

MARTY: That's life. It's a mess. It's not so simple. It's like getting a part, it's not a performance that ends up good or bad, it's both. It's a mess, and that's what makes it what it is.

GIOVANNI: I like clean.

MARTY: Then keep doing what you're doing?

GIOVANNI: How come you know so much all of a sudden?

MARTY: I don't know shit and it's beautiful.

GIOVANNI: And I'm talking to you.

Marty takes a beat.

MARTY: Kelly, Kelly, Kelly, Kelly, Kelly, the mother of my thirteen-year-old son, Kelly. That is the first time I've said her name in three months and it feels great. You know why? Because I love her and I will always love her. And not to take away anything from your friend Vincent, because what he passed on to you that you then passed on to me was amazing. It worked, but let me tell you what it did in the grand scheme of things. Dick! It ends the same way. I love her and I always will. From the bottom of my heart.

GIOVANNI: Oh, good. Things as they should be. Back to square one. I can be me again and you can be you. SHE SUCKS SHE SUCKS SHE SUCKS! Snap out of it.

MARTY: That's not the point.

GIOVANNI: Then what is?

MARTY: It will always hurt. It never goes away. When you say I love you and mean it, that's it for the rest of your life. It always hurts, just less and less as time goes by, but it's never gone. It hurts because it's supposed to hurt. That's life and staying away from it because of what I just went through and might go through again with someone else is chicken shit.

GIOVANNI: You calling me chicken shit?

MARTY: If you'll accept it, then yes I am.

Giovanni takes a long beat.

GIOVANNI: Okay, I accept it.

MARTY: That's good.

GIOVANNI: But I got a little ways to go before I can… You know.

MARTY: I understand.

GIOVANNI: Thank you.

MARTY: I love you.

GIOVANNI: I need a breather.

MARTY: That's fine.

GIOVANNI: A break, maybe.

MARTY: Okay.

GIOVANNI: From all the various… The gals… Gather my thoughts a bit, saddle up, and move forward.

MARTY: I'm right here.

GIOVANNI: I do got my mind on one, though.

MARTY: That's good.

GIOVANNI: She's really great.

MARTY: Even better.

GIOVANNI: I may have hurt her feelings.

MARTY: You never know.

GIOVANNI: Forget the breather. I'll find out.

MARTY: Good.

GIOVANNI: Okay, but in the meantime, there's something I need you to do for me.

LIGHTS OUT

SCENE NINE

THE BAR

Marty walks into the bar and sees Layla sitting home.

MARTY: Layla.

She seems pleased.

LAYLA: Giovanni?

MARTY: No, actually, I'm Marty.

LAYLA: Well, you got the wrong gal, Marty. Wait a minute. How do you know my name?

MARTY: I'm a friend of Giovanni's.

LAYLA: That's interesting. Is he meeting you here as well.

MARTY: No.

LAYLA: Am I going to get a prize if I figure this out?

MARTY: No, I'll explain.

LAYLA: Goody.

Marty can't figure out how to put it.

MARTY: Okay, I'm here. Normally I wouldn't be here, but things have changed for me over the last few months, and I am most certainly here. What the hell. You are very pretty, and I'm your date tonight. Giovanni was, but he's not, and that's that.

Layla takes a few beats to process.

LAYLA: This is great.

MARTY: I think so, too.

LAYLA: That was sarcasm.

MARTY: I see.

LAYLA: I mean, I literally can't win.

MARTY: I take it that means you don't find me appealing.

LAYLA: No, I'm sure you're fantastic.

MARTY: I don't know.

LAYLA: Look, I'm going to try and be very candid here.

MARTY: That's acceptable.

LAYLA: I didn't want to be here in the first place. For the first time in my life, and you'll have to excuse my need to speak my mind to a complete and total stranger, but for the first time I don't need anything. Certainly not this. And this isn't even this. It's something else.

Marty waits.

LAYLA: Friend of mine says I got this guy you have got to meet, she might as well have said there's this insurance seminar you gotta check out. Not into it, and not to mention this guy's name is Giovanni. I mean, who names a child Giovanni? This is obviously not the point, but sometimes it can just be the little things. Anyway, here we are, Marty?

MARTY: Yes.

LAYLA: Marty, I'm sure you are excellent. I'm sure you are the cat's claws or scratch or whatever, but I don't know what I'm doing here, and now on top of that, I'm confused and almost offended, but it really has nothing to do with you. You see?

MARTY: I do.

Layla stands up.

MARTY: But you're here. And I think I understand your position, but think of me, if you can. I'm here, and I'm not even someone that someone else thought would be a great guy for you to meet. I'm just here because the great guy couldn't make it. I'm a great guy filler. So for my sake, and you can leave this or take it, but I think you should allow me to buy you a drink.

Layla takes a beat.

MARTY: At the very least, exchange some pleasantries, and who knows…

She sits down.

LAYLA: Who knows. You drink beer?

MARTY: I can.

LAYLA: Let's have a beer.

MARTY: Okay.

A waitress comes by and places a couple of beers on the table.

MARTY: Excellent.

They toast and have a sip.

MARTY: So, what are you doing here?

LAYLA: You don't listen so good, do you?

MARTY: Why show up, I mean? If you were so against it. You're here, you could have said no.

LAYLA: I think I have a few answers.

MARTY: I drink slow.

LAYLA: I guess the answer is that you never really know, right?

MARTY: I would say that.

LAYLA: You did.

MARTY: Right.

LAYLA: I would also say that maybe in life when you don't want to do certain things, it's probably a good idea to immediately move forward and do them.

MARTY: I don't know.

LAYLA: Well, neither do I and that's why I'm saying what I'm saying. I'm certainly not saying it because I believe it.

MARTY: You know, keeping in mind that there's very little chance of anything, let alone this, working out, and by working out, I mean finishing this beer, I'm guessing it would be a good idea to skip making points that we don't believe are valid. Respectfully, of course.

LAYLA: No, that's fair.

MARTY: Nice. Look at us.

Layla smiles.

MARTY: Nice smile by the way.

She smiles again.

MARTY: So?

LAYLA: My good friend, Terrance.

MARTY: Tell me about him.

LAYLA: He says a lot of things that I try really hard to avoid and at the same time believe, but I have the utmost respect for him so I try and do the latter more often than not.

MARTY: You talk funny.

LAYLA: Thank you.

MARTY: Terrance.

LAYLA: Terrance.

MARTY: I like it by the way. I didn't mean I don't.

Layla tips her glass.

MARTY: To Terrance.

They drink.

LAYLA: He really is the best. I'm an actor, or an actress, they changed it a few years ago. I'm supposed to be offended by actress. It's actor now. Female actor.

MARTY: Me, too.

Layla waits.

MARTY: Actor, not offended by actress. But why would I be?

LAYLA: I'm not really either, it's just one of those things.

MARTY: Right.

LAYLA: Anyway, he's my agent.

MARTY: He good?

LAYLA: He's the best.

MARTY: I might need his number.

LAYLA: Rough out there right now.

MARTY: Tell me about it.

LAYLA: You should meet Terrance.

MARTY: I can't wait.

LAYLA: So, aside from being very good at his job, and don't ask me to explain what that means, because I have no idea, but he is, more importantly he's a good friend. Maybe that's what it is. All these people you meet and get to know and throw away and keep, I mean in a business, this business. Maybe that's it. What's the difference? Maybe that's what makes them good or bad or expendable or not. I don't know what I'm saying really.

MARTY: Keep going.

LAYLA: Terrance told me to come here and meet you. Well, not you, whatsisname.

MARTY: You've moved on already.

They drink.

LAYLA: So, here I am, here we are. You?

MARTY: I don't know. I'm here because I'm in a good mood. Because I feel like it might be a good idea for the same reasons you don't believe. And I'm not really sure I believe them either, but I'm here and I have no explanation. I spend a good amount of time thinking about everything, and I've come to the conclusion that all the things I was very confident about, the older I get, just seem to slip further away. So I guess I'm just left with the fact that I know nothing. Things hurt, and I guess they're supposed to. I hate the idea, and surrendering to it, but it's just the way it is, I'm finding. Is this too much? Or too confusing?

LAYLA: Maybe.

MARTY: Sorry.

LAYLA: Let's do something else.

MARTY: Okay.

LAYLA: Only because I like you.

MARTY: You do?

LAYLA: Enough to finish this beer.

They drink.

MARTY: Okay, so what are we doing.

LAYLA: I changed my mind. Let's keep doing what we're doing. I was going to change it up, keep it light, and then I realized I hate that idea. I like it. This. We're talking. I don't even know what your favorite color is.

MARTY: I don't have one.

LAYLA: Good, because I just decided I don't want to talk about it, or anything like it. Let's keep talking like we know each other. It's fun. Who cares if it feels weird or too much. And who cares if we say something stupid.

MARTY: I'll tell you anything you want to know.

Layla thinks. Marty just stares.

LAYLA: What?

Marty just stares.

LAYLA: Say something stupid.

MARTY: Why?

LAYLA: I'll tell you later.

MARTY: Okay. Let's go on a trip together.

LAYLA: Okay. Where?

MARTY: You ever been to Hawaii?

Layla thinks.

LAYLA: No, I have not.

MARTY: Let's go.

LAYLA: Are you serious?

MARTY: I think I am.

LAYLA: You think?

MARTY: No. I'm positive. What difference does it make? I dig you.

LAYLA: You do?

MARTY: I really do and something tells me we should get to some sand.

LAYLA: You know what would be funny?

MARTY: Short people trying to dunk a basketball?

LAYLA: That, too, but no. It would be funny if we really went and got into the sand.

MARTY: With our feet?

LAYLA: Headfirst, even... It would be funny because of Terrance. He had a very fascinating thing happen to him, changed his life. He talked me into this. Well, not this, but...

MARTY: Tell me.

LAYLA: He used to be an actor.

MARTY: You don't say.

LAYLA: I do. And he wasn't very good from what he tells me. Also funny. It's literally the only profession on the planet that people just decide to do. Everyone else takes time or school or both. Actors, they just wake up one day and think, "Hey, I got an idea." But for no reason, *I'll be great at this.* No you won't. You'll be really bad, and no one will tell you the truth, they'll just say, "Ah, get 'em next time."

MARTY: It's like dating.

LAYLA: Totally. Anyway, he gets this gig on Broadway. Just a few lines, turns out he screws up really bad, so that should inform you of the kind of talent he was actually working with. Long story short, he makes a fool of himself and ends up at a dinner table later that night with his agent. You ever hear of the famous hairstylist guy who became a big Hollywood producer?

Marty has not.

LAYLA: Handed his business down to this really sexy handsome guy with a pompadour. Went from sweeping hair to owning a salon and sleeping with Playboy bunnies.

Marty waits.

LAYLA: This is relevant.

MARTY: I don't know.

LAYLA: It is.

MARTY: I'm sure it is, I was saying I don't know about the guy.

LAYLA: Oh. They made a movie of him with Warren Beatty about the shampoo. I mean, the guy. Anyway, what a rant. What I'm getting at is this is kind of what happened to Terrance. Kind of. His agent really fell for him that night, really took a liking. They made friends and he took Terrance under his wing, or wings. Is it both?

MARTY: I think it's just one wing.

LAYLA: Wing. And Terrance became an agent. Great guy, great agent.

MARTY: He have a sister?

LAYLA: Yes.

MARTY: From Philadelphia?

LAYLA: What? You heard this one?

MARTY: I might have.

LAYLA: This isn't an anecdote here. This is a true story I'm telling you and it's relevant. This man's life completely changed because he was in the right place at the right time. So what he said the wrong thing? That's the point, and that's why he is who he is, and that's why I listen. The man has literally changed my life.

MARTY: I like this guy. Should we have another drink?

LAYLA: Yes.

A waitress slams two beers down on the table.

LIGHTS OUT

SCENE TEN

THE COFFEE SHOP

Giovanni walks into the coffee shop and finds Lucy sitting alone. She seems upset.

GIOVANNI: Can I sit?

LUCY: You would look silly standing.

Giovanni sits down.

GIOVANNI: Thank you.

Lucy smiles.

GIOVANNI: That's a different smile.

LUCY: Yup.

GIOVANNI: Yup? That doesn't sound like you.

LUCY: Who's me?

GIOVANNI: I guess I don't know.

She smiles.

GIOVANNI: It's different. I'm not saying I don't like it, I just like the other one better.

Lucy waits.

GIOVANNI: Any chance I might get that one again some time soon?

LUCY: I don't know.

GIOVANNI: Fair enough.

LUCY: Tell you the truth, I like the other one better too, but it's just one of those things. This one, the new one? It means something, just like the other one did.

GIOVANNI: I'm not saying I don't like them both.

LUCY: You already said and that's not the point.

340 • SCOTT CAAN

GIOVANNI: Then what's the point?

LUCY: You tell me.

GIOVANNI: Okay. The point is this…

LUCY: Can I interrupt you?

GIOVANNI: I haven't even started yet.

LUCY: Is that a no?

GIOVANNI: Have I earned the right to be making decisions around the area of what you can or can't do?

LUCY: Absolutely not.

GIOVANNI: I didn't think so.

LUCY: Okay. I want the truth. I don't want a lot of talk. I say that because you're good at it.

GIOVANNI: Thank you.

LUCY: I don't know if that's a compliment. It could have been, not just now, then. Before.

Giovanni looks confused.

LUCY: Forget it. Just tell me the truth. Be honest.

GIOVANNI: I like you.

LUCY: Not good enough.

GIOVANNI: It's God's honest.

LUCY: Then what happened?

GIOVANNI: Nothing happened.

LUCY: Thank God, or I would have been really upset.

GIOVANNI: You're not upset now?

LUCY: You're changing the subject.

GIOVANNI: I'm not.

LUCY: Don't be quick with me.

GIOVANNI: What do you want?

LUCY: Truth.

GIOVANNI: I'm an idiot. What happened? Me. I happened.

LUCY: Well?

GIOVANNI: It won't happen again.

LUCY: Just like that?

GIOVANNI: I'm hoping.

LUCY: Not good enough either.

GIOVANNI: Boy, you're tough.

LUCY: I didn't have to be.

Giovanni waits.

LUCY: I had such a good time with you.

GIOVANNI: Can't we do it again?

LUCY: I'd like that.

GIOVANNI: You wanna get hitched?

LUCY: Excuse me?

GIOVANNI: I'm a true blue kinda guy.

LUCY: You're insane.

GIOVANNI: I just wanna prove to you that I don't have the urge to not call you after a great time in which neither of us took our clothes off. I know you know, you thanked God for Christ's sake, but here, this. I wanna make a point.

LUCY: You are unbelievable.

GIOVANNI: And I think the same about you, so what gives?

LUCY: Hello, is anybody home?

GIOVANNI: I don't appreciate that.

LUCY: And I don't appreciate this.

Lucy gets up.

GIOVANNI: Sit down, you look silly.

LUCY: What the hell is it? I like you! Can't you see that? Why didn't you call me?

Giovanni stands up.

GIOVANNI: I don't know. You see, I got no upside down clue about what the hell I'm doing here. I just asked you to wear my jacket, and I don't even know you. You see this. I don't know. Who does? All I can say is that you're a shine in the rough, okay, and I dig you. I made a mistake. You know sometimes you just think you know who you are but then later you find out something completely different. Life's a goof. What can I say! What can I say? I'll tell you what I can say. I dig you like the trees dig the wind, and I had a small amount of stress behind the way things went down, if you wanna know the truth. I don't wanna get married, I just wanna see you. I don't know. I like the way your eyes look. I made a gigantic error, which I'm willing to cop to here. Come with me is all. That's all I'm saying.

LUCY: I want to, that's what I'm saying, but you can't do that.

GIOVANNI: Which part?

LUCY: Any of it. You gotta sit. You gotta stick around for the ending. You can't just make one the way you think it's gonna go. You gotta play. This is it. This is life. You can't just push the button every time you feel something. That's bullshit.

GIOVANNI: What's the button?

LUCY: The button!

GIOVANNI: I don't know what the button is.

LUCY: The button.

GIOVANNI: Would you stop saying that. They're gonna throw us outta here.

LUCY: Oh, let 'em.

She sits down. Giovanni does, too.

LUCY: You wanna know something?

GIOVANNI: I want to know it all.

LUCY: My mom was in the hospital.

GIOVANNI: When?

LUCY: It doesn't matter. You want to hear about the button or not?

GIOVANNI: Hundred percent.

LUCY: She was sick, so she had the medicine, or the medicine made her sick. I don't know. One or the other.

Giovanni tilts his head.

LUCY: You look like a cat.

Giovanni straightens up.

LUCY: She was on the button. Every time she could feel pain, she could push the button. And I asked her what she wanted. I mean, the woman was dying and that's what you ask, right? I mean, in that situation, that's what comes up. That's what you gotta say. What do you want? Maybe it's gonna be crab legs, who knows. But you know what she says?

GIOVANNI: I don't.

LUCY: She says she wants the button. She wants to go through life and every time she feels pain, she wants to hit the button.

GIOVANNI: Yeah?

LUCY: No. The answer is no. Shit, I'd like a button, we'd all like a button, but that's not life; that's not what it's all about. You can't just hit the button every time something comes up. It's just not the way things work out. You see?

Giovanni takes a beat. And another.

GIOVANNI: I do.

LUCY: Would you kiss me?

GIOVANNI: Do you mind if I cry a little, too?

LUCY: That's fine.

He does both at the same time.

LIGHTS OUT

SCENE ELEVEN

THE STAGE

Terrance walks out onto the stage in an 1800-style war costume.

Lucy and Giovanni sit together watching the performance on one side of the stage with their backs to the audience, and Layla and Marty on the other side, also with their backs to the audience.

Terrance takes a beat, waits, then KABLOOOM! A loud cannon goes off in the distance.

Terrance raises his hand.

TERRANCE: Hark I hear the cannons roar!

LIGHTS OUT

THE END

An Epilogue

Giovanni and Jimmy

Coincidentally, An Epilogue *was produced for the first time simultaneously with the printing of this book by Rattlestick West—Scott Haze, artistic director; David Van Asselt, co–artistic director; Lukas Behnken, managing director—at The Sherry Theater: Center for the Arts in North Hollywood, California, October 2015. It was directed by Kathleen Randazzo; set and lighting design by Paul Howle. The cast was as follows:*

GIOVANNI...............*Joe Pease*
JIMMY...............................*Daniel Irmas*

An Epilogue

SCENE ONE

Lights up, but just a bit, to a wide-open living room. A couch and a coffee table. A loveseat, spiral notepads, and a bunch of pens and pencils scattered around on top of an old wooden desk. An old record player off to the side on a small vintage footstool. An old crate sits next to it filled with records. Either it's the sixties, or the home of a very pretentious artist. No television. No modern technology whatsoever.

A small kitchenette with a butcher's block and a vintage-looking table is set up with a few wooden chairs.

As the lights continue to push up...a man, mid-to-late thirties, scruffy hair and beard. He's visibly upset. He takes a few pacing steps, then sits down on the couch. He flips a coin into the air, catches it, then palms it onto his other hand. He takes a look, then puts the coin away into his pocket. He looks out, studies the walls, then drops his check into his closed fist, resting his head on his hand. He's already defeated. This is JIMMY.

GIOVANNI, Jimmy's best friend. Good-looking, late thirties, Italian American. Heavy Chicago accent. He carefully studies his friend.

JIMMY: Can I afford it?

Giovanni waits.

JIMMY: (*Cont'd*) Good question, right? Pretty loaded. Literally? Sure. Do I have sufficient funds for the aforementioned? Absolutely. But to afford it? A-FORD.

Jimmy leans forward.

JIMMY: She wants me to take her to Paris? She wants babies? Keep doing what you're doing and we'll be just fine? Is that it?

Giovanni continues to study him, but no answer.

JIMMY: Fuck that. Not here. Not today. Nope.

Jimmy quickly stands up and blows right past Giovanni. He heads to a cabinet and begins to search through it.

Giovanni watches him for a second or two.

GIOVANNI: What are you looking for?

Jimmy doesn't even look up.

JIMMY: Weed. I'm looking for weed.

GIOVANNI: You gonna smoke it?

JIMMY: No, I'm gonna eat it. What do you think I'm gonna do with it?

GIOVANNI: I don't know. That's why I asked... And you could, you know?

JIMMY: What? I could what?

GIOVANNI: Eat it. People doing that now. All over the place. Now that it's practically legal. They're making just about everything with it. They got cakes, beverages, lollies.

JIMMY: Really?

Jimmy continues to search.

JIMMY: Lollies, huh?

GIOVANNI: Oh, yeah. One thing to the next. They got it all and I'll tell you what, it's a good thing, because then other people, like the people lookin' for it, for whatever reasons, they don't have to get those terrible coughs and lung problems from smoking it. Everyone's healthy now. And that's fine. I suppose it's good.

Jimmy storms past him again and heads to the other side of the stage. He begins to rifle through the drawers of a desk.

JIMMY: Yeah.

GIOVANNI: Yeah. But I, on a personal level, don't care much for it...I like to smoke it. For a number of reasons. The ritual. I like throwin' it into a pipe and smokin' it up like I'm on some sort of reservation, ya know? Plus, I like to know what I'm getting into. You take a puff, you wait and see. Now takin' a bite on the other hand? What do you know? I'll tell you what you know. Nothing. Zip. You really can't tell what from what. Next thing you know, not to mention it's thirty minutes later and you already moved on to do something that you didn't care to be stoned for, and *boom*, it hits you like a ton of something big, and here we go. You're off, and you don't know when you might be back on.

Jimmy looks stressed. He can't find it.

GIOVANNI: What's the matter with you? You're bouncing off and all over the place.

JIMMY: Can you get someone to get me some weed?

GIOVANNI: Sure. What's with the sudden urge?

JIMMY: I need to calm down.

GIOVANNI: That's fine. Sit down. Let us gather. I just got here. I have some things, you have some things. We'll sort through all.

Jimmy sits down and takes a deep breath. Giovanni checks him out. Jimmy tries to concentrate on his breathing. It's not working.

He pushes out a few fast breaths and then sucks in deep like he's about to submerge himself under water.

GIOVANNI: Okay. That's good... (*He waits.*) Why don't you go ahead and exhale.

Jimmy exhales a giant sigh.

GIOVANNI: Okay, nice. Now. Something wrong with you, something you'd like to discuss, in English, that needs assistance? Besides the obvious of needing to calm down.

JIMMY: Yes, I think so.

He waits.

GIOVANNI: Okay, I'm here. What is it?

Jimmy thinks.

JIMMY: I don't know.

GIOVANNI: What do you mean? How could you not know?

JIMMY: I mean, I know. Of course I know. I'm just not so sure. It's a lot.

GIOVANNI: Okay, you're gonna have to slow down, or speed up, or something, 'cause I don't know either.

JIMMY: Okay. This morning I thought it was one thing, which I'm pretty sure it still is, but now I'm starting to think that maybe it's a lot of different things.

Giovanni thinks. Jimmy snaps a finger.

JIMMY: Come to think of it, I'm actually positive it's one thing for sure, but it also might be something else is what I'm saying. I mean, that's the thing, though, right? Who knows what's what when you're this worked up? In general even. Worked up or not.

Giovanni thinks some more.

GIOVANNI: Okay. What's bothering you the least? Let's start backward.

JIMMY: Why backward?

GIOVANNI: It's unconventional and you're you.

Jimmy thinks.

JIMMY: Okay. First things last?

GIOVANNI: Something like that. Why not?

Jimmy starts to think. Giovanni waits. Jimmy pops up.

JIMMY: Okay. I got it. A woman moves into your home.

GIOVANNI: My home or yours?

JIMMY: This is general here. It's neither one of our homes.

GIOVANNI: That's good. Less confusing. Go ahead.

JIMMY: Okay. She decides, you both decide, to share space. Now, this space just happens to be yours.

Giovanni wants to ask a question.

JIMMY: Not yours, literally, not mine. The general.

GIOVANNI: Okay.

JIMMY: Okay. Now, all of a sudden, over time, and not that much, over the course of whatever, a switch begins to happen. You with me?

GIOVANNI: I'm right here.

JIMMY: This is something.

GIOVANNI: I just said I'm right here.

JIMMY: Okay. This switch. This event. This occurrence or whatever...

GIOVANNI: Go ahead.

JIMMY: All these things that used to be mine, out of the blue, and within a short period of time, have slowly, or maybe not so slowly, started to become ours. Not us. THE GENERAL. The general mine becomes the general ours. Now that gets tricky all in itself, but that's not even what I'm saying. I'm talking about scales. I'm talking about give and receive. I am talking about equality. Sure, she comes home, maybe she throws a new blanket on the bed, maybe she buys a coffee machine. Why not? And I say, "Thank you." But come on. You see what's happening?

GIOVANNI: I believe I have potential, but right this second, no.

JIMMY: Having a woman move in with you is like the worst deal in the history of bad deals. Think about it. She gets a new house, new furniture, new place to put all her shit, and what do you get in return? Love? Supprt? Occasional affection. But what the fuck? She's still getting all that shit, too. Nothing's changed, except mine becomes ours, and *I* just became *we*. For what? I mean, I was just having sex with you, regularly, for free, and now I'm paying for it. Do you see this? I mean, what the hell is going on here?

GIOVANNI: I think what's going on here, and keep in mind this is just my opinion, but that being said...this is how it works. Someone has to be the Masculine and someone has to be the Feminine. I mean, everyone plays a part. You move in, she moves in. Someone wears pants, and "generally," that's bullshit, but fine. Generally, the one wearing those very pants wakes up every morning and puts money in 'em. It's in the drawer, right next to the side of the bed where the pants are.

Jimmy takes it in.

GIOVANNI: You'd like to be taken care of?

JIMMY: Absolutely not.

GIOVANNI: That's what I'm saying.

JIMMY: No. That's what I'm saying. No. That's exactly what I'm saying. I could never do that.

GIOVANNI: You couldn't do what?

JIMMY: I could never be that kind of person. I could never move into your house and all a sudden start uttering the words *we*, or *us*, or *ours*. I mean how do you get the balls to do that?

Giovanni sits down on the couch.

JIMMY: (*Cont'd*) What? You just come in, sit on someone's couch, and— when it feels appropriate—you name it *ours*? You had nothing to do with procuring that couch. You don't even have a clue of how it got there, but now it belongs to you? This is bullshit. How can a person do that?

Giovanni stands up.

GIOVANNI: I couldn't, and that's the point. That's not my part to play, and as it is, neither is it yours. That's it right there. And that's the way it works. You got a solution to that, then I don't know what? Let's call somebody. But if not, let's do the right thing here. Let's call it what it is. Women are from one place, and we're from somewhere else. And I don't mean to sound like a pig, because Lord knows I'm not, because sometimes things are actually reversed. She plays him and he plays her. But one, I'm old fashioned. And two, I got muscles and I choose to be what I am. I hold the door, you act like a lady. I pick up the check, you rub my feet. That's just what I prefer.

Giovanni sits back down on the couch.

JIMMY: I prefer the same, that's not what I'm saying.

GIOVANNI: I think the truth is, you're not so sure about what you're saying.

JIMMY: Is that so terrible?

Giovanni picks up a magazine.

GIOVANNI: That's a whole other conversation. I mean, you ask me if it's okay to speak not knowing what's coming out. I'm saying that's a bad thing. But that's way off topic here, and we can't afford that. Not at this point. I got shit going on and you do, too. What the fuck am I talking about?

JIMMY: I don't know.

Giovanni takes a second to gather. He puts down the magazine, snaps, and points at Jimmy.

GIOVANNI: You want to live alone?

Jimmy thinks about it.

GIOVANNI: It's not a thinker. Spit it out.

JIMMY: No. I don't.

GIOVANNI: Right. Neither do I. In theory. You love your girl?

JIMMY: Very much.

GIOVANNI: Right. Problem solved.

JIMMY: Just like that?

GIOVANNI: Absolutely. What did I just say? People like to live alone. That's a choice. That's fine. It's not mine. We're still, in theory, but it's not yours either. What do we get, you ask? We get company. I like company. I like to take a bite and say, "Hey, taste this. It's pretty good. What do you think, woman?" I'm pretty sure they like the same thing. They get the same thing, plus a house and some new shit. But, really, all they're after—the good ones, I mean, at the end of the day, is some sort of legitimacy in their little community of females. Big deal. Ask me to explain that I can't.

JIMMY: I don't want to live alone.

GIOVANNI: Right! Of course you don't, so what the hell are we talking about here?

JIMMY: I'm not sure.

GIOVANNI: Well, let's go on ahead and really get to the bottom, 'cause leave alone the fact I got stuff, too, if this is what's bothering you the least, and you're this worked up, and as a result it's having the same effect on me. We might need some stronger drugs.

JIMMY: Okay, but now I'm maybe not so sure about what's bothering me the least.

GIOVANNI: I see.

JIMMY: I'm confused.

GIOVANNI: I can see that, too. And, for the record—and I'm not saying I'm up for it, but pot might not be the best detangler, if you know what I mean. Eating it, smoking it, stickin' it up your nose. You think you're confused now?

Jimmy gathers himself.

JIMMY: No. I think it's best if we stick to the plan.

Giovanni nods.

GIOVANNI: That's fine, too.

Jimmy pulls a quarter out of his pocket. He flips it into the air, catches it, and palms it onto his other hand. He looks down at the coin.

JIMMY: Shit.

GIOVANNI: Is that for the dope?

Jimmy nods his head.

JIMMY: Something else.

GIOVANNI: Okay. But I warned you.

Giovanni pulls his phone out of his pocket and dials a number.

JIMMY: What are you doing?

Giovanni puts up a finger silencing him and then puts the phone up to his ear.

JIMMY: (*Cont'd*) How could you call someone right now? Inappropriate.

Giovanni puts his finger again.

GIOVANNI: (*Into phone*) Hey, Bobby. It's Giovanni Botigliero. I'm good. Yeah, really good. You? How's the family? That's fantastic. Really good to hear. How old is he now? Seven years old? Wow. Amazing. Time really does fly. Well, that's really great. Hey, can you bring me some weed? I can meet you over at the canyon store over there on Laurel. Thirty minutes? Okay, I'll see you in a bit.

He hangs up the phone and puts it back into his pocket.

LIGHTS OUT

SCENE TWO

Giovanni stands up.

GIOVANNI: Okay, look. I'm gonna tell you something, and this has something to do with what I wanted to tell you in the first place when I got here, so we can kill a few birds 'with one stone. Also good, because I gotta go meet this drug dealer in a few minutes.

He checks his watch again.

JIMMY: You want a drink?

GIOVANNI: What drink? An adult drink? I just said I'm gonna drive.

JIMMY: A juice. It's noon.

GIOVANNI: A juice, I'll have.

Jimmy heads over to the kitchen. Giovanni follows.

GIOVANNI: Okay. So, this guy I know. Marty. Really exceptional guy. Real gem. You know I don't say that, 'less it's true.

Jimmy nods.

GIOVANNI: So, he's been up, down, and all through the ringer, this guy. He's got an ex with a new boyfriend living with his teenage son, and the guy's name is Enrique, and he drives a hog. Now I got nothing against Spaniards, or motorcycles, for that matter, but the combination living with your ex, and looking after your teenage boy can be very disconcerting, to say the least. He's had a tough go is what I'm getting at. Meanwhile, and through all this crap, he sees people.

Jimmy pours some juice.

JIMMY: People?

GIOVANNI: People. Doctors. Shrinks. What do I know who he sees? The point is this. Come to find out, this guy, Marty, he does a lot of things, or was doing a boatload of things that got him right where he was by no fault of no one else. You see?

JIMMY: You want ice?

GIOVANNI: A little.

Jimmy gets ice for the juice.

GIOVANNI: (*Cont'd*) What was I sayin'? My friend, Marty. His whole life he's been doing... Stuff.

Giovanni pauses to think.

GIOVANNI: (*Cont'd*) Stuff. Bad decision making. Acting out or whatever, now this is the people talking, the doctors, and what have you, all this stuff that, now get this, the stuff he's doing, or was doing, was exactly what got him where he ended up.

Jimmy's trying to follow. He hands over the drink. Giovanni takes the beverage.

GIOVANNI: (*Cont'd*) Thank you. Let me put it like this. It's like he's saying all I ever wanted to do, my whole life, is join the circus. Meanwhile, he beats the shit out of a clown every time he gets the chance.

Jimmy is confused.

GIOVANNI: (*Cont'd*) I can do better. It's like all he ever wanted was to wear a cop uniform, but he can't stop breaking the law.

Jimmy still doesn't get it.

JIMMY: He's a dirty cop with a thing for clowns?

GIOVANNI: No, he's a fuckin' actor, and that's got nothing to do with anything. He did it to himself. He fucked himself. His parents fucked him, so now he fucks himself. Subconsciously, I'm saying. Picked the wrong gal, got rid of the right one, made a left when he should have gone straight, but deep down he knew better. His actions got him where he is, or was. He's doing better now.

Jimmy starts to put it together.

JIMMY: Well, that's good to hear.

GIOVANNI: Nothing's wrong is what I'm saying. You got a great girl. Don't let your parents fuck it up.

JIMMY: They're dead.

GIOVANNI: You don't think I know that?

JIMMY: You saying I should see people?

GIOVANNI: What?

JIMMY: A doctor?

GIOVANNI: No. You don't need it. You got me, and I got Marty. He already paid for it. Which brings me to what I was going to say before. It always swings back. I like that.

Giovanni stands back and presents himself.

GIOVANNI: (*Cont'd*) I'm gonna be an actor.

JIMMY: Really?

GIOVANNI: What do you think?

JIMMY: I think you could do great.

GIOVANNI: Personality plus, right?

JIMMY: Always. I think that's great. You gonna take some classes?

GIOVANNI: No. I'm too old for that. And I'm feeling on top of the world. I heard those people can really knock you down, and I don't need that. Not right now. I've got rhythm. Or momentum, or both. But that's it. I'm on top of the world. This guy, Marty, got me thinking. I got all the answers, always have, but no direction. I'm good with the girls, but that's what they are. Girls. I want a Woman. It's time to stop playin' mid-twenties and move. I want a career. I want what you got. Imagine that.

JIMMY: You don't, trust me.

GIOVANNI: Why don't I?

JIMMY: For several reasons, but for one, I think I'm having a midlife crisis around the very thing you are presently contemplating becoming a part of. And even if I'm not, it sucks—whatever it is. I'm pretty sure it's a midlife crisis, though.

GIOVANNI: Hold on. Slow down. You can't say that.

JIMMY: I just did.

GIOVANNI: You can't. You have any idea how that sounds? To me. I'm listening, and I'm telling you that's no good. Let us dissect. Midlife? You're not even forty. That would mean you're only planning to go to eighty. Not even eighty. We can't have that. You're going in early.

A moment.

GIOVANNI: (*Cont'd*) We need that dope.

Giovanni puts his drink down and starts for the door.

GIOVANNI: (*Cont'd*) I'll be back.

JIMMY: Wait.

GIOVANNI: Wait, what? I gotta meet this guy.

JIMMY: Just wait.

GIOVANNI: I can't. You're talkin' dots and dashes. You got me in circles over here. I gotta meet this guy. What the fuck?

JIMMY: Just...there's an order here. I want to get to it, but it has to be in time. *My* time. The *right* time. When I'm ready, I'll know. Just wait. I'm not talking hours. Could be seconds.

Giovanni waits.

JIMMY: (*Cont'd*) I have a process...I think.

Giovanni looks at his watch.

LIGHTS OUT

SCENE THREE

Lights up. Jimmy steps up to Giovanni. He puts his hands on Giovanni's shoulders and looks him dead in the eye.

JIMMY: I'm ready. You ready?

GIOVANNI: Loaded question that...

JIMMY: Just say yes.

GIOVANNI: Okay.

JIMMY: Someone is coming here today.

Jimmy looks down to his wrist. He's not wearing a watch.

JIMMY: (*Cont'd*) At six p.m. sharp to discuss the future. My future. It is, without question, what's bothering me the most, but also, without question, strongly connected to the least...it's all connected, is what I'm saying.

GIOVANNI: Okay.

JIMMY: His name is Dean, and he works for the Network.

GIOVANNI: The TV people you write the show for?

JIMMY: Yes.

GIOVANNI: Your boss?

JIMMY: Don't ever say that again. I'm an artist. I don't have a boss, or shouldn't, but for all intents and purposes, yes, that's him.

GIOVANNI: This is good.

JIMMY: No.

GIOVANNI: Maybe for me.

JIMMY: You won't be here, unfortunately. Sorry.

GIOVANNI: That's fine. I got connections, too.

JIMMY: I'm gonna quit my job.

GIOVANNI: I heard you the first time.

JIMMY: I was pretty sure of that, but you did just ask me to repeat it.

GIOVANNI: What the hell are you talking about?

360 • SCOTT CAAN

Jimmy takes his hands off of Giovanni and backs away.

JIMMY: Well, I guess I'm talking about a lot of things. I'm talking about losing my mind. I'm talking about quality of life. I'm talking about babies. I'm talking about trips to Paris. I'm talking about making a decision that could potentially undo un-do-able damage.

Giovanni ponders.

GIOVANNI: Nope. That's a double...something or other. That doesn't work, I don't think.

JIMMY: I can't take it anymore.

GIOVANNI: Hold on.

JIMMY: For what?

GIOVANNI: Well, take it anymore, as in can't, would imply that there is, in fact, something you have been taking.

JIMMY: Oh, I've been taking.

GIOVANNI: Taking what, though?

JIMMY: I don't even know where to start.

GIOVANNI: Well, figure it out because, as far I know, you got a job that most law-abiding citizens would kill for.

JIMMY: As far as you know? How far is that?

GIOVANNI: I don't know, but two years ago you were broke. You got a roof now. Clothing. A toaster. I remember, not too deep back in the past, you trying to spread stale peanut butter on a slice of wheat with a plastic spork. It didn't work. You know how much bread we destroyed?

JIMMY: I wasn't this miserable.

GIOVANNI: We fucked up a lot of bread.

JIMMY: What? You gotta be hungry to be miserable?

GIOVANNI: Where's this coming from? Since when are you miserable? And to say you weren't something when it's two years behind is one thing.

JIMMY: Look at me.

GIOVANNI: Okay.

JIMMY: Well?

GIOVANNI: You're handsome. What the fuck?

JIMMY: I have dreams. All of a sudden. Very nasty and scary dreams. Dreams where I kill people. Dreams where people are trying to kill me. I have dreams that I'm having sex with lots of women.

GIOVANNI: You can't throw that in there with the other stuff. It doesn't go.

JIMMY: Sure, it does. All my ex-girlfriends lined up in a row. And I'm crying, and I'm forced to have sex with them in front of my current girlfriend, and she's crying, too.

GIOVANNI: Obviously.

JIMMY: Then there's this one I keep having with my mother...

GIOVANNI: Okay, that's it. I draw the line there. Not only is she your mother, but she's dead. Killing, sex, whatever it is, it's no good, I'm sure, and I get the point.

JIMMY: I'm miserable. I've never been so unhappy. Not when I was broke, not when I was lonely, not ever. One thing, and one thing only, my entire life has made sense to me, and that's been my work.

GIOVANNI: Respectfully, and I love ya, but do you have any idea how pretentious that just sounded?

JIMMY: Shit. Yes, I do. As a rule, usually before I say something pretentious I like to preface with what I'm about to say is going to sound really pretentious, because it generally exonerates the comment from sounding really pretentious, but I skipped that because I'm really out of sorts.

Jimmy pauses.

GIOVANNI: Still is what it is.

JIMMY: Fine, but it's the truth. And right now, at this point, it's beyond not making sense.

GIOVANNI: The comment or the work?

JIMMY: Life. Any of it. The work? I hate it. Everything about it. I hate what I'm doing, I hate the people I'm doing it for—and, most important, as a result, I'm starting to hate myself. Not to mention I'm destroying other things that have no business being destroyed. She wants babies? No shit. That's a woman's right. Paris is obviously something else, and I hate the French, but I suppose she deserves that, too. It's just a trip. Big fuckin' deal.

Giovanni is perplexed. Jimmy begins to pace.

JIMMY: *(Cont'd)* It's just not worth it. It can't be. Not for all the money in the world... Well, maybe for all the money in the world. An arbitrary number obviously, and a fantasy to top it off, so no. I don't know. I'm very confused is ultimately what I'm saying.

Giovanni takes a moment to process.

JIMMY: *(Cont'd)* Look. I mean, look. You. What? You've come in with this newfound ambition for the arts. And I don't want to piss on that. I think that's great. I think you'd make a fantastic actor. Hey. These people on television? You want to know something? They suck. A lot. All of 'em. Even the ones that bitch. Especially the ones that bitch. Fuck the training. You don't need it. Just be you. But whatever you do, and this is a warning, don't, under any circumstances, and I know this is going to sound pretentious, but never sign something that has the potential to fuck with your artistic integrity. It's no good. Trust me.

GIOVANNI: Are you done?

JIMMY: Life.

GIOVANNI: What about it?

JIMMY: I don't want to make the wrong move here. I mean, that's it, right?

GIOVANNI: That's what, right?

JIMMY: Life. Everything. It's all there in the moment. Whatever that specific moment is. Here's this space. This box. What you do next will affect everything. I don't know. Maybe I ask for more money, get rich, travel to France, and make babies. Maybe I tell them to get fucked and they sue me. Maybe they just let me go, I doubt it, but maybe. I'm rolling the dice here, either way, and let me tell you, it's a very scary roll. What do I want? Unfortunately, this is not an A-to-B situation. The line's a mess. What I say could potentially inform everything else to come. Maybe the troubles of my relationship go away if I'm happy. Maybe things get worse if I'm broke. Maybe it's just nice to have a paying job. I really don't know. It's really up to me.

Giovanni checks his watch.

GIOVANNI: I gotta go.

JIMMY: Wait.

GIOVANNI: Hey. I gotta go get this bag, come back, we gotta get high, come to a conclusion, and then sober up all before six. You gotta let me go.

JIMMY: Hurry up.

LIGHTS OUT

SCENE FOUR

Lights up. Giovanni and Jimmy sharing a joint. They sit on the floor.

GIOVANNI: How do you feel?

Jimmy thinks.

JIMMY: Stoned.

GIOVANNI: That's good.

JIMMY: And a little paranoid. Maybe this was a bad idea.

GIOVANNI: It was, but not because of the paranoia. That'll pass.

JIMMY: Right.

GIOVANNI: Isn't that funny?

Jimmy's head pops up.

JIMMY: What? What's funny?

GIOVANNI: Relax.

JIMMY: Wait. Why was it a bad idea?

GIOVANNI: Jesus, you're a mess.

JIMMY: What the fuck's funny?

GIOVANNI: You. This. It was a bad idea, because that's what drugs are. Bad. A bad idea.

Jimmy stands.

JIMMY: Well, why didn't you say that before? I knew it. Why the hell do I listen to you?

GIOVANNI: Me?

JIMMY: Myself, you, both of us. Why didn't you tell me this before?

GIOVANNI: Because I was in the same position with you. It's always a good idea when it's an idea, and that's what's so funny, it never is once you're doing it.

JIMMY: That's funny to you?

GIOVANNI: Kind of, yes, but what's funnier, and all I was trying to say before you started to short was the fact that is passes. It always does. That's the thing about mind-altering substances. You got stages. Especially as an adult. You're a kid, you don't have stages because your brains still forming into complex mush, but as an adult, you move around up top. One minute something's good and then the next you're a fuckin' mess. But it comes around is what I'm saying, so everything's fine.

Jimmy looks confused.

GIOVANNI: But, as a rule, drugs are bad, and I will try to remember that, as a rule, next time I'm not thinking clearly, but I have to say, and warn, that it's a pretty confusing and difficult thing to pull off. Obviously.

JIMMY: You need to stop talking.

GIOVANNI: No shit?

A long pause.

JIMMY: Okay. Ask me a question.

Giovanni thinks.

GIOVANNI: You like the Jets or the Packers next week?

Jimmy gives him a look.

GIOVANNI: What do I know? Ask you a question?

JIMMY: I need to be guided here.

GIOVANNI: We didn't eat peyote for Christ's sakes. It's a little weed. What the hell's the matter with you?

JIMMY: It's the confused, and I need help stage, okay?

GIOVANNI: Fine. What are we doing?

JIMMY: We're figuring it out. Good question.

GIOVANNI: Okay. What do we have?

JIMMY: We have a job.

GIOVANNI: The rest of the world's broke.

JIMMY: Don't do that.

GIOVANNI: What?

JIMMY: I don't want to be thinking about other people. Certainly, not the rest of the world. That's too much. Let's be selfish here. Fuck everyone. What I have and what I want are the only things that matter.

GIOVANNI: Fine. I'm here, too, for the record.

JIMMY: That's fine. I can accept that. What we need is what's what here, and nothing else. Fair?

GIOVANNI: Not to the rest of the world, but fine. I can go with that.

JIMMY: Good.

GIOVANNI: For now. Okay. What do you want?

JIMMY: Wait. I'm not done with what I have.

GIOVANNI: Go ahead.

JIMMY: I got a girl. A job and a girl. Now you can ask me what I want.

GIOVANNI: You know you are making me feel very unnecessary.

JIMMY: That's bullshit. I need you. Now ask me what I want.

Giovanni plays along.

GIOVANNI: What do you want?

JIMMY: Do I have to choose between the two? Girl or job?

GIOVANNI: I don't think so.

JIMMY: That's not helpful. I need definitive answers. Or questions. Both.

GIOVANNI: Okay, then, no. That's fuckin' ridiculous. Why would you have to choose between the two?

JIMMY: I don't know. That's why I'm asking you. See?

Jimmy reaches for the joint and starts to relight it. Giovanni pulls it away from him.

GIOVANNI: Absolutely not. That is a bad idea.

JIMMY: No. It's good. I'm on a roll now. We're getting somewhere.

GIOVANNI: Right. You want to start over? Go back to the beginning? Do the whole thing all over again? We'll spend the day being paranoid. Come on. What did we just say? Let's take advantage. This is the good stage. The selfish part. Only good cause of the potential results. Let's think. We got time, but not enough.

Jimmy scratches his head.

LIGHTS OUT

SCENE FIVE

Lights up. Giovanni sits back into the couch. Jimmy storms on to the stage.

JIMMY: Okay. I got an idea.

GIOVANNI: Great.

JIMMY: Let's run it down. You be the guy, and I'll be me.

GIOVANNI: I'm not familiar with this stage. What are we talking about?

JIMMY: You be the guy. My B-O-S-S. And I'll be me. This is great. Who needs acting class? This is gonna be good. For everyone.

GIOVANNI: I'm the guy?

JIMMY: You practice acting, and I'll do life.

GIOVANNI: Okay. What's my name?

JIMMY: Mr. Dean.

Giovanni thinks.

GIOVANNI: I don't think so.

JIMMY: What do you mean you don't think so?

GIOVANNI: Doesn't suit me. Do I look like a Dean?

JIMMY: Not necessarily, but that's not the point.

GIOVANNI: Well, sure it is. If this is for both of us, then let's keep it honest. I don't think I'm right for the part. And I'm no guru, but I imagine that's not the best start for handing in a worthy performance. I don't need to go to acting class to learn that one.

JIMMY: You telling me you always gotta be perfect for the part? That's not acting. What are you, Gregory Peck?

GIOVANNI: Who?

JIMMY: Forget it. You can pick your name. What is it?

Giovanni thinks.

GIOVANNI: How about Frank? I look like a Frank, don't I?

JIMMY: You do. Fine. Frank it is.

GIOVANNI: All right. And I'm the boss of this place? This television programming network? I'm the boss?

JIMMY: Yes, you are the boss.

GIOVANNI: The big boss.

JIMMY: That's right.

Giovanni stretches out a bit.

GIOVANNI: You got a tie I can borrow?

JIMMY: Are you fucking kidding me?

GIOVANNI: Just the opposite. You want me to take this seriously? I have a process.

JIMMY: A process? You have a process?

GIOVANNI: That's correct.

JIMMY: That's ridiculous.

GIOVANNI: Oh, really? The exercise itself is fucking genius, but me wanting to do my part to service everyone, including myself, makes it ridiculous. I'm offended, and would prefer to go back to being a friend giving mediocre advice. I don't need the insults.

JIMMY: You want a tie?

GIOVANNI: Yes, I do. I would like that.

Jimmy storms offstage.

Giovanni walks around in a circle and does his best impression of an actor getting into character.

Jimmy returns with a red tie.

GIOVANNI: Red?

Jimmy throws him a look.

GIOVANNI: I'm kidding. Red is fine. It will do the trick.

Giovanni takes the tie and to puts it on.

JIMMY: Should we sit?

GIOVANNI: It's your house.

JIMMY: Are you going to continue to be this difficult?

GIOVANNI: It's your house. I'm in character here. I'm the guy. My name's Frank, and I'm being respectful. I don't know. Maybe he's not that type of guy. Maybe he's the kind of guy who just sits. It's your house. I'm here. You decide what we do.

JIMMY: Okay, fine. That's enough. Sitting or not. Skip that part. We start now.

GIOVANNI: How's the tie look?

JIMMY: Amazing.

GIOVANNI: Thank you.

JIMMY: Okay, good. You ready?

GIOVANNI: Yes, I am.

JIMMY: Okay.

Jimmy takes a second to settle into the act.

JIMMY: How are you, Frank?

GIOVANNI: Hold on. Can I just say one more thing, and then we'll start.

JIMMY: What?

GIOVANNI: I would suggest…two things, actually. Don't ask him how he is. Let's just assume he lives on the west side, as most of these types do these days, and let's also assume he's pissed that he had to make the drive all the way over here. In rush hour. Why he's agreed to do this? We don't know. Or you do and you've chosen not to share. Either way, I say never look a gift horse in the kisser. Don't bring that up, either, is also what I'm saying.

JIMMY: Fine.

GIOVANNI: That's not it.

JIMMY: Go.

GIOVANNI: Second and more important, I don't think you should call him Frank.

JIMMY: No shit. I agree. His fucking name is Dean.

GIOVANNI: No, it's Mr. Dean. You said Frank. How are you, Frank?

JIMMY: That's because you said you didn't like Mr. Dean. You said you like Frank.

GIOVANNI: I know that, but now I'm saying, as Frank, I would like to think that I deserve some respect here. So, given all the above mentioned, my name is Frank…

Giovanni pauses to come up with a name.

GIOVANNI: Duke George the third.

JIMMY: Frank Duke George the third.

GIOVANNI: That's correct.

JIMMY: And you're not being difficult, huh?

GIOVANNI: No, I'm not.

JIMMY: Okay, Mr. Duke George the third.

GIOVANNI: Call me Frank, kid.

Jimmy bites his fist.

GIOVANNI: Okay, now, I'm fucking with you. I'm sorry. Let's go. For real now.

Jimmy gets his bearings.

JIMMY: Okay. How are you, sir?

Giovanni makes a face. Disapproving.

JIMMY: Don't make a face. We have to start with pleasantries. How are you, how ya been…anything can end with him pissed that he had to drive here.

GIOVANNI: In rush hour.

JIMMY: Yes. In rush hour. I have to start with something.

GIOVANNI: Fine.

JIMMY: Fine.

Jimmy takes a breath. Giovanni waves him on.

JIMMY: So.

GIOVANNI: So?

JIMMY: Well, Mr. George. I don't want to write on the show anymore.

GIOVANNI: Oh, no?

JIMMY: No.

GIOVANNI: Why's that?

JIMMY: Well, for a lot of reasons.

GIOVANNI: Start with number one, please. I mean, I'm here.

JIMMY: Okay. Well, I feel like I'm dying inside.

GIOVANNI: Don't be so dramatic.

JIMMY: What? Is that you or him talking?

GIOVANNI: That's both of us. Dying inside? What are you, a broad? Men don't die inside… Well, maybe we do, we're just not supposed to admit it.

JIMMY: It's the truth.

GIOVANNI: Fine. Be more specific.

JIMMY: Okay.

GIOVANNI: And less dramatic for Christ's sakes.

Jimmy waits. Frustrated.

GIOVANNI: Okay. I'm in character now. From here out. No more advice. You're on your own. So, what's the problem with writing this particular show?

JIMMY: Respectfully…

GIOVANNI: Yes.

JIMMY: It's just not my thing.

GIOVANNI: Not your thing. What does that mean?

JIMMY: It means that when I decided to be a writer, this is not what I signed up for.

GIOVANNI: Quite the contrary. This is exactly what you signed up for. I have your signature to prove it.

JIMMY: But I didn't know what I was actually getting into.

GIOVANNI: Then why'd you sign?

JIMMY: Because I was broke, and I needed the money.

GIOVANNI: So, now that you have that, and you are no longer broke, you think it's fair to just tell me that you no longer wish to be of service?

Not to mention the thing's a hit, and all you can come up with as reasoning is that it's just not your thing.

JIMMY: Jesus, you're tough.

GIOVANNI: No, you're just weak.

JIMMY: Excuse me?

GIOVANNI: Tell me something. I'm here. I'm listening. You want out, you're dying inside...I want to know why? Tell me what's so bad. Explain to me why. Let's imagine I'm a compassionate man. Forget that. Imagine I'm not, because I'm not. Tell me something that makes sense. The entire world's lookin' for a way to rub some change together. People are eating dirt. You're getting rich with a fuckin' typewriter living in the hills. What the fuck is your problem? This I want to know.

JIMMY: Go easy, would ya?

GIOVANNI: Absolutely not. No one's happy, okay. That's just the way it is. Okay? That's life. Happiness is for children. Adults don't smile. Not unless they're on something. You want to feel like you did when you decided to become a writer? Then kill yourself and try again. It don't work like that. Things are tough, relationships are tough, life's a fuck, and that's just the way that it is.

JIMMY: Why are you saying this?

GIOVANNI: I don't know, but I'm getting all of a sudden very emotional, and I don't like it. This either. Fuck this game.

Giovanni rips off the tie.

LIGHTS OUT

SCENE SIX

Lights up. Giovanni scratches his head. Jimmy flips the coin into the air again. Catches it and looks.

JIMMY: Okay. Here's what I say. I say you're better off living a short life where you actually did something you cared about. So you were hungry. Fine. Food's overrated. So is everything else.

Giovanni picks up the joint out of the ashtray and lights it back up.

JIMMY: We gotta do the right thing. Something that wakes you up. Whatever it is. The thing that makes you move. Or else it's just an exercise. A really long one, and eventually you forget why you're doing anything at all.

Giovanni exhales and offers him the joint.

JIMMY: No, thank you.

GIOVANNI: So, what? Just have a blast? I seen those people. They do drugs and sleep with teenagers. I'm personally in the process of avoiding that very cliché.

JIMMY: Right, because you're smart. Fun? I don't know what that means. And the problem with sleeping with, or even spending time with young girls, is that they haven't gotten to the point in life where they've realized, being with someone crazy is not all that it's cracked up to be.

GIOVANNI: I don't understand that.

JIMMY: You have to be intelligent, is what I'm saying. If shooting dope and jumping off buildings is what floats your boat, that's not a great argument. Gotta be something behind that, and I'm guessing it's not something good.

GIOVANNI: I don't like either of those things.

JIMMY: Luckily, neither do I. But I'm getting close, and that's the problem. So what? I gotta figure it out. For me. You say this person, that person, to the rest of the planet, sorry, I can't speak for them. I can only do me, and this is how I feel. My aunt calls me, "I love the show, so clever how the guy did the thing with the knife, and how they figured it out with the liquid and the other thing."

374 • SCOTT CAAN

JIMMY: No. The other one. The dopey one on my mom's side. Aunt Barbara's the one who always told me I can do anything, which I also don't like because my brother listened and he ended up with two broken arms. Anyway, she thinks it's great. The show. The other Aunt. The dopey one on my mom's side. "Aren't you happy, you must be so happy…" No, I'm not happy. I wanna kill myself. "Why? You should just be happy you have a job in this economy, and I think it's great! Shape up." I say, "Okay. I'll get right on shaping up." But what I'm really thinking is, *Where do you get the fucking nerve?* It's like a monkey talking to a giraffe. They don't go. They can't communicate. One's over here, the other's down there. "Why can't you just be happy for the things you have?" Because I'm an unhappy person. It's all relative, ya fuckin' dope.

Giovanni makes a face.

JIMMY: I'm sorry, but it's true. I'm me, and she's my aunt. What am I gonna do?

Giovanni ponders the question.

GIOVANNI: That's a good question.

JIMMY: Right.

GIOVANNI: Shit. Now, I'm paranoid. I hate this part.

JIMMY: Let me ask you a question, and this one needs an answer.

GIOVANNI: Fine.

JIMMY: What happens if you tell Carl Lewis he can't run anymore?

GIOVANNI: He's a hundred. Where's he running?

JIMMY: Not now. Then. When he wasn't a hundred.

GIOVANNI: I don't know. What are we talking about?

JIMMY: Carl Lewis in his prime. They come over to his house, sit him down, and they tell him he can't run or jump. Or, better, they tell him he can run, but just a little, or you can jump, but just not so high.

GIOVANNI: Why would they do this?

JIMMY: They wouldn't, but what if they did?

GIOVANNI: I don't know.

JIMMY: He's not happy, I'll guarantee you that. He does not enjoy the prospect of future. His own, I mean. This I know.

GIOVANNI: No. He shoots dope and jumps off a building, maybe.

JIMMY: Exactly.

GIOVANNI: We don't want that. I get it. You're Carl Lewis, and these people are the Russians.

JIMMY: Right.

Jimmy stops to think.

JIMMY: (*Cont'd*) I think maybe you're mixing up your Olympics.

They both think.

JIMMY: (*Cont'd*) Wait. Maybe not. What year…?

GIOVANNI: Whatever. I get it. I'm saying. These people. This thing. You.

Jimmy takes a beat.

JIMMY: These people. This machine. They don't have hearts. There's no pulse. They don't give a shit about feelings. You know why? Because they don't have them. They don't have feelings, they don't have friends, and they don't have families. It's actually a prerequisite. I know this sounds crazy, but I'm pretty sure, in order to be an executive at one of the big television networks, you have to take a class on how to ignore compassion.

GIOVANNI: Ignore…

JIMMY: Compassion. Your own, I mean. Look it. The lead actor on our show lost his mom, got addicted to methadone, and had knee surgery, all in the same month. He didn't miss an episode. These people are monsters. They just want you to keep doing what you're doing and they don't care how you feel about doing it. They want you to keep on, or they want you dead.

GIOVANNI: Well, being dead sucks. That I do know.

JIMMY: Yes, it does.

Jimmy paces around a bit. He stops.

JIMMY: My girl.

GIOVANNI: What about her?

JIMMY: The poor thing. Look what she has to deal with. I couldn't deal with me. Not on a regular basis. No way.

Giovanni thinks on it. Jimmy paces a few more steps and then snaps to.

JIMMY: That's it. I got it. Patience. That's what I get. She gets a couch and I get patience. A lot of it.

GIOVANNI: Seems fair.

JIMMY: Look at me. I've gone and jammed it all together. It's not her. It's me. She wants me to think about babies and trips to Paris. I can't even breathe. You can't travel dead. You can't make babies if you're not alive, can you?

GIOVANNI: I'm pretty sure, no.

Jimmy realizes he's come up with something. He looks Giovanni right in the eye.

JIMMY: Thank you.

Jimmy grabs a notebook and a pen off of the coffee table and begins to write.

LIGHTS OUT

SCENE SEVEN

Lights up. Jimmy is passed out on the couch. Giovanni sits on a chair in the middle of the living room.

He holds up the notebook Jimmy was writing in, faces the audience, and begins his performance.

GIOVANNI: Here's the thing. The problem. I was down a bit. Like for cash, ya know. Nothing had really gotten this serious yet. Like in life, I'm saying. Things had worked out up till this point, and then all of a sudden they don't. Here I am enjoying my life. Come to find out people don't do this. Enjoy their life, I'm saying. But I don't know from that so that wasn't me. But now. Look at this. Here I am stuck and I want to rip these people apart. I really do got the urge to do bad things. Why? 'Cause they got no souls. They got no intention of doing it right. Or at least to the best of their ability. Who knows if they got any anyhow. The problem is I agreed to be with these people. Be a part of something. I said I need the dough, too. So, in a way, I understand the move, but you can't sit in it. At least I can't. Not anymore. Or not for too long. It's all our problems now because we signed up. We said, "Okay. I'll play along, but just for a bit. I'll feel it out." We didn't know, though. We didn't know that once you settle in, it's hard to come back. Who wants to start over anyway? Not me. But maybe. Who knows? I get this deep gut move where I wanna kill these people. I imagine it up real good in my head. Some kinda torture, but where it's just the two of us, and I get my way with no way out. This one guy. The ring leader of this soulless group. The guy with the flute up front who scares people with threats of no more money. That's it, though. Again. Money. We move for it. We break for it. We sell our original dreams for it. We take the blueprints we set up, and turn 'em into something else to fit the way. We trade our heroes for homes and speedboats that don't work anyway and we teach our kids that creativity and passions for someone else. Or that it just plain ain't. Period. That's the performance. That's the heartbreak. Life.

Jimmy slowly wakes up and notices Giovanni holding the notebook.

JIMMY: What are you doing?

Giovanni quickly puts the notebook down and starts to tidy up a bit.

GIOVANNI: You, ah...you fell asleep over there. I thought I'd give the place the once-over while you napped.

JIMMY: That's nice of you.

GIOVANNI: Yeah. I wanted to let you sleep. Clear your head, or cloud it, whatever it needed given the forthcoming events here.

Jimmy sits up.

JIMMY: I had a crazy dream.

GIOVANNI: Oh, yeah?

JIMMY: What time is it?

GIOVANNI: You seem calm.

JIMMY: I might be. Maybe I'm just tired.

GIOVANNI: You slept.

JIMMY: Right.

Giovanni checks his watch.

GIOVANNI: It's twenty-till.

Jimmy waits.

GIOVANNI: Till it's time.

Jimmy gathers his thoughts.

JIMMY: I dreamed...

GIOVANNI: Dreamt.

JIMMY: What?

GIOVANNI: You dream you dreamt.

Jimmy waves it off.

JIMMY: I was about to kill this guy. Mr. Dean. Like I had him. He had nowhere to go. First, I was in prison, but in this really small cage. Like one of those Abu Ghraib torture boxes. I was begging him to let me out, on the count of being so uncomfortable, and the anxiety. Fuck, it was awful. Anyway, after a lot of pleading, he finally let me out.

Then we started to have this intellectual conversation about whether or not it was acceptable, and/or legal, that he kept me in the little box. He made some points. Mine were more valid than his. I thought so anyway, Then somehow I got a hold of him, and we ended up on this big stage. My girl was there with my parents, and a bunch of my ex-girlfriends. They were all eating popcorn. And I, in a very articulate way, was threatening this guy. Very detailed. I'll bounce your head off of this thing. I'll kill your dog with a pen. Whatever. But he listened. He was listening, but not just because he was scared, like he really understood and cared about what I had to say all of a sudden. I don't know. Maybe he was just scared.

Giovanni waits.

GIOVANNI: Did you kill him?

JIMMY: No. I didn't have to for some reason.

GIOVANNI: So, then what?

JIMMY: I don't know. Maybe we ate something. I woke up.

They both sit with the dream for a bit.

All of a sudden, Jimmy pulls the quarter out of his pocket. He flips it into the air and palms it. He looks at the coin, forces a smile, then tosses the quarter behind his back.

Giovanni goes back to tidying up the room.

Jimmy pulls out his phone. Dials a number.

JIMMY: (*Into phone*) Hell, yes. Can I get the number for Air France, please?

Jimmy writes down the number on the notebook Giovanni was reading from.

JIMMY: (*Phone*) Thank you.

Jimmy hangs up the phone, then looks up to Giovanni. He holds up the notebook and gestures to Giovanni. Almost seeking approval for the text written in the notebook.

Giovanni takes a beat. Thinks about it.

GIOVANNI: A bit pretentious, maybe.

JIMMY: Paris or my words?

Giovanni smiles.

GIOVANNI: Paris is fantastic.

Jimmy agrees with a nod.

A KNOCK ON THE DOOR.

GIOVANNI: He's early.

JIMMY: Shit.

Jimmy stands up and heads for the door.

GIOVANNI: I can be the maid.

JIMMY: No, you be you. It's fine.

GIOVANNI: I can do an accent. I got a really good Cuban thing I could do.

JIMMY: No. You're just on your way out. Everything's cool. I'm calm. I got this.

Giovanni gives the thumbs up.

GIOVANNI: You're gonna be fine. You're gonna do the right thing. Whatever that is. For you.

Jimmy smiles.

JIMMY: Hey.

GIOVANNI: Yeah.

JIMMY: You're gonna be fine, too. You're gonna be great, and you're gonna be fine.

GIOVANNI: Always. That's me. Never lost to be found.

JIMMY: The future, I'm saying. For you.

Giovanni points to the door.

GIOVANNI: I don't know. I might actually be on the fence all of a sudden. I'm in transition. I'm up in the air. One minute I'm one way, the other minute, who knows? I'm really lookin' for the right thing, and if working for these people might be in the cards, the right thing deck, then let's play. But first things first. I gotta see what's what. Ya dig?

JIMMY: I think so.

A KNOCK AT THE DOOR.

Jimmy smiles. They share a knowing look.

JIMMY: Just a second.

Jimmy takes a few beats for himself, and then reaches for the door.

Giovanni follows him.

GIOVANNI: I think maybe the stage might be my thing.

LIGHTS OUT

THE END

Day In Life

Day In Life

SCENE ONE

A PARK

A grown man, TOM, sits alone on a park bench. He looks out. Stares into the abyss, something eating at him.

A few seconds pass.

Another grown man, DALE, slowly steps up to the bench, sits down, and takes out a newspaper.

Subtle acknowledgement of each other's existence.

Then after a few silent beats, Tom motions down to a sack next to his feet.

TOM: I got Danish.

Dale, seemingly disgusted by the thought, brushes it off and rolls his eyes. He starts to read his paper.

Tom takes it in.

TOM: I didn't mean to offend you.

Dale tries to brush it off. Goes back to his paper.

TOM: What's this now?

Dale puts his paper down.

DALE: Can you just never mind, please?

TOM: Stop.

DALE: Stop what?

TOM: I can't. There's no never mind. In fact, just the opposite. I mind.

DALE: Well. that's gonna have to be what it is, I'm afraid. I'm me, you're you, and that's that.

TOM: I say no.

DALE: You say no?

TOM: You some kinda parakeet? Yes. I say no.

DALE: Can you please?

TOM: No! You please. That's what I say to you. You please. Do you a favor? No. How bout me?

DALE: It is nothing, okay. I say it is nothing, then that is what it is.

TOM: No, no, no. I say no, it's not okay. I don't mean this is the end or nothing silly like that. But it's a thing. You don't like Danish? That's one thing, but if it's something else I gotta know. Not because of anything special, but just because. I say it's important. Or could be.

DALE: But it's not. That is what I am reassuring you of. It couldn't be important because it's not.

TOM: To you maybe.

DALE: To you, I'm saying.

TOM: But to you it could be?

Dale thinks about it.

DALE: I suppose it could, to me, be something important.

TOM: Well, that's no good is what I'm saying. All for one here. I mean, what gives?

DALE: There is nothing special.

TOM: How could you say that? Sure it is. You just said so.

DALE: What did I just say?

TOM: Hey, I'm just thinking, that's all. I'm thinking. I got things. Always do. You know this about me.

DALE: I do.

TOM: Am I a team player?

DALE: Always since I've known you.

TOM: Okay then.

DALE: All right.

TOM: Okay.

They both wait.

DALE: You okay?

TOM: No, I'm not okay. You want something else?

DALE: Like what?

TOM: We can get what we want. That's the beauty of it.

DALE: I'm good.

TOM: Okay.

DALE: For now.

TOM: Obviously for now. This I know. That changes and I don't know what. Just so we're clear.

DALE: I got no problems.

TOM: That's not true.

DALE: Okay. I got problems, but what the hell are we talking about? I get it. You don't like that I don't like the idea of what you are offering, and further, I understand. It's not a spot anyone would like or choose to be in. We are who we are. We like whatever we like, but I'm assuming the aforementioned has its hyphens or discrepencies or whatever. Here's what I'm saying, and I'm saying it right now. Forget what happened. Forget the Danish. We get along, do we not?

TOM: Of course we do, that's what I'm saying.

DALE: Okay, we're saying the same thing. What's eating you, no pun intended?

TOM: Me?

DALE: Who am I talking to?

TOM: Okay.

DALE: Okay?

TOM: Okay, fine. You want to know the truth?

DALE: No. Lie to me. What am I, a broad?

TOM: Things change.

DALE: Sure they do.

TOM: Well, that's what I'm afraid of.

DALE: I don't like Danish.

TOM: But why? That's what I'm saying. I don't know this. I know a lot, but this is something I don't. How do you think that is? For me, I mean. To take, I'm saying.

DALE: Fine, and I'm saying that there's gotta be something getting at you special, because I mean, what the hell are we talking about here?

TOM: Things are different.

DALE: With what?

Tom seems very affected by something. He takes a beat to get it up.

TOM: Okay.

DALE: Okay?

TOM: I'm gonna have a hard time being specific here, but I'm gonna try my best. I'm gonna give it a try.

DALE: Go ahead.

TOM: Okay. Example.

DALE: All right.

TOM: You remember the days when a guy... Now I'm talking a guy's guy... A real chip. I'm talking about the kinda guy you share a sandwich with. A bench. Guy who's got you covered when the roof's gone. You know what I'm saying?

DALE: Sure.

TOM: There was a time, and it wasn't too long ago is what I'm saying, that this type of guy would wait downstairs with a cigar. Laughing. Blowing tobacco. Just waiting for the outcome.

Dale is confused.

TOM: Now they got the very same guy siting there in the room while the baby's coming right out. Can you believe this shit?

Dale waits.

TOM: Are we men or are we men?

DALE: You wanna know why I don't like Danish?

TOM: I think that would be a nice thing to hear.

DALE: Reminds me of things.

TOM: Okay.

DALE: Not to mention, it's not the manliest of snacks.

TOM: That all depends.

DALE: I disagree, but that's not the point.

TOM: What's the point then?

DALE: Long time ago.

TOM: I assumed.

Dale takes a minute to piece together what he's going to say.

DALE: I'm sitting in the can, right? The can for kids, I mean.

TOM: Juvenile can.

DALE: That's right.

TOM: And?

DALE: And I was feeling a certain way. I had also, the previous week, seen this kid on the other end of the room get some sort of smuggled chocolate item, that at the time I coveted, and also imagined a good idea for the next time for myself. So, here I was. Having asked for a smuggled chocolate bar personally, but here comes my old man and what does he do? Out of his pocket he pulls a Danish. Not also, but instead of. I'm obviously upset at the sight of the thing. But here he is. Sweating. Like some kinda animal. He apparently had to run to get the thing, and he had already lost a good amount of his hair at this point, and he really thought he was doing something good but it turned out to be a real problem. And wrong for what I was going for. Thing explodes all over the place when he rips it out of the package. Guy's got it all coming down his face, the Danish I mean, sweat and Danish. Curly, pathetic little hairs mixed in from the poor guy's balding head. The guards are looking at me like, "Hey stupid, next time tell him to bring a chocolate bar like a human being." I've given them a look back like, "Thats what I did." This is all subtext by the way. The conversation with the guard, I mean. Anyway, the guy was a mess. My father, I'm saying now. Took a long look at him and that's when I realized I was on my own. For several reasons. Several things. Next thing I know, here we are.

TOM: I see.

DALE: We're saying the same thing, I think.

TOM: I see that. But different.

DALE: Right. Different.

TOM: But the same.

DALE: I think so, yes.

TOM: That's okay.

Dale nods.

TOM: I mean, I like that.

Dale nods again.

TOM: This guy does that, this one used to be like this. Things happen. Change.

DALE: That's right.

Tom thinks to himself.

TOM: When were you in the can for kids.

DALE: When I was a kid.

TOM: Right.

LIGHTS OUT

SCENE TWO

LIGHTS UP

The guys are on the bench.

DALE: The kid's a jerk.

TOM: Which kid?

DALE: This one. Which kid? Who are we talking about?

TOM: That's what I ask.

DALE: That's what I'm saying. You don't know who we're talking about, we got trouble. And I'm not just talking about the troubles of misunderstanding, which believe me, I'm well aware is a thing. But no! I'm talking about the miscommunication of what we are as people. I say I like something and you say you can dig it too, what the hell, we're on the same page, if not, at least a similar one. But you say "What are you talking about," I say we got a serious problem. One that goes beyond just the simplicity of we don't got the same taste. You see this?

TOM: No, I don't.

DALE: You know who I'm talking about?

TOM: I think so?

DALE: Well, that's better. It's certainly not one hundred percent, but it's better than nothing.

TOM: You're getting me a little muffed up here.

DALE: I can see that.

TOM: Sorry.

DALE: It's fine.

TOM: Okay.

DALE: This guy. Or kid…

Tom waits. He's confused.

DALE: See, you don't know.

TOM: That's correct.

Dale reaches into his pocket and pulls out his cell phone. He seems startled as he looks at the caller ID.

TOM: What? What is it?

DALE: Nothing. It's the hospital. For a second, I thought my mom was dying again. Probably just about my back.

He puts the phone back into his pocket.

DALE: So, this is what I'm saying. I'm talking about a kid who I find to be a jerk. Who he is or who he is not, for that matter, is no longer very relevant. Because my feelings about the guy, or kid, aren't really so strong that I even care to get into it. But this? We are very close friends. Would you say that?

TOM: I would. Sure. I'd say that.

DALE: Okay. We have to understand each other. That is what I'm saying. You good with that?

TOM: Yes, I am.

DALE: This guy don't matter.

TOM: This kid.

DALE: Right. Guy, kid. Human being, for all intents and purposes.

TOM: He don't matter.

DALE: Right. It's you and me. Or me and you. However it goes.

TOM: I got it.

DALE: Good, so tell me something.

TOM: I'm good.

DALE: That's good.

TOM: You been good?

DALE: Aside from this ballbuster I got for a nephew, yes, I'm good.

TOM: That's the guy.

DALE: Yes it is.

TOM: We're on track.

DALE: Yes. Which makes me very happy, but what I am, however, not happy about is this ball-breaking kid I got for a nephew that I pulled the very unlucky card of looking after.

TOM: What did he do?

DALE: He didn't do nothing if you can believe it, but I still got all this crap behind the nothing he didn't do. Let me explain.

TOM: You hungry?

DALE: Always.

TOM: We'll get something.

DALE: One hundred percent.

TOM: So this kid.

DALE: This fucking kid.

TOM: How about a nice melted?

DALE: What?

TOM: I'm sorry. I'm right with you, but the idea of a nice something melted together with cheese just got a hold of me, and my mouth started to water for something melted. But I'm with you.

DALE: Now you got me. Melted what?

Tom thinks.

TOM: I don't know.

Dale thinks.

DALE: We'll figure it out. We'll get to it. Anyhow.

TOM: The kid.

DALE: Right. This little jerk of a kid, who if I didn't mention, is some kind of a special jerk.

TOM: You did. And he didn't do nothing and you are catching the suffering.

DALE: Right. This little putz. First of all, I gotta watch this kid like a hawk. Now, not because that's my style in which I choose to look after someone, no, it's because of my instructions. And let me just add on top of everything else, I am not, nor have I ever been, one to deal with instructions in the first place. It's just not who I am. This little jerk got a set of little jerk parents, one of which I am related to, who decides it's gonna be okay to skip town for the rest of the year and leave the aforementioned little jerk kid with me. With instructions of all things.

TOM: Some nerve.

DALE: No shit, right? I mean, what do they think this is? What am I? A jerk? A jerk watcher? The watcher of jerk kids? When did I earn this?

TOM: Why'd you accept all this? That's the thing I'm wondering.

DALE: Because I'm a nice guy, and I wasn't in the know of what a little jerk they were handing off.

TOM: You got duped.

DALE: I was duped. Yes! This is what happened.

TOM: It's bullshit.

DALE: That's right. You gotta be out in the open about this stuff. Forget about duping me. For the kid's sake. You gonna teach this kid that it's okay passing people off to other people without telling them the truth about what they're getting handed over? That's no lesson for a kid. Life's short and tough, that's what the kid should be learning. There's no time for leading people down the wrong path. Am I right?

TOM: Yes. Absolutely. Not to mention, he's a jerk to begin with. The kid needs a positive influence. Maybe that's what you were doing. I mean, taking the gig to begin with. Not a gig. You know what I mean.

DALE: No, you're right. That's exactly what it is. A gig with no pay, crappy food, and a jerk kid.

TOM: Where'd they go?

Dale seems confused.

TOM: Those jerk parents? Respectfully, I mean.

DALE: He is my brother.

TOM: That's why I said.

DALE: Thank you. Get this. They went abroad. Now what the fuck is that?

TOM: The fucking nerve. Abroad?

DALE: Right.

TOM: Like it ain't enough they're gonna dump this little punk in your lap, they gotta go abroad on top of it all. Pick a place. I'm sorry, but I hate that shit. Be specific. If it's Paris, say Paris. That's life. Details. Abroad? Do me a favor.

DALE: Thank you.

TOM: Some nerve, I'm telling you what. Anyhow, I'm sorry, I just get… It upsets me. That's all.

DALE: It's fine, I get it.

TOM: So, what's this kid's problem.

DALE: Now that's an excellent question. It's unfortunately one that I'm afraid I'm not gonna be able to answer. He's got plenty of them, I can only assume. I mean, I love my brother, I suppose, but he's not grand prize at the end of the day. Things are what they are. He never won no awards for being a mensch or anything like that. I'm not sure he even place in the bespoke event. Ever.

TOM: Wait a minute.

DALE: For what?

TOM: Bespoke? I don't think that's right.

DALE: Sure it is. We spoke about it before. Or I did. Either way. Spoken about before. Bespoke.

TOM: I don't think so.

DALE: In any case, I'm talking about something that I believe you understand?

TOM: Yes.

DALE: Right. This kid and my brother, and you know what they say about apples.

TOM: I know what they say, believe you me.

DALE: They say a lot, okay, and this kid's rotten, trust me.

TOM: I just gotta say that it all starts somewhere.

DALE: Right.

TOM: Not to interrupt, but I do get what the fuck you're laying down.

DALE: Right?

TOM: I mean, here you got jerk-off kids running around with jerkoff parents and everyone's going the same way. They got no choice. It's like some sort of cycle or something that ain't got no end because it's impossible that there could even be one, given the circumstances.

DALE: Fucking A.

TOM: I mean, how are you gonna change something that doesn't... You know what I mean? Things don't change. You're talking about apples? Trees? It is what it is. This is this. It's not something else. Trees grow toward the sky and that's that.

DALE: It's got roots.

TOM: That's what I'm saying. That's exactly what I'm saying. Roots.

DALE: It is what it is.

TOM: And it ain't to be messed with. Nothing to do but watch it. Like bad TV. Which reminds me of something else, but later. This kid.

DALE: I'm really upset.

TOM: I can see that.

DALE: I try to be a good guy to this kid.

TOM: I can imagine. You do nice things.

DALE: I'm looking after him.

TOM: All you ask for is what?

DALE: Exactly. What the hell am I saying here? I'm not telling him to do what it takes for me to have one of those stickers. You know the stickers? My kid did this and he's the best at something. They got them for uncles too, I'm sure. My nephew's the smartest kid in the bunch. I'm not asking him to get me one of those.

TOM: No. You're talking common decency. You do for me, I do for you.

DALE: That's exactly right.

TOM: And what does he do? He moves around like the jerk kid that he is and leaves you with egg on your face, cause whatever he done, and believe me, I'm looking forward to finding out, but whatever he done, or did not do for that matter, now you gotta go and explain it to this jerk kid's parents. Respectfully.

DALE: I can't win.

TOM: You try to do something nice for someone.

DALE: I tell ya what.

TOM: I'm disgusted. Let's find some food and forget about it.

LIGHTS OUT

SCENE THREE

LIGHTS UP

The guys sit on the bench. Tom seems to be on a thought, Dale looks through the paper.

TOM: I got something.

Dale puts the paper down.

DALE: Go ahead.

TOM: I'm processing it now, so I gotta see.

DALE: Do that. You see. See what happens. I'm right here.

Tom waits. Dale feeds a bird.

TOM: Okay.

DALE: You got it?

TOM: It's important, I think. I'm pretty sure, is what I'm saying.

DALE: That's fine.

TOM: Everything good with you?

DALE: Today? Yes. Today, everything is good with me.

TOM: I'm happy to hear that.

DALE: Happy to say it. It's today. Today is today.

TOM: Yes, it is.

DALE: It's not tomorrow.

TOM: Right. Cause who knows.

DALE: Nobody got a fucking clue and that's my point.

TOM: My point, too.

DALE: Here we are.

TOM: So.

DALE: Right.

TOM: I got something.

DALE: You said.

TOM: It's a… What do you call it? Percolating.

DALE: Good word.

TOM: I like it.

DALE: You used it.

TOM: That's my point.

DALE: You hungry?

TOM: You know I am, but I'm saying something here.

DALE: You sure?

TOM: Don't be wise.

DALE: How about something sweet? Like a nice milkshake with all the stuff.

Tom thinks.

TOM: Like a couple of kids.

DALE: Could be nice.

TOM: I'm in, but listen.

DALE: Go ahead.

TOM: Explain something to me.

DALE: Okay.

TOM: You ever thought we'd get here?

DALE: Where are we?

TOM: That's kinda what I'm getting at. I don't know, also, what I'm saying. When you're young, you don't think.

DALE: About anything.

TOM: Right. Kind of. I mean, you're thinking but it's all bullshit. I mean, what the hell do you know?

DALE: Zero, and that's why you're not thinking.

TOM: Right. But here. This place. Take a look. This is it. We made it here and as far as I'm concerned, or rather, what I think is this. What do we got? Same shit. We made it here on the assumption that we actually had somewhere to go.

DALE: What are you doing? Trying to depress me?

TOM: I'm not trying, but if that's what's happening, I'm really sorry.

DALE: We really don't gotta do this.

TOM: No. We don't gotta do nothing. We didn't even have to make it here. Here being where? I have no clue. But truth be told, we don't gotta do nothing.

DALE: Except eat, maybe.

TOM: Fine, that we gotta do, but that's about it.

DALE: Sleep.

TOM: I don't know. People don't, sometimes. People like us, even, and that's something else. Something else that comes up upon the discussion of what we don't have to do.

DALE: So we don't gotta do nothing and that's that.

TOM: But that's what I'm saying. We did it this far. We made it here and also what I'm saying, what I'm directed you toward, is the fact that nothing's changed. There's no pot. No gold. No silver. I didn't even catch a bronze through all this crap. What do I got? What do we got? We're just here. That's it. It's like making it all the way to no place.

DALE: That's it?

TOM: Just about.

DALE: That's what you've come up with?

TOM: Pretty much.

Dale just nods his head.

LIGHTS OUT

SCENE FOUR

LIGHTS UP

Tom points a finger.

TOM: Here's what I'm thinking.

DALE: Okay.

TOM: We could do something.

DALE: We could.

TOM: No, I'm saying we could like we oughtta.

DALE: That's fine, too.

TOM: It's half-baked at this point, as most things are.

DALE: You know what I'm thinking?

TOM: Out of the blue?

DALE: No, I been thinking it.

TOM: No, I'm saying like right now. Now's the time? At of all the times to be thinking something, you choose now?

DALE: What's wrong with that?

TOM: Nothing. I just think it's quite a coincidence is all. Here we are, two gents sitting in the park.

DALE: Right.

TOM: You don't find that to be interesting?

DALE: What part?

TOM: We both got our own separate ways of going about stuff, right?

DALE: Sure.

TOM: Just a couple of thinkers. I'm thinking this, you're thinking that.

DALE: What's the point?

TOM: I don't know, but I'm thinking something's happening. With us, I mean. Together.

Dale waits.

TOM: Maybe not together, but at the same time, for sure.

Dale waits again. Tom seems off in thought.

DALE: I'm thinking I'd like to kill that little Chinese guy that works at the deli.

TOM: That's… That is what it is.

DALE: This little fuck. Like I deserve the treatment I get from the guy. What did I do? I ordered a bagel, and at the very same time, I said easy on the cheese. Now I get it, this isn't a bagel shop. This guy doesn't spread cream cheese for a living, but he sells fucking bagels.

TOM: It's part of what he does.

DALE: Exactly. What the fuck? I didn't give him the job. I didn't say, "Hey, come on over here downtown and open a deli." I didn't tell him to sell bagels and offer spreads. Did I do that?

Dale waits for a response.

DALE: I'm asking you.

TOM: No, you didn't.

DALE: Right. I did not. Certainly not. I didn't say that. I wasn't even a piece of the puzzle. What do I know this guy from, Adam? I loved here. I made it through all the bullshit, right?

TOM: As far as I'm concerned.

DALE: Then go easy on the fucking cream cheese. What gives?

TOM: People, man.

DALE: People is right. What the hell is the matter with this place. And just so you know, I got no problems with the guy coming from China. He can be from wherever he chooses. I got no problems with this.

TOM: People are touchy.

DALE: So fucking touchy. I mean, what the hell's the problem.

TOM: I don't know.

DALE: He's Chinese. If he wasn't, I wouldn't say so. You got a problem with that?

TOM: I don't.

DALE: Right.

TOM: Right.

DALE: People got problems, that's all I'm saying. Cream cheese aside, people got problems.

Tom waits.

DALE: I'm sorry, you were saying?

Tom is spinning.

TOM: We gotta do it.

DALE: The guy?

TOM: Forget the guy. I mean, he's certainly part of the problem, but no. We gotta start something. We gotta take all the shit that gets us the way we get and make a move. An official move.

DALE: Do something, you're saying.

TOM: That's exactly what I'm saying. Goddamn right. You up for it?

DALE: I wouldn't mind a little nosh first.

TOM: That we could do, but this is important.

DALE: So is nourishment.

TOM: I'm not gonna argue.

DALE: Fine. So whaddya wanna do?

TOM: That's an excellent question.

Dale waits.

DALE: You got an answer?

TOM: Not just yet, but it's cooking.

DALE: All right. We got time.

TOM: I don't know. I mean, I'm not so sure is what I'm saying.

LIGHTS OUT

SCENE FIVE

LIGHTS UP

Dale stares at Tom like he's waiting for bad news.

TOM: I get some real bad thoughts sometimes.

DALE: Sure.

TOM: I mean it.

DALE: Who you talking to? I don't know.

TOM: That's what I'm saying. Maybe you don't.

DALE: We're different, is what you're getting at.

TOM: No. That is certainly not what I was getting at, but things come up, and here we are.

DALE: Oh, I see. What? You got some sorta thing with me now?

TOM: What?

DALE: Like what?

TOM: Nothing. What are you talking about?

DALE: No. What are you talking about? What the hell did I do? What am I doing? Yeah, I talk some shit, but all of a sudden, out of the blue, I'm the bad guy? I don't like this guy, I don't like this guy, so what, now I'm some kinda jerk? Some fucking outsider now, all of a sudden?

TOM: Wait a minute.

DALE: How much time you think I got?

TOM: You're getting me all wrong here.

DALE: No. I think maybe quite the opposite. That's how you got me. We playing sides now? What the fuck? I care about a very few things if you wanna know the truth, and if I gotta start explaining what they are, I think, and although a matter of opinion, I'm dealing with truth here, my truth. What gives?

TOM: You got it all... I didn't. Backward. Zip it, would ya?

DALE: What did I say?

TOM: A lot. Now slow down for a second.

DALE: Hey, I got two speeds.

TOM: Well, give me the other.

DALE: I'm right here.

TOM: We ain't no different.

DALE: You sure?

TOM: That's not what I'm saying.

DALE: I got feelings.

TOM: As do I. Now, go easy. I'll buy us a nice something on the way outta here later.

DALE: What are we talking about?

TOM: Maybe something hardy.

DALE: I'm a meat and potatoes kinda guy.

TOM: Look.

DALE: I like what I like.

TOM: We good?

DALE: As far as I'm concerned, that's never a question. Never has been.

TOM: Good. Cause I don't want it to be. Got me all twisted over here.

DALE: Not my intention.

TOM: We good?

DALE: Yes.

TOM: Fine. Jesus. Too early for this. What time you got?

Dale looks at his watch. He might not have one.

DALE: Maybe lunch at best. You thinking now?

TOM: No. Too heavy, now listen to me.

DALE: What the hell else am I doing?

Dale waits. Tom puts it together.

TOM: I got these dreams.

DALE: Please. Dreams. I used to have 'em so bad I'd stay up. Like on purpose. Anything but what is what I was thinking. Bad too.

TOM: No, I'm talking daytime. I know what you're saying, but I'm talking something else. Daytime, maybe even in the night too, but nothing where I'm out, like off in...

DALE: Dreams.

TOM: No, no, no. Like here. Here we are. I'm looking out. You see that?

DALE: What are we looking at?

TOM: Fantastic question, but for these purposes, just pick something. It doesn't matter.

They both look ahead.

DALE: Okay.

TOM: Like this. I'm awake. You awake?

DALE: I'm pretty sure.

TOM: That's what I'm talking about. Just looking out and I'm thinking about death. Not just my own, I mean there's that too. But here I am, here we are, and all we're doing is looking, and like I said, it don't matter at what. You're looking at this, me at that. I'm thinking things. Bad things.

DALE: Always?

TOM: A good amount.

DALE: Right.

TOM: I'm killing people.

DALE: Why?

TOM: I don't know and that's my point. I'm playing out scenarios on the count of something I can't quite get a hold of. I'm doing bad things. Very bad things. To people. Objects, even. Why? I say this to say there ain't no reason. I mean, is there a reason to be upset?

DALE: Always.

TOM: Right. But if that ain't enough, I'm trying to pull from it.

DALE: Take it further you mean?

TOM: That's exactly what I mean. One thought leads to the next and then... Then I don't know what. I'm just off.

Dale takes a beat to remind himself of something.

DALE: I ever tell you about that time I killed that pair of poodles?

TOM: What? No. You did that?

DALE: No. Not really. That's probably why I never told you about it because it was a figment of my imagination. But I assume we're on the same page here is why I'm bringing it up.

TOM: You killed poodles?

DALE: Are you listening to me?

TOM: Yes.

DALE: Then you would know I never killed a pair of poodles.

TOM: What did you do to them?

DALE: I didn't do nothing to 'em.

TOM: Then what did you do?

DALE: I didn't do nothing. Boy, are you dense. Listen.

TOM: I am.

DALE: I'm saying I get the thinking things. Death. Looking out at whatever you're looking at and making up death. Or bad. Or both.

TOM: Dreaming.

DALE: Right. But not at night, although it could happen at night.

TOM: Just as likely.

DALE: I get it, and that's what I'm saying. I'm also saying I didn't kill no pair of poodles. I did however think very deeply about it, on the count of this pit bull that I had when I was a kid that didn't do nothing to the aforementioned pair of poodles. But I thought they were gonna and from here is where I make all my decisions.

TOM: Wait a minute. I'm all muffled up here.

DALE: I see these bug, puffy white things standing on a stoop. You with me?

TOM: Yes.

DALE: I'm young. This explains the choice of dog. Mine, I mean. I got this pit bull that looks like it could eat a pair of poodles like it was a starter, which reminds me, I wouldn't mind a nice clams casino before we get into our steak, but forget that.

TOM: For now?

DALE: Yes, for now. Anyhow. I got this dog, Pete, or Woody, something tough. It was a while ago, and I'm not so sure, but here's these two white, puffy fucks sitting on a stoop. They got some fairy for a caretaker, and I don't got no problem with no one else's choice to do what they do. None of my business, but when I say fairy, I mean this guy, he's floating around like it's Christmas or some other thing, and he's got these white labradoodles or poodles, whatever the fuck they are, sitting on a stoop. Leash-less.

TOM: That's not okay.

DALE: Not slightly. I mean, what kinda world is this? You can't act like that. It's bad enough you're dancing around like there's something to be happy about, which there is not, but let's add insult to the whole thing. Get a leash. Do yourself a favor. Do the dog a favor.

TOM: Not to mention what you already mentioned, but on top of it all, and to top it all off... There's a pit bull walking around. And fucking bulldogs. What do I know? Shepards.

DALE: (*Mispronounced*) Rottweilers.

TOM: German animals roaming the streets like it's nothing.

DALE: Put a leash on your dog.

TOM: For crying out loud.

DALE: You see what I'm saying?

TOM: The nerve of these people.

DALE: This is not a safe place. Stop dancing around like a fairy, buy a pair of pants that fit, and put a leash on the goddamn poodle.

TOM: Like we're asking for something.

DALE: This is how it starts.

TOM: It's always something.

DALE: I'm sorry, but I get so upset.

TOM: I understand. Trust me, I do.

Dale takes a deep breath.

DALE: All right. So next thing I know, I'm imagining things.

TOM: How could you not be?

DALE: I am. And it's not good.

TOM: It couldn't be.

DALE: Right? So here I am, imagining. It's really something what you can do up there.

TOM: That's my whole goddamned point.

DALE: I know, and that's why I'm saying.

TOM: So, what happens?

DALE: I'll tell ya.

TOM: Go ahead.

DALE: These two puffs, these careless dopey show-dogs I can only imagine, and I'm imagining, cause none of this is actually happening, but these white puff snowy-looking things mosey on over. Like they ain't got a care in the world.

TOM: Putz dogs.

DALE: No shit. All the while, the dancing fairy oblivious, he don't come to until I'm six ways into pulling, pushing, and trying to scream the pair away. I'm holding a killing machine! Get those dogs outta here. So by the time he notices, this goofy kid, my Woody's got a hold a these two and he's making a mess. I don't need to get into the details.

TOM: I get it.

DALE: I know you do. It's a disaster. Worst day of everybody's life, or so I'm imagining, but then next thing I know, I'm in court. Court? What do I know what they do, but I'm in court.

TOM: Dog court.

DALE: Some fucking thing.

TOM: I can imagine.

DALE: Oh, I imagine it good. They got a judge and everything, and he don't like German dogs, he don't like bulldogs, and he certainly don't got no compassion for my Petey, or Woody. Whatever. You see what I'm saying.

TOM: I do.

DALE: Here's this poor pit bull, still on my leash. I mean, I'm the one who was doing it right in the first place.

TOM: You don't gotta tell me. You're following the rules. Rules of the streets. I'm sure there's a law, but you're doing right by the planet.

DALE: Damn right I am.

They both take a break. Tom nods his head in disgust.

DALE: Anyhow, this goofy judge goes ahead and gives my dog the chair. Behind what?

TOM: Doing right.

Dale nods his head.

DALE: Right?

TOM: Just being a dog. That's all.

DALE: Doing what he's supposed to be doing.

TOM: Protection, as far as Woody's concerned. And now this.

DALE: This sentence. For what?

TOM: Makes me sick.

DALE: Exactly what it did to me.

TOM: I'd like to find that judge.

DALE: That was next. Believe you me, that was part of the fantasy as well. But first. I camp out, couple days later, rifle up, and put a few in the twins. The poodles, I mean.

TOM: Same thing I would have done.

DALE: Under the circumstances, what the hell else you gonna do?

TOM: I tell you what. This place is something else.

A beat. Contemplating. Both men.

DALE: Anyhow, I know what you mean. The dreaming. What have you. That's why I bring it up.

They both take a beat. Take it all in.

TOM: Whatever happened to that pit bull?

DALE: He died of old age, I believe.

TOM: Sad nonetheless.

DALE: Yeah. He was a good kid.

LIGHTS OUT

SCENE SIX

LIGHTS UP

The guys and the bench.

TOM: We're all going to hell in a handbasket.

Dale takes it in.

DALE: What is that?

TOM: What's what?

DALE: You doin' quotes now?

TOM: What's that mean?

DALE: I'm asking you.

TOM: You?

DALE: No, you. You doin' other people's stuff now. It's come to this? This? This is what it's come to. I don't like it.

TOM: You don't like it. Why is that?

DALE: Hey. Stick to one thing at a time here.

TOM: You hungry?

DALE: Don't do that.

TOM: What am I doing?

DALE: Don't be a cliché. Don't say things.

TOM: What am I doing?

DALE: You're breaking apart. Be a man, for Christ's sake.

TOM: Where the… What? Who do you think you are?

DALE: You got something to say? Say it. Don't do this.

TOM: I'm breaking apart?

DALE: That's what I said.

TOM: Why'd you say it?

DALE: You know goddamn well why I said it. Now man up. That's enough. This is it. You wanna say something? Go ahead. I'm right here. You hungry?

TOM: Yes, I'm hungry.

DALE: Bullshit. Speak. Don't give me no puke about what someone else said.

TOM: What the hell is this?

DALE: This? This is it? Stand up.

TOM: No chance.

DALE: I mean like in the sense of something else. God knows I'm not asking you to move.

TOM: Then what are you asking?

DALE: I'm asking for what any living human that's gone this far would be asking. All we got is a bunch of people running around, saying the same shit. They're doing the same shit. Wearing the same shit. That I don't care so much about, but you see what I'm barking.

Tom thinks about it.

TOM: Be original?

DALE: Goddamn right.

TOM: So we're saying the same thing.

DALE: Bullshit. I don't want to hear it.

TOM: You got no choice.

DALE: Yes, I do, and so do you. Get up. Stay seated, obviously, but get off your ass. We made it this far, no?

TOM: Yes.

DALE: Be you. That's what I'm saying. You wanna bitch? I can do it with the best of them, but do it right.

TOM: You being so tough.

DALE: Tough is tough.

TOM: Whose is that?

DALE: Mine, and that's the point.

Tom thinks about it.

DALE: I mean, I've had it up to here.

TOM: Okay.

DALE: Okay? Cause okay's okay.

TOM: Fine, I get it.

DALE: Go ahead.

Tom thinks about it.

TOM: This guy.

DALE: Me?

TOM: No, not you. Who we talking about? I'm busting at the seams? Yes. This is true. This is where I am. You want me to do something else? I'm stuck. This motherfucker.

DALE: What's his name?

Tom takes a second to think about it.

TOM: Let's call him Peter.

DALE: That his name?

TOM: No. But I'd like to protect the innocent, and I particularly don't like the name Pedro, so let's use it.

DALE: Fine.

TOM: This cocksucker.

DALE: Go easy, but now you're talking.

TOM: A penguin, I'm talking.

DALE: Come again?

TOM: A suit. You know?

DALE: Sure.

TOM: One of these guys that follows the rules, and that's why we're talking about the same thing. Or was. Before, I mean. This guy, I tell you what.

DALE: Go ahead.

TOM: No. He's even worse than someone following rules, because he don't gotta. He could do something special, but he chooses to be a penguin, and I'd like him dead.

DALE: I know a guy.

TOM: No, no, no. Those days are over for me. That's all we need, a stint in the can.

DALE: I could make a phone call is what I'm saying.

TOM: What is this, a movie? What are we doing here?

DALE: Look, would ya? What are we talking about? I'm saying I could. This penguin, he need to die behind being the kinda guy that don't deserve to be here? Here being this earth? Maybe he does. Deserve that, I mean. To not exist. But that's not what I'm saying. I'm talking about a phone call. One in which he gets something knocked around. Or maybe a slight cut. I'm not saying a hospital cut. No. Something fixable with some band-aids and maybe a solution of sorts.

Tom seems to be turned around.

DALE: Stick with me here.

TOM: I'm trying.

DALE: Well, try harder, cause no one's taking a trip to the can here. Certainly not behind some phone call about some penguin who's giving you the itch.

TOM: I really can't stand this kid. I mean, I believe I've done the right thing.

DALE: Which is what?

TOM: Separation. I made a clean break, or separation as to not have to mingle with this here penguin jerk. I mean, that's the right thing. People. This life. You can choose to do bad things, then what? Leads you to worse things. The can, this thing, that thing. I mean, truth be told, nothing's worse than that. The can, I mean. Or what. Life. People. We can just deal with who we gotta deal with, and beyond that, if we can't, ya just don't. Am I right or am I right?

DALE: We're saying the same thing and I'm not saying nothing no more.

TOM: Good. So fuck this penguin. I'm doing the right thing.

DALE: Yes you are.

TOM: Goddamn suits.

DALE: That was never us.

TOM: And that's that.

DALE: We are who we are.

TOM: And they for they.

DALE: Absolutely.

A beat. Dale's thinking.

TOM: What are you thinking?

DALE: Something unusual.

TOM: What unusual? Like a snail?

DALE: No. Nothing French, please.

TOM: Yeah.

DALE: A nice plate of cheeses maybe.

TOM: That's unusual?

DALE: For me it is.

Tom nods in agreement.

LIGHTS OUT

SCENE SEVEN

LIGHTS UP

They sit in silence for a few beats.

Tom turns to Dale.

DALE: I got nothing.
TOM: Yeah.

They sit in some more silence.

DALE: Nothing's doing?
TOM: I guess not.

Tom spots something off and away.

DALE: What? What is it?
TOM: Just thinking.

Dale understands.

DALE: Yeah.

LIGHTS OUT

416 • SCOTT CAAN

SCENE EIGHT

LIGHTS UP

After a few silent beats, Dale looks out.

DALE: Sky's getting dark.

TOM: Nah, we got awhile.

Dale takes a look.

DALE: I don't know.

A sad moment.

TOM: So what, that's it?

DALE: Think so.

Tom puts his head down.

TOM: Yeah.

DALE: You know what I'm thinking?

TOM: Something sweet?

DALE: No, no. Not that. I'm thinking something else.

TOM: This place?

DALE: Yeah, maybe. To think…

TOM: 'Bout what?

DALE: I'm getting to it.

TOM: Sorry.

DALE: To think…

TOM: I ain't saying nothing.

DALE: To think that was the highlight of my life.

TOM: What was?

DALE: Whatever it is. Whatever it was. That's what I'm thinking. What if,
you know?

Tom takes it in.

DALE: This time when we ran with those kids, or that broad, although everything changed when she had the kid, but whatever it is. The time we smoked that dope and came home without any clothes. The girl that broke her nose. Whatever it is I'm saying. The stolen cop car, the fire on the seventh floor. Whatever we did. This is all human specific, but whatever it is. That was it. The highlight of my life. Whatever it is for you.

TOM: What are you thinking?

DALE: I'm thinking maybe it ain't even happened yet. That's what I'm thinking.

TOM: I like that.

DALE: Me, too. I think that maybe that's why I'm saying it. Or hoping it.

TOM: Be nice.

DALE: Right?

TOM: What's next?

DALE: That's what I'm saying, we don't know.

Tom takes it in.

TOM: I'd like to take a trip, ya know?

DALE: Nah. Not for me.

TOM: Yeah. Something nice where the wind gets a hold, you know?

DALE: I'm not much for airplanes, or the people that fly 'em for that matter.

TOM: So maybe we drive. Find some place that's automobile friendly and take a few days. Put your feet up. Forget the city and everything else. A nice change, but maybe for just a bit.

Dale is thinking about it.

TOM: Maybe before it's too… I don't know. Something different, that's all.

DALE: Sounds good.

Dale stands up, stretches out his back.

TOM: Tomorrow?

DALE: Yeah. I'll see you tomorrow.

Dale slowly walks offstage holding his lower back.

Tom looks out.

LIGHTS OUT

THE END